Travels along the U.S./Mexico Divide

CHARLES D. THOMPSON JR.

# BORDER ODYSSEY

UNIVERSITY OF TEXAS PRESS      AUSTIN

Copyright © 2015 by the University of Texas Press
All rights reserved
Printed in the United States of America
First edition, 2015

Requests for permission to reproduce material
from this work should be sent to:
  Permissions
  University of Texas Press
  P.O. Box 7819
  Austin, TX 78713-7819
  http://utpress.utexas.edu/index.php/rp-form

♾ The paper used in this book meets the minimum requirements of ANSI/NISO Z39.48-1992
(R1997) (Permanence of Paper).

LIBRARY OF CONGRESS
CATALOGING-IN-PUBLICATION DATA
Thompson, Charles D., Jr. (Charles Dillard),
1956– author.
   Border odyssey : travels along the US/
Mexico divide / Charles D. Thompson, Jr.
— First edition.
       pages     cm
   Includes bibliographical references and
index.
   ISBN 978-0-292-75663-2 (cloth : alk.
paper)
   1. Mexican-American Border Region. 2.
United States—Foreign relations—Mexico.
3. Mexico—Foreign relations—United
States. 4. Thompson, Charles D., Jr.
(Charles Dillard)—Travel. I. Title.
   F787.T47 2015
   972'.1—dc23     2014031549
doi:10.7560/756632

*For the border crossers.*

*For the monarchs.*

*For my parents.*

*For Hope.*

*Something there is that doesn't love a wall*
*That wants it down.*

ROBERT FROST,
"MENDING WALL" (1913)

*Mr. Gorbachev, tear down this wall.*

PRESIDENT RONALD REAGAN,
BERLIN, 1987

*Complete the danged fence.*

SENATOR JOHN MCCAIN,
ARIZONA, 2010

*Yea, though I walk through the Valley of the Shadow of Death, I will fear no evil.*

PSALM 23:4 (KJV)

CONTENTS

# ONE

# Evidence of Things Not Seen

CIUDAD JUAREZ, SONORA, MEXICO

NEARLY TWO HUNDRED PEOPLE, NONE OF THEM YOUNGER THAN seventy-five, crowded around us. My wife Hope and I had accompanied our friend Poncho to visit these Braceros on a Sunday morning in Benito Juarez Park in Ciudad Juarez, Mexico. When I asked if I might take some photos of them—regular candid shots is what I had in mind—they began moving toward us, surrounding us, getting so close that each individual face filled the frame. They formed a line with each one waiting his turn, each set of eyes asking that I not leave anyone out. They had me for the entire morning.

Years earlier they had been given visas and invited to work in the United States. Our country had asked them to come because we needed their strong arms. In 1942, officials began a federal program to import these laborers, calling them Braceros. They came as replacements for our soldiers and factory workers during the Second World War, and they remained as field hands after the war. The program lasted until 1964. During its twenty-two years some 4.6 million men signed contracts and traveled north of the border to work. After 1964, the United States no longer needed them and told them to go home. There was no letter of thanks, and government officials said they would send their retirement money later.

The Braceros had waited patiently, trusting they would be paid the benefits they had earned. But now they were old and no retirement checks had arrived. Half a century had passed. They were demonstrating in the park because they wanted the world to know they were still waiting. They seemed gratified that someone, anyone, would be willing to document their presence in this park.

As I looked through the camera lens at their lined faces, I imagined them all as young farmworkers. They had been faithful in giving some of their best years to work in our fields. Now too old to work, they had gathered in this park every Sun-

Modesto Zurita Estrada, just one of the heroes at the Braceros' Sunday gathering in Ciudad Juarez.

day for years. They had pledged to one another to continue until they were too old even to do that. The ones still able to continue stood together peacefully once a week a few miles from the U.S./Mexico border, calling attention to the injustice of it all.

The day we arrived in 2010, the old Braceros held signs and propped placards on a nearby fence, while one hoisted a Mexican flag. They stood strong, shoulder to shoulder, an unlikely group of protesters: old men in cowboy hats and caps with various logos. They stood silently; there were no chants. Alongside them were some family members: wives, widows, and a few supporters, including a faithful retired professor named Manuel Robles who helped them stay organized. Now I held each of them in my frame, and for the briefest of moments each gazed back, his face telling volumes.

Occasionally over the years a reporter from Mexico had happened by to write an article. During election season a politician or two had sometimes discovered them again. That day they stood in line waiting their turn to stare into my lens as if this alone could rescue them from the grasp of anonymity. Their faces were like road maps, with lines of experience from crisscrossing the border and working in the sun written on their skin. I focused and clicked away, asking Hope to write down their names alongside descriptions in my notebook. "White cowboy hat; red checked western shirt," I said aloud as I snapped the shutter. "Black Marlboro cap, glasses, green striped shirt." We would match the descriptions with the names and photos later.

I noticed that some held up laminated cards and photocopies of papers in their photos. They were copies of decades-old identification cards and work visas showing they had entered the United States legally. These pictures were of proud men in their twenties, all of them ambitious farm people dressed up and staring solemnly into the camera just before they left for the U.S. Were these the last portraits some of them had taken before now? Some had died, and their names were on a banner propped up temporarily at the Juárez statue. The remaining ones were like veterans of a forgotten war who knew their ranks were dwindling.

I had to tell them I possessed no official means to help them. I stepped onto a park bench and projected my voice above the crowd encircling me, speaking in Spanish and offering them as much respect as possible. "Ladies and gentlemen, I want you to know that I'm not with the United States government." But even as I said that, I realized that as a citizen, I did in fact have some accountability in this—as every American has. I knew I didn't want to give them false hopes, though I didn't want to shirk my responsibility either. I continued, "I teach at a university in the U.S. and my wife and I are here at the invitation of our friend, Professor

Luis Alfonso Herrera Robles from the University of Juarez." Poncho, as he is known to his friends, is a sociologist who for years has been going to the park, first with his parents to serve coffee and *pan dulce*, and later working with his mentor Professor Robles to record their stories on tape and to document their cause. Poncho believed my photographs could help and had told this to the Braceros. Poncho and I had talked before we arrived of collaborating on a photo and oral history project, one that we have since pursued and finished. But I knew in the Braceros' presence that day that my work was a long way from getting their money for them.

"It's so important that you are here," I announced in my strongest voice. "It's an honor for my wife and me to stand with you here today and to join with you as you demand justice. We will try our best to spread the word about you and use the photographs to help. We hope to bring copies back to you as well. Please continue your struggle for what you know is right. *Sí se puede!*" The crowd erupted in applause. I got down off the bench and went back to the line. I framed the next person in my viewfinder, and he stared back at the camera with a stony but kind face as I snapped the shutter. "Black cowboy hat, glasses, mustache, yellow striped shirt," I said to Hope. She wrote down his name as I moved to the next in line.

# TWO

# The Border Etched in Bones

JUAREZ, EL PASO, AND THE DAVIS MOUNTAINS

I HAD NEVER IMAGINED WHEN WE FIRST PLANNED OUR TRIP that such a scene would be waiting for us in Ciudad Juarez, the difficult place Chuck Bowden titled *Murder City*, the place where tens of thousands of people had been killed over the past decade, the place where thousands of young women working in maquiladoras had been disappeared, trafficked, or murdered, giving Mexican "femicide" its grisly meaning. We never dreamed that in the place where men and boys had turned up bloodied on streets, some decapitated, some hanging from bridges, we would find an unlikely group of elders demonstrating so openly and with such courage for a cause that has nothing to do with drug cartels or murders.

It became clear after days of traveling along the U.S./ Mexico border that the *fron-*

The border wall adorned with artwork by the late Alfred J. Quiroz in Nogales, Sonora, Mexico.

*tera* was more multifaceted and profound than anything we could have invented about it from afar, particularly in a place where fear influences how we imagine it, and how could there not be fear of Juarez? Deeper understanding was exactly what we had hoped for by going there; still we could never have planned or even imagined that scene with the Braceros in the park. Maps had been only outlines, stark lines drawn in two dimensions. Going there made possible varied colors and detail, texture and depth that I'm still trying to fathom.

We had thought we might spend our time in Juarez behind walls at the university and that Poncho might not let us venture beyond them. Instead, he had filled our days with exploration. By the time we met the Braceros on a Sunday morning in May, we had driven all over Juarez, meeting a variety of people, including migrant farmworkers on both sides of the border, priests, activists, and even a bride and groom getting married in a Mexican hotel. What had seemed a single image of violence had been transformed into faces of dozens of people whose eyes I had looked into and whose stories I'd written down. What had sounded from the outside like a stark cry of fear and hopelessness now seemed like a chorus of human voices calling us to deeper understanding and even encouraging us to help rebuild relations between our two countries. Then what?

I had no solutions to our diplomatic challenges, but I did have stories that had convinced me we had gotten the border all wrong. I had images in my camera and words written down in my notebook, and they called to me, they urged me to give something back. The Braceros' stories had been the result of only one morning of dozens spent along the border, and before I finished there would be many more that would weigh on me until I could release them again. Stories are the opposite of walls: they demand release, retelling, showing, connecting, each image chipping away at boundaries. Walls are full stops. But stories are like commas, always making possible the next clause.

Walls between humans have never worked anyway, whether the Great Wall of China, the Berlin Wall, Jerusalem's West Bank wall, or even the ugly fence constructed between two Virginia neighbors that I had seen plastered with "no trespassing" signs. All were and are futile attempts to block out problems that need to be addressed head on. Hadn't the strategy of building walls proved faulty back when medieval castles were under siege? Boiling oil and showers of arrows raining down on intruders might have worked for a night or two, but they never proved to be good long-range strategies, especially when the water and food began running low. It seemed to me that only the defense contractors who build and maintain border walls could be pleased with our new distinction of having the best fence in the world.

Before our trip when Hope and I traced the single black line from the Gulf of Mexico to the Pacific on maps, highlighting in yellow the dotted lines signifying back roads closest to the border, everything had looked so clear and unambiguous on paper. What had been a single line in the landscape in satellite photos had now become multidimensional, messy, and human in all the best and worst senses. Even the physical wall itself had been painted, filled with graffiti, blowtorched, and cut. We saw that in some places the fence had just stopped mid-hill, leaving unexplained gaps. I realized these complications would have to be included in my telling of the story of the border. It would be chaotic at times, come out in fits and starts, and be nonlinear, but in the telling I knew that no matter how lost I was in its confusion and danger, I always had the option of heading back to the line to regroup. Maps aren't places themselves, but they provide a useful fiction to guide us through the realities otherwise impossible to contain.

| | | |

AFTER SAYING OUR GOOD-BYES in the Juarez Park, Diego, one of Poncho's colleagues, drove us across the bridge and back to El Paso in his family's Toyota van. He had a pass that allowed him to cross the border for a day, and he had an errand to run in the U.S., so he volunteered to take us back. As we neared the border bridge, we pulled into one of the dozen lines of traffic waiting to go north. While we had walked into

Mexico on foot without being questioned three days earlier, the return trip was much more complicated and time-consuming. Diego considered us lucky to sit in line for what he predicted would be two hours. As we waited and talked, dozens of small-time entrepreneurs meandered on foot through the parked traffic, some selling ice cream in pushcarts, others hawking newspapers, Chiclets, roasted nuts, huge placards of religious icons, jewelry, and more. Three indigenous women, Tarahumaras wearing long colorful skirts and no shoes, had only their outstretched hands to offer and walked through traffic pleading with their eyes for money. This border carnival in the hot sun on pavement was repeated every day. It provided the crossers some sense of community and distraction as they waited, sometimes from morning until night.

We reached the electronic sensing devices near the U.S. Customs entrance. We handed our passports to Diego and waited some more, making sure not to say anything critical about the border or immigration, or even to joke, as we had heard that the sophisticated detection devices monitored even the sounds inside vehicles. When we finally got to the inspection station, a dark-uniformed customs agent approached Diego's car door, took the passports, and, seeing that we were American, looked over at me to ask what we had been doing in Ciudad Juarez. I could see he was wearing a bulletproof vest and knew that he had to be sweating inside it.

"We were guests of the College of Chihuahua and the University of Juarez. We both gave talks at a conference for grad students. I showed my film about immigration to students and faculty there." All of that was true. It would have sounded ludicrous to go into my additional reasons for traveling the border: the stories, images in the park, and all the rest.

The young, stocky white guard looked at me and shook his head. "You're lucky to be alive," he said, looking back at our papers. He chuckled a little, handed the passports back, and added, "Just kidding." We knew that he wasn't.

The university had put us up in a Best Western with palm trees and a pool. Three fancy wedding parties took place in the hotel that weekend.

The brides and their attendants wore long pastel formal dresses, the men dark suits and pointy boots. They danced to live bands into the night as we sat by the pool and listened to the music. Meanwhile, twenty-four young men and boys were murdered during the weekend in the streets of the city. Territorial fights in the drug wars, Diego surmised, just the kind of danger the officer was talking about. So I knew what the guard meant about luck, but we had also seen what was on the other side of fear, an entirely different reason to feel lucky.

We had parked our car in a border lot in El Paso watched over by several disheveled Latino men who played cards in a little shack at the entrance. They told us that they slept there all night and let in no one but the car owners. We didn't worry about the rental car. After all, we knew that statistics show El Paso had long been one of America's safest cities. When three days later we shouted our return greetings from Diego's car window at the gate, they looked back from what looked like the same card game, remembered us at a glance, and waved us through. Clearly there had not been a lot of gringos parking their cars and walking into Ciudad Juarez.

We thanked Diego for the hours he had just spent taking us across the bridge, got our bags, and loaded them into our trunk. We waved good-bye, started the Chevrolet, and drove mostly in silence through the peaceful and deserted El Paso downtown. We found our way quickly to I-10 East and drove to a Texas state park where we would stay for the night. We started talking about what we had just been through, knowing we still had over a thousand miles to cover and much more exploring along the way.

That afternoon we arrived at the lodge at Fort Davis and went hiking. Up in the Davis Mountains, about fifty miles from the border, we saw signs along a trail that warned of mountain lions that stalk small children or women hiking alone. I had heard about the big cats bringing down men my size by jumping off ledges onto them from behind. But I didn't worry too much as we hiked. After Juarez, a threat I could understand as part of nature was almost welcome. At least there were instructions about what to do. Never walk alone. Make noise. Try to look larger and more menacing than you might feel. But I noted that none of those signs said not to go.

At the border everything was different. There, authorities wanted us to stay away. The border is a dangerous place and there's nothing to be done about it. You're lucky to be alive if you make it out. They might as well have had signs that said as much. But our trip along the border was our push back against all that.

We weren't trying to be foolhardy. While heeding the travel warnings as well as we could, we had wanted to find an alternative to the narrative of danger that we've all become accustomed to. We were trying to do something to help change the vision and the conversation about border fears. We knew there had to be something more to immigration discussions than just to repeat over and over again that we should make the wall stronger and crack down on illegal immigrants. It seemed every politician always began any talk about immigration with a nod toward "strengthening the border." We were after an alternative narrative.

After you walk a trail with your own feet, talk with others along the way, breathe the air, touch the rocks, smell the plants, see the clouds above you, and even keep watch for the mountain lions, a trail and the places it traverses become part of you. You return with your own memories and maybe a few pains, and the place gets etched into your bones. This book is my telling about the border from my bones: my discoveries and frights, new friendships and hauntings, pains and possibilities, all gained because we ignored warnings to stay away.

Why tell it? First of all, the border belongs to all of us. Like the underlining of a sentence, the border wall is a line beneath our country that emphasizes what we believe about ourselves—at least officially. I was afraid that if we weren't careful, the wall could start to define us, and we could become the people of the wall, overpowering all that I grew up believing, eclipsing even the symbol of a crowned lady holding a torch. I decided to face our fears by going there, hoping to replace fears with understanding.

Looking back now at the whole trip, I'm happy to say we lived through the experience, though "understanding" might be too strong a word. I can say that the border taught me about possibilities beyond a single stark line, all gained from listening firsthand to those who, like the Braceros, live the *frontera* and bear its consequences. I returned home with a complicated set of images, experiences, and stories that needed retelling. But simple lines couldn't begin to contain them. Perhaps that is the major point of it all. Simple lines can't contain people either.

# THREE

# Traveling the Valley of the Shadow

WHIPPOORWILL FARM, PITTSBORO,
NORTH CAROLINA

MY BORDER ODYSSEY BEGAN THREE DECADES AGO IN A blackberry field on my farm in North Carolina. In 1986, the border crossed me. Five men, all of them *campesinos* whose livelihoods had dwindled to nearly nothing in the so-called lost decade in Mexico, had left the state of Nayarit and joined a river of *Mexicanos* flowing northward. The five arrived first in tomato fields in Florida. Then, responding to a call for *pollera* workers sent by chicken plant managers to their network of family and friends, they had found themselves in Pittsboro, North Carolina, on a chicken-butchering line thousands of miles from their homes—and in a county where almost no others besides blacks and whites had lived and worked for the past two centuries.

They found ready work in the Chatham County plant called Townsend Poultry. They found trailers and old rental houses to move into where they lived as groups of men. Hardly any women or children came at first. The new immigrants worked long hours. They ate. They slept. They sent money back to Mexico. Eventually some of them started a soccer league. One began making hammocks and selling them on the side. Later the *tiendas* would come to sell them Mexican foods and phone cards.

Families would come, too. The border crept northward.

Their jobs were to slaughter, pluck, and cut up chickens in near-freezing temperatures, and then package them for shipping to stores and restaurants. Every day dozens of trucks arrived at Townsend filled with cages of white birds. The roadsides in the county were littered with white feathers so thick they would look like snow. Men carried the cages from the trucks inside, where people moved like machines, repeating the same motion all day, standing in ice water, turning live birds into parts lined up on plastic-wrapped Styrofoam trays. Every day refrigerated trucks left with chilled chicken parts in waxed cardboard boxes, some stamped with Townsend's name, some with grocery chain name brands, some heading to restaurants.

The company officials wouldn't let me into the plant because of rules about nonemployees, but people who worked there told me what went on inside. Plus, I could smell the plant some two miles away from our home on the days that winds blew from the east, especially those days

*The border wall and a Border Patrol vehicle behind a lettuce field near Jacumba, California.*

when they irrigated the fields around the plant with the bloodied and soiled water used in rinsing the slaughtered chickens. So I knew.

At first we started seeing the men in grocery stores. I nodded and said hello to those I passed. They kept their heads and their voices down, but they nodded back. They knew not to cause any ruckus, or even to talk loud, in public. They confined themselves to the shadows. But residents were quite aware that they had arrived. People said things like, "Nobody works harder than those Mexicans." Several years passed before my need for farm help would send me to the plant.

When I got there I told a Townsend foreman named Joe, a friend of a friend, that I needed help harvesting blackberries that afternoon at my farm. He asked for directions and agreed to take the message to the workers on his shift. I'd hired several high school students for a few months, but when the temperatures started rising, they found other jobs. Two of them were working behind the counter at Hardee's in town. Another got a job in a convenience store. Maybe the farm experience helped them. Regardless, they weren't coming back.

That afternoon, on a hot day in June 1986, five men—Faustino, Librado, Eusebio, Luis, and Juan—came into my life. I didn't know it then, but they were about to change much more than my farm labor situation.

They were driving an old blue Impala, and they emerged from the wide old car still wearing black rubber boots and the long white lab coats bloodied and stained from working in the freezing water, feathers, and blood and guts they had endured since arriving from Mexico. I could see how relieved they were to be outside as they looked around at the landscape. We exchanged greetings and handshakes, though the conversation was halting due to our language barrier. Hope, whom I had married just a year earlier, spoke fluent Spanish from childhood, and she fortunately arrived just then from her agricultural research job in town and began to help with translation. Encouraged by her language abilities, the men relaxed and let out their stories. They said they had not been on a small farm since leaving Mexico.

The men explained that they were all from the same small rural community and came from farming backgrounds. Faustino was Eusebio's son. The rest were in the United States without family. They lived together in one house. Though they had not harvested *moras,* as I learned blackberries are called in Spanish, before, they certainly knew how to work on a farm and how to pick. There would be no learning curve. I felt a sense of relief wash over me, experiencing a feeling of being rescued that I'm sure has been shared by thousands of other farmers before and since.

I offered two dollars over the hourly wage at the plant, reasoning that organic food should pay a living wage for those who harvest it, even if just for a few hours a week. But they declined, because they wanted to be paid by the flat of berries so that working hard would get them more money per hour, and they wanted to start right away. Making money, I learned quickly, was the only reason they were in North Carolina. They wanted to send back every penny they could to their families. They always arrived when they said they would and hurried to the fields to make as much money as possible. After a while they were doing the work without any instructions. I could leave to make deliveries and know that they would start without me.

I began to look forward to our times together two afternoons a week. I wanted to know the details about their lives in Mexico. I worked on my basic Spanish skills as they told me their stories of farm losses and searches for stability in marginal U.S. jobs. I took a dictionary to the field. Though surely I lost many of the particulars in the clumsy conversations between us, the details I was able to glean were profound. They told me their personal border stories, of the pain of leaving families behind, of crossings by night, of swimming the Rio Bravo, of being caught and deported—all for the opportunity to work in the chicken plant.

I also realized that these men were not rootless vagabonds traveling the United States to seek work wherever they could find it, but hardworking farmers with small landholdings of their own. They had families waiting for them back home. They were highly skilled in the craft of agriculture. They just couldn't afford to stay home and farm. No matter how hard they worked, their land could not provide their families with a living anymore.

Over time, Librado and Faustino started working with me on Sundays, too. They repaired motors, sharpened tools, built fences, and cut firewood. They knew carpentry and painting. While their work was good for my farm and helped them financially, the unfairness of it all began to weigh on me. Their invaluable local knowledge and skills had been uprooted and moved thousands of miles from their own land, and they had become "illegal" in the process.

I started to ask hard questions, like why I had been able to buy a farm (albeit with some resistance from the entrenched agricultural establishment), find a market for specialty products, and then hire other farmers from Mexico, some of them older and much more experienced than I, to work for me. I began to realize our agricultural system is two-tiered at best, with clear winners and losers, and that even as I sold my products in the college town of Chapel Hill at a premium, jobs on factory farms and processing plants—jobs mostly held by immigrants—were on the rise. Huge agricultural industries had reached into the small-farm economy in Mexico and plucked out its farmers even as I went into the business. I realized it was no coincidence that farm people were headed north to survive just as jobs in an industrializing agriculture awaited them.

Slowly I grasped that I was drawn more to the losers of globalizing agriculture than to winning at the game of local farming myself. I joined a delegation to a Mexican farming village led by a group called Witness for Peace. Hope and I helped host two different refugees through the Carolina Interfaith Task Force on Central America. I studied Spanish harder. When my questions began to outweigh my answers, I realized I needed to go back to school. And I was accepted into graduate school at UNC–Chapel Hill.

After nine years of relative success on the farm—thanks in large part to my Latin American farm neighbors—Hope and I sold our land and I entered graduate school full-time. Listening to and interpreting stories of migration and farm labor became my guiding work as I sought to hear from those who had experienced it firsthand. For my dissertation research, Hope, our seven-year-old son, and I moved to rural Guatemala, where we lived in the village of a refugee we had first helped sponsor in North Carolina. When I returned I joined the board of Student Action with Farmworkers, an organization housed at the Center for Documentary Studies at Duke University. Eventually that connection led me to a job at the same center, where I've taught since 2000.

As part of my work, my students and I have written about, recorded, and filmed hundreds of farmworker stories, including border crossings and harrowing tales of sacrifice. Though not every border crosser's story begins with agriculture, those are the stories I have gravitated to and continue to be moved by. Today more than 150,000 migrant farmworkers pass through North Carolina every year harvesting crops ranging from Christmas trees to apples to sweet potatoes to strawberries. Many of the workers are undocumented and unprotected. Tens of thousands more work in meat processing. No state is untouched by this great movement of the poor and displaced. Wherever there is agriculture, there are border crossings and farm refugees. More than two million people across the nation fall within this category. That doesn't include those who try to come here to work and fail, or those who die in the desert trying to get here.

In the twenty-plus years since I left farming in 1993, the United States has done little to improve the lives of farmworkers, and instead has made their lives more perilous. When the North American Free Trade Agreement passed in 1994, some said it would help people in Mexico get jobs. But that didn't come true for the types of people I've worked with. From what I've witnessed, NAFTA helped to uproot people from their farms and villages, and when they arrived at the border to work in reassembly plants, they found the pay so paltry that many had to keep moving north. In the same year that NAFTA passed, the United States began to erect over seven hundred miles of border wall and surveillance technologies in key locations. That tells you something.

But as any hydro engineer knows, it is impossible to stop the flow of any stream for long; you can only redirect it at best. So the walls we built

in the populated areas ultimately created a channeling effect that directed the flow of migrants toward deserts and dangerous deep-river crossings. Our government called the first initiative Operation Gatekeeper. It
sent migrants into more dangerous places, and deaths in the desert began to mount.[1] We learned most of the dead were poor rural people from
Mexico and Central America, people who didn't know about surviving
in deserts or even about maps in some cases.

Meanwhile, Department of Labor representatives I've met say they
had too few inspectors to patrol the fields, check farmworker housing,
or regulate meat-processing labor standards. Abuses went unreported.
Wages stagnated. And millions of undocumented people have kept doing our dirtiest and most dangerous work without protections, often
without their basic human rights safeguarded.

When the terrorist attacks of September 11 brought more funding for
barriers and surveillance, the situation got worse at the border, not exactly
for the terrorists, who were not in Mexico to begin with, but definitely for
the migrants. By building a bigger wall and adding surveillance and new
agents, we had created a new hell for the border crossers and new money-
making opportunities for human traffickers as our prohibition made migration more dangerous, expensive, and corrupt, but also more profitable
for some. Since 2001, Congress has failed to pass legislation including the
AgJOBS Bill and the Secure Borders, Economic Opportunity, and Immigration Reform Act—bipartisan bills ostensibly designed to address the
problems of farmworkers and other immigrants. Instead, our legislators
have lowered tariffs paid by international food corporations and allowed
U.S. companies buoyed by taxpayer subsidies to undercut Mexican farm
prices. We sent tens of thousands of new guards to the borderlands, creating a border military-industrial complex that did little to win the war on
drugs, but we did start catching and deporting hundreds of thousands of
poor people fleeing their failing rural economies.

For me, all these complexities of the border linked directly back to

---

1. Jeremy Harding, "The Deaths Map," 8–9.

the five farmworkers who first taught me about international agriculture. As I continued to study, I decided I had to go to the border to see it firsthand.

When the Gates Foundation funded a major service-learning initiative at Duke University in 2006, I jumped at the chance to begin a program of study concentrating on migration and the border, calling it "Duke-Engage on the Border/*Encuentros de la Frontera*." Since then, dozens of students in this program have volunteered in Tucson and Nogales, Sonora. We have partnered with organizations such as BorderLinks, No More Deaths, Human Rights Coalition, and Humane Borders, all humanitarian groups located in Tucson. We have gone to the wall, met migrants, attended federal immigration court, heard from Border Patrol officers, and even met with the Pima County, Arizona, coroner whose job is to identify the bodies of migrants brought in from the desert. We have also stayed as guests in the homes of people whose lives on both sides of the border are caught up in the world of NAFTA, maquiladoras, and life on both sides of the border. And we have connected all of this back to fields in North Carolina.

|    |    |    |    |

BACK IN 1986 WHEN the farmworkers and I were working togeth-er, Faustino pulled out an envelope with some forms and asked if I would sign papers for him and the other four workers. I had heard only a little about the Immigration Reform and Control Act (IRCA) at that time, but he explained as I pored over the forms that if immigrant work-ers could show they had been gainfully employed for three years and kept a clean record, they could apply for a green card and eventually the right to apply for citizenship. President Reagan had signed the bill into law only a month before. When I pointed out that they had not worked full-time for me, they said they simply needed someone to confirm they were working, contributing to the economy, and acting as good mem-bers of the community. I had no trouble signing and did so that day for

all five. Though Eusebio, Faustino's father, died shortly thereafter and Librado went back to
Mexico to be with his family on

A flophouse in Altar, Sonora, where migrants hoping to cross the U.S. border
sleep while waiting for their guides.

their rancho, the other three got their green cards. Faustino's children
attended public school and wanted to go on to community college.

I saw Faustino at a benefit concert for a local elementary school years
after IRCA changed his life. He had become a member of the PTA in
nearby Silk Hope, North Carolina, and was helping to raise money for
his children's school. He still worked in a chicken plant, he said. He also
had purchased an old house and was fixing it up. His children were learning and growing in the local schools, and he seemed elated.

Then he mentioned our farm. He had driven by and realized, much to
his disappointment, that the new owners had let the fields go fallow. A
spec house had gone up in the corner of what used to be the blackberry
field. "*Muy feo*," he said about the land, "Very ugly." I realized again how
much he had cared about the place. I shared his disappointment to see
it going down, but I still knew I'd made the right decision to study the

questions I'd been working on. I thanked him again for all that he had done to help the farm succeed. We shook hands and then embraced and said good-bye. His children ran up to Faustino then, and at his urging they turned to address me—in perfect English.

|   |   |   |   |

THREE DECADES AFTER first meeting Faustino and his companions, I was on my way to the border, and Hope was game to go with me. Having grown up in San Antonio and traveled many times to Mexico as a child, she wanted to see the border again and visit some of the places she had gone to years before. She was quick to add, though, that this was really my trip. She knew I had to do it, and she would be there to support me. That was all the encouragement I needed.

# FOUR

# Two Kinds of Flight

## HARLINGEN AND BOCA CHICA, TEXAS

ON MAY 17, 2010, HOPE AND I WERE SITTING PASSIVELY IN A Southwest Airlines jet as it whisked us to the Harlingen, Texas, airport. From there we would drive a rental car to the easternmost point on the border. Though we were in a climate-controlled environment encased in a shiny metal fuselage thirty thousand feet from the ground and traveling some five hundred miles per hour, everything about the border suddenly seemed present to me in a way that no amount of preparation, reading, or

Two strawberry harvesters, Efrain and Lorenzo, wait in Altar, Sonora, before crossing the desert on their way to the California fields.

talking had achieved. We would be touching down in Texas in a matter of hours—with no time to acclimate.

There would be a change of time zone, climate, and sleeping quarters. We would be on the border by nightfall to stay on a ranch within a stone's throw of the Rio Grande in an old rustic house with no climate (or crime) control. But there was no going back now. We would head directly to Boca Chica, the easternmost point on the borderline, the "little mouth" of the Rio Grande, where we would begin our travel by road from the Gulf Stream waters to the Pacific Ocean. We would follow the southern border through four states, traveling the official divide between two nations as different from one another as any two juxtaposed on the planet. Our trip, of course, would be nothing like the plight of migrants traveling on foot. I could never pretend our trip would resemble riding on the tops of trains or in the backs of trucks through Mexico or walking on foot through a desert at night. We wouldn't have to wait for days for the right moment, the right *coyote* to smuggle us across. We would travel the border unhidden from the law and in charge of our own plans, arriving first by plane.

I had no idea when I first started planning all of this that there was an airport so close to our starting point. But after a search of Southwest Airlines destinations, we found on our map a symbol of a plane in the center of Harlingen. The airport serves the popular Padre Island beach resort and nearby Rio Grande valley cities. For us it would mean a quicker arrival to Boca Chica, and my hope was to see the border's beginning before sunset.

The middle of May seemed early enough to avoid the summer heat and storms, but the longer into the afternoon we awaited our connection in Houston, the darker the thunderheads became. Clouds of dramatic purple, yellow, and black began to swirl around the terminal, sending flights banking far to the north. Our plane arrived from Houston two hours late. Then we had to wait out even more storms before we could take off. My plans to take photos before dark seemed foiled, but the appointments I'd made for the following days were too tight to change. We didn't board the plane for Harlingen until 5 p.m. The sun would set at

7:30. We had a one-hour flight and an additional hour's drive from the airport to the Gulf.

With our senses dulled from waiting hours in the terminal, we sat reading silently for most of the flight. Then as the plane began to descend over flat agricultural fields, I started to awaken to my surroundings. I turned to a friendly looking woman in her early sixties seated across from our row. She met my eyes and smiled. "Do you live near here?" I asked.

She had graying blonde hair braided down her back and wore jeans and a T-shirt. Yes, she said, she had lived most of her life in Harlingen, and she now was raising three grandchildren living there with her. She was a nurse, she said, and had a job at the hospital. I asked her how she liked living in Harlingen.

"I'm getting out of here as quickly as I can," she replied. "I was a nurse in Vietnam. I've seen combat and boys sent back with horrible wounds, damaged, never able to recover mentally. I've seen a lot of war violence in my time. I don't want to see any more of that. And I want my grandchildren to grow up somewhere else. As soon as I'm able, we're moving to Chicago."

Before I could ask for more details, she asked about our travel. I stumbled over my answer. "Why are we here? Uh, we've come to see the border for ourselves, to learn about the border wall, to meet people along the way, particularly agricultural workers." I felt naive and idealistic as soon as I opened my mouth, as though I failed to understand the dangers, as though we intended to sing "Kumbaya" while holding hands across the border. "It's a rough place. Y'all be careful out there," she cautioned. I thanked her, trying to show that I really did know what she meant, but I deserved the lecture for not having an answer better prepared.

With her dressing-down still hanging heavy in the air, the wheels of the 737 bounced once and then touched down for good as the engines roared. The plane slowed on the runway before coming to a stop at the small terminal. As we rose from our seats and got our bags from overhead, the nurse wished us well, and we thanked her. Then we rushed past the other gates and jogged toward the baggage claim and the Dollar rental car office. The sun was already low in the sky but still above the horizon. I knew we had little time, but I thought we should go for it. We ran toward the rental car exit where the warmth and the humidity wafting through the doors told us what was to come.

Before the trip I had purchased a number of maps, including the 167-page *Texas Atlas and Gazetteer*. But never having been to that side of the Gulf before, and suspecting there was likely to be no cell reception and no way to access GPS, I thought we had better ask for exact directions just in case. It turned out that the Latino attendant at Dollar knew Boca Chica well.

"Just take Route 4 and when you get to the sand, turn right. You can't miss it. I go down there some. It's a good fishing spot."

Another man standing in line, an air conditioning technician in a tan uniform with his name above the pocket, perked up at the thought of casting a line. He asked some details. Fortunately the attendant answered and I didn't have to explain that we didn't have fishing rods with us, that all I was taking was a camera. We also had to get out of there quick. I tried to tell the attendant our trip details privately.

"The rental has to be one-way. I need to leave the car in Tucson," I said in a lowered voice.

"It's a lot more expensive to do a trip that way," he replied, trying to talk us out of it.

"We just don't have time to make it back here. Returning the car would add another thousand miles and several more days, maybe a week, to our trip." I also believed backtracking would be anticlimactic. We just wanted to make the trip from east to west and then fly back to North Carolina. I didn't mention that the car was about to see some real action.

Sand. Gulf. Fishing. A road that runs into beach. That didn't sound bad at all, even if the seasoned former Army nurse had just told us she was getting the hell out of the borderlands as soon as she could. Already two types of flight, one a promising arrival by plane, and the other a grandmother trying to run away from Harlingen to Chicago, and we hadn't even left the airport.

# FIVE

# Of Roads, Fences, and Neighbors

FROM MY LIBRARY IN NORTH CAROLINA

JOHN STEINBECK'S BOOKS ABOUT AGRICULTURAL WORKERS, including *The Grapes of Wrath*, *In Dubious Battle*, and *Of Mice and Men*, have been seminal to my understanding of farm work. But his book *Travels with Charley*, a tale of his cross-country trip with his dog, is the one that most helped me understand my odyssey. He went on his journey, he said, because he felt distant from this country. Though he had worked as a farmworker advocate and written dozens of works that captured the 1930s as well as anyone, Steinbeck said he was out of touch. Without travel, writing dies, he said.

Steinbeck wrote, "An American writer, writing about America" needs to soak in more than one can learn from "books and

A bus stop with a billboard beside the border wall in Nogales, Sonora. The crosses mounted on the wall are for remembering migrants who died attempting to make it to the United States.

newspapers." A writer has to get moving. Though he had traveled much while young, he had lately lived too much in one place. "I had not heard the speech of America, smelled the grass, the trees, the sewage, seen its hills and water, its color and quality of light. . . . In short, I was writing about something I did not know about, and it seems to me that in a so-called writer this is criminal."

In 1962, Steinbeck left in his truck "Rocinante" to see the country. Rounding the West and heading south to Louisiana, he drove directly into the land of blatant racism. There he picked up a hitchhiker who spewed epithets. Steinbeck stopped and made him get out, and the man screamed "Nigger lover" at him as he drove away. Steinbeck would continue through the South, ending his sojourn at Abingdon, Virginia, near where I grew up.

Steinbeck would have understood our trip, though not many others did. No travel guides would have dared recommend it. Tour groups had canceled their itineraries anywhere near the border. The State Department had renewed travel warnings for the entire border region. Friends cautioned us to avoid the risk. Family members wanted reassurances about our safety, and some asked hard questions we couldn't answer. But I listened to the quixotic voices like Steinbeck's instead. His plan had been simply to hop into his truck and circumnavigate the nation without much of an itinerary. He called his journey "clear, concise, and reasonable," and then named his truck after Don Quixote's horse and began to wander the countryside, a knight errant. He said, "After years of struggle, we find that we do not take a trip, but a trip takes us." The struggle he referred to is one with ourselves, as happens when we try to give up control and trust in the motive even when everything else is shaky.

| | | |

I REMEMBER USING the phrase "good fences make good neighbors" a few times in casual conversations back when I was first starting our farm. I must have been drawn to the cliché's apparent nod to self-reliance and ownership, its allusion to agriculture and the hard work that farm fences symbolize. I thought I agreed with it. But in 1985, shortly before the Latino men started working for me, I read Robert Frost's full poem, "Mending Wall." Frost states, "Something there is that doesn't love a wall" and quotes his neighbor saying, "Good fences make good neighbors," but then he calls it into question. "I wonder / If I could put a notion in his head: / 'Why do they make good neighbors? Isn't it / Where there are cows? But here there are no cows. / Before I built a wall I'd ask to know / What I was walling in or walling out / And to whom I was like to give offense." I had been completely wrong about the line. If you build a fence for anything other than cattle, Frost believed, you contain as much as you keep out.

When I returned to the poem again in the context of our border travels several decades later, I realized that the "*something* there is," complex even for Frost to put into words, was why I was going south. That "something" urged me on with the same heartfelt feeling that made Ronald Reagan's memorable "Mr. Gorbachev, tear down this wall" resonate with so many Americans.

Though many times our country had failed miserably at promoting freedom here and abroad, President Reagan's speech at the Berlin Wall had been a shining moment that touched on America's best ideals. What citizen could disagree? We stood for tearing down walls between people. Something there is—deep down in America, in Americans— that doesn't love a wall. Travel is more our style. If nothing else, we, "the huddled masses, the wretched refuse of teeming shores," know what it means to be on the move. Our dreams are in motion.

# SIX

# Boca Chica Sunset

BROWNSVILLE, TEXAS

HOPE NAVIGATED US TO THE BOCA CHICA HIGHWAY, BUT THE traffic was thick and the stoplights frequent. As soon as we found an opening I sped up, running yellow lights and a few red ones to get out of Harlingen. At first we were on a highway crowded with businesses and fast-food places, followed by a two-lane stretch with scattered houses and mailboxes, then ranches, then nothing but marsh and sand and no people at all. The sky turned a brilliant pink and the witching hour arrived. I pushed the gas pedal harder.

We were doing eighty miles per hour down the spit of land toward Boca when the red ball of the sun left us. Though now filled with color, the sky was darkening by the minute. When you get to the sand, the agent had said, go right. I repeated the simple directions aloud as we neared the south of Brazos Island, the last barrier island in Texas. We were in a small car, a Chevrolet Cruze, not advertised as an all-terrain vehicle.

When we hit sand, I braked, but we were still doing fifty when the pavement ended. Before we had a chance to think we were bumping over the uneven terrain of the beach, and I started turning right almost by instinct, heading south. When

the car began to bog down, I knew I had turned south way too soon. The Chevy's tires sank deep into the sand; the car lurched and lost speed fast.

The Boca Chica beach at the Rio Grande and the rented Chevy Cruze at sunset.

Luckily I hadn't braked too hard and momentum kept us plowing ahead. Fishtailing and dodging around two trucks backed up toward the water, I steered the car to the hard sand near the breakers. Fishermen in the surf and others sitting on their tailgates looked up, and a few waved just as the tires gripped the smoother track and we forged ahead. We waved back, wishing we could have stopped. Half a minute later we were doing forty miles per hour and bouncing along on tracks of shells and hard sand. The sky was graying.

"Slow down," Hope shouted as we bottomed out a few times on rough spots. I was still a little crazed from navigating all the traffic and the impossible challenge of beating the setting sun. "I've been planning this trip for months and I've got to get some pictures while we still have light," I answered. My old digital Olympus camera wasn't great at night-time shooting. "Besides," I said, "There are two types of vehicles that can go anywhere: a tank and a rental car!" She held on. I gripped the steering wheel and gave the shocks a workout.

At the most intense moment of driving, when the wheels seemed to leave the sand at one point, I got a cellphone call, and seeing the number I felt I had to answer. Hearing Spanish on the other end, I shouted back a line or two about being at Boca Chica. Then the call went dead. Though we had never met, I knew the voice had to belong to Santiago, the ranch hand we were supposed to meet by 8:00. It was 7:30 already and all we had time to say was "*hasta pronto!*"

The Boca Chica of the Rio Grande as it is called on the U.S. side, or Rio Bravo as it is known in Mexico, was some two miles away, but as we barreled down the beach we began to see a lighthouse whirling its beacon over the little river in the distance. Rushing toward it, we came to a stop in the corner formed by the Gulf and the Rio. "Little mouth" is exactly right; there is nothing *grande* at all about it. I jumped out of the car and went for my camera in the back seat. There was just enough light left to get a few shots. Having missed the last good light by some twenty minutes, the dusky colors post-sunset would have to do.

Only after I'd taken some pictures did I start to breathe deeply and take in the scene. The gentle rhythm of the Gulf waves and the mild ocean breeze, along with the view in front of us of three Mexican fishermen, likely a father and two sons, casting a net, calmed my nerves almost instantly. I let my shoulders drop and took off my shoes, as if to let my stress run out of my legs and into the sand. The sand was cool and soft, the waves gentle, the water inviting.

While planning the trip, I'd imagined confrontations in a no-man's-land with border guards in black uniforms, fences, spotlights, motion detectors, and signs warning of dire consequences: violators will be prosecuted, no photographs! Instead, we found only hand-net fishermen casting in the surf, a pickup with its doors open, a family gathered around a fire, the simple lighthouse whirling its modest light, and our rental car—the only vehicle visible anywhere in sight on the U.S. side. We stood taking pictures in the last of red sky at night, gentle waves washing ashore, the color and the gentle sounds all making me want to sit down and rest.

The tide was at its lowest at 7:30—I had known that from reading on-line charts, so that part of our timing was perfect. This made the channel seem so shallow that I likely could have waded into Mexico without getting my underwear wet. Somewhere out in front of me in the water was the international line, but there were no markers. I cooled my feet in the gentle surf. "Perfect for swimming," I said to Hope. The fishermen seemed oblivious to us as they continued casting in our direction, now only fifty yards away, not looking even when I attempted to call out to them. They kept coming up empty, reaching back, and casting the twirling net again. A motorboat passed near them, heading from river to Gulf, and turned toward the north. Either nationality could take a boat into the channel. The turn at the end, either north or south at Boca Chica into national waters, was the restricted part. No one was there to check anyway. We were the only Americans present, with our Chevrolet on a deserted beach. We could have been in a car commercial. For those few moments all seemed right with the world.

Except that it wasn't. Just a few hundred miles to our east lay the damaged Deepwater Horizon oil rig that had exploded one month before, killing eleven, injuring seventeen. It was still pumping at least fifty thousand barrels of oil per day into the same body of water my feet were in. And at points westward on the borderline there was untold turmoil. But at that moment none of it seemed real.

I could have stayed for hours, building a fire and watching the darkening waves and the fishermen until they quit. For a few moments I breathed in the salt air and did nothing. The rise and fall of my body kept time with the waves. Then one last shot with my camera: pink one direction, fishermen another, lighthouse beam passing across breakers, dark.

# SEVEN

# The Ghosts of Palmito Ranch

RIO BRAVO NEAR BOCA CHICA

"SANTIAGO'S WAITING FOR US," HOPE REMINDED ME. "WE'VE got to go." We started the car, found the hardened tracks, and headed back toward pavement. All the U.S. fishermen had gone home and there were no other cars on the beach. At the blacktop we got a phone signal again, and Hope called the number. Santiago answered on the first ring. He said he was on Route 4 at a spot we had whizzed past less than an hour before. He said he would be waiting in an old Ford pickup at the end of the dirt road near the Texas historical marker.

It had been impossible to see much of anything running eighty on the way in, but heading back, the metal sign under a grove of mesquite caught the headlights. I pulled off for

Santiago, with his assault rifle, peers into the Rio Grande at Palmito Hill Ranch.

a few seconds to take a photo of that old marker, not knowing whether I would get another chance. The marker's text began, "Battle of Palmito Ranch, The last land engagement of the Civil War was fought near this site . . ." I read it by our headlights, knowing that this was the ranch where we would be staying the night. Then just as my camera flash lit up the dusk, I saw Santiago up the road, standing at his truck and waving to us.

I had wanted to camp out in a tent on our first night in Brazos Island State Park at the south end of the Texas outer banks, though there were no camping facilities anywhere nearby—just sand and salt marsh. Hope and I had different views about it. I didn't want to sleep in a motel in Brownsville. She hated the thought of mosquitoes and no bathrooms. I argued that the Union forces had camped at Brazos Island prior to their confrontation with Confederates at the last battle. The area was so historically important, I said, and besides we would have a mosquito net on our tent. That argument got me nowhere. Then one phone call changed everything.

For several nights in March we had sat together at the kitchen table looking at maps and making calls, searching for places to stay along the border route. I called the number of a bed-and-breakfast in Del Rio, Texas, anticipating we might be there on the fourth night of the trip. Until then, most arrangements had been tentative. Then I reached Sarah Boone.

Hailing from Alabama, Sarah exuded a sense of warmth that made me want to tell her everything. When she asked why we were interested in going to Del Rio, I gave her my whole clumsy spiel. "We're traveling the full length of the border to help us understand immigration and the border wall, and get to know what people who live near the border think about their lives and the places surrounding them. I'm especially concerned about farmworkers where I live and I wanted to make a pilgrimage to the border for education, for connection, and in tribute to them."

I said it all in one breath and braced for her reaction, knowing it could cause her to go silent or worse. I had already endured a not-so-friendly response from a B&B owner in Marfa, Texas, who blurted out, "They should all be deported." She was the same one who said that the Gulf oil spill had been natural and harmless—her husband worked on cleaning up oil spills. Further dialogue had been impossible. So I cringed a little as I awaited Sarah's response.

She nearly shouted into the phone, "Honey, I love what you're doing and I want to help you! I'm going to give you a discount for our place and I'm part of a whole border network all along where I can get you in touch with people and find places to stay and I'll help introduce you to them, too. Send me something in writing about you and your trip. And give me a few days. For starters, I've got a great guy I can put you in touch with at Brownsville." I couldn't believe our luck. I got off the phone pumping my fist, and told Hope, "It looks like you won't be camping in a mosquito marsh after all!"

As promised, emails from Sarah with contact information began to arrive the next day, along with copies of her notes to her friends, many of them including her glowing introduction. One email included a spreadsheet with names, addresses, and phone numbers, along with Sarah's commentary on all of them. The list existed nowhere else; she had made this one for us with people she had met. "Many of these folks are friends of mine; these are excellent resource people who can help you get to know the border firsthand." Suddenly she had turned maps and websites into people, and she was making appointments with us and for us. Overnight, Sarah had become our border angel.

The contact list spread from the Gulf of Mexico to California. Names of mayors, priests, human rights activists, environmentalists, journalists, and others in small border towns accompanied lists of places to stay and eat. The names included several professors—people whose scholarship encompasses border and immigration studies. Professor Tony Zavaleta of Brownsville was one of them.

Tony's first message to Sarah conveyed pure Texas hospitality: "They are welcome to stay at my ranch house which has charm, electricity, a toilet, beds, a refrigerator and telephone." In follow-ups with Tony, I learned he was dedicated to the border, both as the director of the Center for Border and Transnational Studies at the University of Texas at Brownsville and as the owner of Palmito Ranch, the southernmost ranch in the entire United States. With his older relatives passed away, he had become the sole caretaker of this important historical place that few have heard of. Santiago, meeting us on Route 4, was his ranch hand and host when Tony couldn't be there.

After planning to stay with us, Tony was called away unexpectedly by his work. Apologizing profusely, he assured me that Santiago was both savvy about life on the border and a good cook. "He will take care of you for the night." Once Tony learned that we spoke Spanish, he was confident we would get along fine.

When we drove up next to Santiago's beat-up but stout four-wheel-drive pickup, it made our rental car look like a shiny toy. I could tell by the truck's knobby tires that the road we were headed to could demand something more substantial than a sedan made for pavement. But the car had already passed the sand dune test. How much worse could it get?

Santiago, sixty-eight, was built like his truck: worn but strong. He was beside our car and reaching in to shake hands before we could get out to meet him. Packing a black 9 mm pistol clearly visible in a belt holster on his side, he smiled and said, "Buenas noches, bienvenidos a Palmito!" A minute later we were following him down the dirt road to the Palmito entrance. The banged-up truck had a Texas tag; on the tailgate was a cartoon of the "Virgencita de Guadalupe," and on the bumper was an old black-and-white sticker that read, "No border wall." Someone had tried to scrape it off, but it was still legible.

Santiago stopped and opened the gate, and we pulled into the driveway behind him. We cut through tough, dry weeds that scraped the bottom of the car like they were made of steel. I wondered if they were taking the paint off the sides as I tried only half-successfully to straddle the deep ruts carved by hard rains. You could tell that cars as low as ours hadn't entered the road for years.

| | | |

I HAD NEVER HEARD of the Battle of Palmito Ranch, I confessed to Tony when we first talked on the phone. When he began telling the story, I was riveted. The place had been in his family for seven generations, he said. His ancestors had lived there tending their goats and corn when Civil War troops began shooting at one another in the field out in front of the house.

He also told me details from stories he had written about the numerous ghosts he and others had seen around his place. Dozens of them have appeared here, he said, including an apparition of La Llorona, the crying woman who had allegedly killed her children and now wandered forever looking for them, a Maya king who had died on a knoll overlooking the Rio Bravo after traveling there from Mesoamerica, and, connected to the battle, a number of black Union troops killed here.

I asked him if he had seen any ghosts himself. "All the time," he replied. He also had physical evidence. One day an Indian-head penny had appeared on his porch—minted in 1865. Another appeared the next day—it was from 1863. No one could have come onto the porch without his knowing it, he said. After exhausting every other possibility, Tony was convinced that soldiers killed in the Civil War battle had left them as a message. I'd heard of ghost sightings like he described at other battlefields; they seem especially commonplace where there are unresolved deaths and no closure. Palmito Ranch—actually the whole border—seemed rife with the unsettled. Of course there would be stories of ghosts.

The last battle of the Civil War was fought there on May 12 and 13, 1865, an entire month after Lee surrendered to Grant at Appomattox on April 9. It ended in a Confederate victory—an ultimately meaningless one, but a clear victory nonetheless. There were at least sixteen Union casualties and over a hundred more captured, all for naught.

The conflict began when three Union regiments—the Sixty-Second U.S. Colored Troops made up of free blacks and former slaves, the

Second Texas Union Cavalry, and the Thirty-Fourth Indiana Volunteer Infantry—were mustered from their camp on Brazos Island at Boca Chica and sent toward Brownsville, Texas. Their commander, Colonel Theodore H. Barrett, had set his sights on taking possession of a Confederate trading post at a Mexican border boomtown named Bagdad, located across the river near Matamoros. According to the historian Jeffrey Hunt, Barrett wanted to enhance his reputation before the war ended, though his maneuver was "in direct violation of orders from headquarters."[1] Barrett believed he could wrap up the skirmish fast and with minimal casualties. Colonel Rip Ford, commanding officer of the Second Texas Cavalry of the CSA, at Bagdad, begged to differ.

The only strategic justification for the battle was to end the shipments of munitions, medicines, and supplies from Mexico still flooding across the river into Confederate camps near Brownsville. Union troops had already blockaded the flow of war materiel in the East. Even the routes on the Mississippi River had been stopped. Bagdad, however, was still sending shipments into the Confederacy. With Union troops ordered to keep clear of the border so as to prevent any conflicts with Mexico, rebel troops had moved into a location south of the Rio Grande and the port had flourished. By the spring of 1865, Bagdad had become the South's main seaport, and the Second Texas Cavalry was stationed there to protect it.

The river was much deeper then—before drought, irrigation, and municipalities siphoned off the Rio's water upstream. Blockade-runner ships anchored at Bagdad hauled Confederate cotton into the Gulf and eventually to England, returning from Europe with every type of good available for resale. Professional traders took advantage of the flowing water and money, and the town mushroomed. Over twenty thousand people lived in Bagdad's makeshift shanties in its heyday. Bars and brothels opened there as well. Local critics compared Bagdad to the biblical Sodom and Gomorrah.

---

1. Jeffrey W. Hunt, *The Last Battle of the Civil War: Palmetto Ranch*, 2.

By mid-May officers on both sides surely knew of Lee's surrender a month earlier, but the Confederates held on in Bagdad because of the economic importance of the site, and they saw the potential of the place after the war's end. Commerce, they surmised, would be as important in the war's aftermath as it had been during it. They were not about to abandon the site because of the surrender in faraway Virginia. This was about the economy beyond the war.

Barrett's main unit was the Sixty-Second U.S. Colored Troops, a group of 250 infantry. Some of them had once worked under the whip on plantations, and now they fought in uniform for the U.S. government—for freedom. Some of the survivors would go on after the war to make a name for themselves as Buffalo Soldiers. When first conscripted these soldiers had served in the First Missouri Colored Infantry stationed in Louisiana, one of the worst assignments possible in the U.S. military due to the heat, humidity, and mosquitoes. After many died of disease in the swamps, the surviving troops were transferred to Brownsville—not exactly a healthy climate either—to serve out the remainder of the war. Even in May we welcomed air conditioning in our car in the morning. We could only imagine how their woolen uniforms and high boots must have felt as the troops marched across the wetlands in close formation toward Bagdad.

Also fighting for the Union that day was the unit some called the Texas Yankees—the Second Texas Union Cavalry. Though the Texas Confederates hated former slaves, they hated Texas Yankee whites even more. To the Texas rebels, the Texas Union loyalists were homegrown traitors. But many of these particular Texans had no cause to fight against the Union. Some were of Mexican origin and had even fought for President Benito Juárez, defending Mexico against the invading French. Some were small landholders or sharecroppers who had chosen to be annexed by the United States in 1848 following the Mexican-American War. When the slaveholders of Texas and their allies revolted against Lincoln and the North, these former Mexicans had no reason to join them. In fact, many had more in common with the slaves than the owners. After living through Mexico's difficult times, inclusion in the United States was likely a good deal for them.

Joining these units of blacks, Latinos, and Texas white Yankees was the Thirty-Fourth Indiana Volunteer Infantry, an all-white unit of farm boys from the Midwest. When combined, these Union troops reflected perhaps the greatest ethnic diversity ever fielded during the Civil War. Tragically, however, this assortment of troops was on a suicide mission for Barrett's vainglory.

Adding to the strangeness of the scene, Mexican nationals and even French soldiers were also on site that day in 1865. At that time, the democratically elected Juárez was in exile in Paso del Norte, later called Ciudad Juarez. The French-born self-appointed emperor, Maximilian, who had deposed Juárez, had taken power. His reign was at its apex in 1865. Ignoring France's insistence that he step down, Maximilian pushed north to the Rio and gained control of all of Mexico. Though his influence would soon wane, Maximilian's soldiers stood at the ready near Bagdad, making sure they lost no territory in the American battle. They only observed that day, but as Mexico had already seen American land-grabbing in decades prior, they had just cause for being there.

As the first foot soldiers in the Yankee units reached the river without cavalry support, Ford's Confederate cavalry charged across the water, outflanked them, and then bore down on the Colored Troops, killing at least sixteen and capturing over a hundred more. This sent the Union forces retreating back toward Padre Island. As the Northern troops fell back, the rebel cavalry overtook them at Palmito Hill, routing the lines and sending the whipped Union force back toward the Gulf. The Union cavalry never gained ground.

The mission Barrett had thought would be a cakewalk ended in bitter defeat. Some of the Indiana infantry troops wrote that the whole debacle was a humiliation for them—a sad ending to a stellar fighting record throughout the war. We have no known written record left by members of the black regiment. But as the ghost stories collected on the Zavaleta ranch reveal, they apparently haven't let us forget they were there.

Some of Tony's ancestors at Palmito Ranch had been born in Mexico, but by the time of the battle they were U.S. residents, having gone nowhere. Following continuous skirmishes and then a full-blown war in the years between 1845 and 1848, the U.S. border had been pushed over eighteen hundred miles southward to its Rio Grande location, all by force. Mexico had once extended all the way to what is now California's northern border. Now the river some two thousand miles south of there was the line. In 1865, the Rio Grande was back in the middle of conflict, and the family who owned the ranch beside it could only wait out one of the strangest battles ever to take place on U.S. soil.

When the U.S. Civil War's end finally came to Texas—helped along by the presence of large numbers of Union soldiers who arrived to clean things up following the battle—some Confederates went to Mexico and volunteered for Maximilian's army. But even with their help, Maximilian failed to stand against the renewed Juarista forces that had been boosted back to power by both a popular domestic uprising and financial aid from the U.S. government. Maximilian was captured and executed by firing squad in 1867. Since then Mexico has remained under home rule and the border at the Rio has not moved. But that is not to say it has been stable.

|   |   |   |   |

JACINTO, A PRESENT-DAY HUICHOL SHAMAN, had visited the ranch at Tony's invitation a few years before us. It didn't take long for him to make contact with the spirits there; he went into a trance as soon as he stepped onto the deck. He saw scores of spirits wandering across Palmito Hill and told Professor Zavaleta the following: "There are spirits everywhere, and some are very old. There are *indios* like me and a prince of Mayan people." Tony recalled Jacinto's report in writing: "There are *negritos*, called buffalo soldiers as well as many other people who lived

2. Ibid.

and died there. I can see that there was once a time when great armies roamed this place. . . . A great battle ensued—white against black—while a third army observed the carnage from the southern bank of the river but did not engage."[2]

Jacinto asked the legion of wandering souls why they had chosen Palmito. They replied that the ranch is a portal between the past and present, a place where much remains untold and unsettled. Traveling through the passage were the ghosts of indigenous peoples, Tejanos, Mexicans, Americans, Northern and Southern, black and white, all of whom had died somewhere on the site, Jacinto reported. He saw soldiers of three armies; some spoke English, some Spanish, and some French. Along the banks of the lower Rio Grande valley, Tony concluded, "Life, suffering, and death are equally guaranteed."[3]

We approached the old unpainted wooden house after dark and climbed the stairs to the deck where Tony had found the coins. Having read the ghost stories before arriving, my senses were primed for possible sightings. I had no idea what would be in store for us that night. Part of me was eager to find out.

---

3. Antonio Zavaleta, "The Ghosts of Historic Palmito Hill Ranch," 3.

# EIGHT

# El Ranchero

BROWNSVILLE, TEXAS AND MATAMOROS,
TAMAULIPAS

RAISED WITH TELEVISION WESTERNS LIKE *BONANZA*, MY
childhood dreams of ranches contained pretty expanses of rolling hills with grass, plenty of water, and enough high-dollar
cattle to pay all the bills. The ranch hands were white men, rug-
gedly handsome cowboys who spoke English with a twang, and
who would fight for the American flag at the drop of a hat. Few
of the melodramas mentioned the fact that the whole cowboy
or *vaquero* culture was of Mexican origin. Usually there were no
Mexican cowboy good guys at all. Most of the Latinos I saw on
TV were desperados.

Palmito Ranch belied all that. As Santiago helped carry our
bags across the deck and inside the dusty house filled with
mounted deer heads, skulls and bones of animals, old house and
ranch implements, and Catholic relics all covered with layers of
dust, it was obvious the place had not been invented by Hollywood. And Santiago was no television ranch hand.

Tony's family had possessed Palmito Ranch before there
were deeds to local land, and for generations, whether Mexican,
American, or both, they had scraped a living from the sandy
and hard soil where today even steely scrub brush struggles to

survive. They raised goats and cattle, and tried to coax corn and beans
and chilies from the unforgiving
ground. After they could no longer

Santiago stands by the old chimney
where he saw a man disappear at Palmito Hill Ranch, Boca Chica, Texas.

hold on as ranchers, the family moved away, hiring caretakers like Santiago to look after the place. The family still visits when they can, but the
crops and livestock were long gone and the last chapter of the ranch's
history of agriculture had all but ended.

| | | |

THERE HAD BEEN FEWER than two thousand Mexican *rancheros*
living in the sparse Tejas state when the first English-speaking white
squatters started arriving there around 1820. Some settlers came from

southern slaveholding areas to expand their cotton fields. Some sought land for cattle and soon adopted agricultural skills perfected over the generations by traditional Mexican *vaqueros* living in the area. But, as Americans are wont to do, they ramped up everything, increased the numbers of head of livestock per acre, plowed up some marginal land and planted wheat, corn, and cotton, and eventually engaged in huge cattle drives across the open country northward to supply meat to eastern markets. The small *rancheros* used to open grazing had little say as the newcomer farmers built fences and wore out the land, and the cattlemen increased their livestock numbers and overgrazed the native grasses.

Mexico's new government, which had only won its independence from Spain in 1810, tried to ward off the American onslaught by offering land grants in Tejas to additional Mexican settlers. But the resulting trickle northward into Tejas met a flood of Americans arriving by the 1830s, and they, along with the original Mexican settlers, got swept along with the tide. When the state was made part of the United States, so were the area's inhabitants. That Palmito Ranch was still intact, still held by the same family for generations, and now recognized as a Texas Century Ranch, was a tribute both to the grit of the earliest *rancheros* and to their descendants' efforts to cling to what they had wrought by hand.

| | | |

WE PUT OUR BAGS in our bedroom and at Santiago's beckoning, sat down at the kitchen table. Santiago gave us beer and bottled water he had just purchased in town. Palmito Ranch had a well, but they were unsure about the water's safety. An old windmill that once pumped groundwater still worked, and the tank still held hundreds of gallons, but we didn't drink it. It is remarkable that any water could be pumped out of the ground at all with the river so precarious that some had taken to calling it the Rio *Seco* (dry). The dried brush covering the ranch was a sign of how little moisture was in the fields. Some mesquite trees hung on, but that was due to nature's perseverance, not agriculture's.

Santiago set to work preparing food on the propane gas stovetop—beans, steak, sautéed peppers and onions, and tortillas. He accepted no help. As we sat and watched, I noticed the day's Matamoros newspaper on the table nearby was nearly covered with photos of bloodied bodies. "Four Men Executed," the headline said in Spanish. It was a sickening sight, especially on the dinner table.

Four unidentified men, likely small-time drug runners connected to the cartels, had been murdered in the streets of Matamoros the day before our arrival—just ten miles to the south of where we would be sleeping. I gestured toward the grisly photos and asked Santiago what he thought. He knew nothing of the details, he said, but guessed that they were more than nameless thugs now lying in the gutter. They were someone's sons, husbands, or fathers, he said, but there was no justice for them in Mexico. Drug gangs can just kill these guys and no one prosecutes them.

Maybe their families had failed at farming or ranching somewhere in rural Mexico, he said, and they had made a decision to leave all that. Maybe their fathers had already left for the United States and the youths had grown up without men in their lives. Maybe that was why they took some wrong turns. Maybe they had been kidnapped, trafficked, and made to work for the drug lords. But that was only speculation, as the newspaper could only report that the victims had met their demise at the point of unknown guns, their faces mutilated, unidentifiable. All that the reporter could say was that it was likely drug-related. There was no digging deeper into the deaths—too many journalists had already died for their work.

The victims had no identification on them, the paper said. Thus the victims' families might never learn what had happened. Forensics teams were already overburdened. Refrigerated trucks serving as makeshift morgues were full of the unidentified and unclaimed. As many as sixty thousand people had met their demise in modern Mexican drug wars, and too many had ended up *sin nombre*, nameless bodies waiting to be identified so they might be interred.

I thought again of Jacinto's trance, his trip into the netherworld, and the hordes of borderland ghosts he'd seen at the ranch. Weren't these new deaths similar in that people had died in questionable circumstances? If so, would their souls wander? The portal at Palmito couldn't possibly support the uncounted thousands who had died at the border. Not even Jacinto could decipher the cacophony of voices.

As the *bistek* sizzled a few more minutes in the pan over the gas fire, Santiago began showing us around the room. There were longhorn cattle skulls, mounted deer heads taken as hunters' prizes over the generations, dried armadillo shells, snake skins, and Civil War artifacts dug up by years of plowing the fields—swords, bullets, bits from bridles—and a femur Santiago said was "*humano!*" Hope gasped. Pictures of saints stared down at the bones and blessed them, whether animal or human. The bones lay among the weapons of war, together telling of the ranch's connection to nature, layers of history, religion, death, and the afterlife, all in piles. Eating a meal in that setting meant swallowing both human struggle and mortality.

Well after sundown the old weatherboard house remained hot. We sweated as we talked and ate, gazing around at the memorabilia along the walls. The air hung with humidity, houseflies, and our mix of emotions and thoughts of battles and blood and ghosts. Thanks to the strange amenity of air travel, we had gone from the cushioned seats of an air-conditioned jet to seeing old fishing nets cast into tranquil Gulf waters, to death scenes, battlefields, and Mexican food simmering on a gas burner under a bare lightbulb—all spoken in Spanish, on the same day we had left home, as the image of the *Virgen* of Guadalupe above the door looked upon us with her benevolent, all-knowing smile.

The food was perfect. As we washed it down with another Tecate beer Santiago pulled out of a cooler of ice, we asked him about his life. He was eager to share. He had started working in restaurants when he first arrived in the United States and had learned his excellent cooking skills that way. He had crossed the border back when immigration had been a little easier, back before the high fences and the increased Border Patrol numbers.

He had grown up on a *rancho* but later trained as a palace guard for the president of Mexico in the late 1960s. He joined the police force with the idealism of youth, but then was forced to see government corruption up close. Already disillusioned, he quit the force for good, he said, when military snipers, and then a whole cadre of government soldiers, shot into a crowd of unarmed students demonstrating near the palace in 1968. Santiago witnessed the killing of hundreds of innocents, a tragedy that outraged the world. The "Tlatelolco Massacre" was the worst in the era of unrest of the 1960s, yet the Mexican government refused to investigate. To this day, no one knows exactly how many died there. Santiago left Mexico soon after, angry and jaded. Arriving in Texas, he took odd jobs and later obtained a green card thanks to the immigration reform law known as IRCA of 1986. Since then he had encountered a number of roadblocks in his efforts to obtain his citizenship, mostly financial in nature. Almost thirty years later, his green card, which he pulled from his wallet, was all he had to show us. Though well past retirement age, his job on the ranch and his meager savings were his sole sources of income. He received no Social Security payments.

His story about citizenship echoed those of many Mexican and Central American immigrants I've met over the years. They wait in line fifteen or twenty years for their papers—if they enter the country with a visa, that is. If they come in without one, *como mojado* as they say, there has been almost nothing they can do to gain legal status. Even with a green card and waiting for so many years, Santiago says he still can't pull together the thousands of dollars to pay lawyers. The government charges five hundred dollars, but the legal fees can be twenty times that. So he continued to live like millions of others who have crossed: betwixt and between, in the borderlands of citizenship.

After our meal, Santiago plugged in the new freestanding swamp-cooler air conditioner Tony had just purchased for our stay. After sweating through supper, we were eager to see if it worked. Santiago would sleep in the next room without the machine, he said. Worse, we realized the hot air exhaust from our room was not vented outdoors but blasted heat into the rest of the house, including where Santiago would be sleep-ing. We protested, but he would have it no other way. We were the guests. He was there to make us comfortable.

Before we turned in, Santiago ducked into his room and came back quickly. He had another bit of assurance to offer us for the night, he said, and held up a black, semiautomatic assault rifle. He smiled and hugged it close. "This is my sleeping companion for the night," he said. "Don't worry about anything bothering you. I've got this." Then he promised we would all shoot that and other guns the next morning for fun, and turned to enter his bedroom.

"Sorry, Santiago, I've got one more thing to ask," I said, then brought up the ghost sightings Tony had written about. Santiago replied, "I don't worry about any ghost but the Holy Ghost!" Then he said good night again. We thanked him for his hospitality and the incredible meal and went into our room. I lay down with the slightly cooler air blowing di-rectly on my skin and a box fan going full blast from the corner. I drifted in and out of sleep, sweating through the night, feeling that if I were go-ing to see my first ghost, this would be the time.

| | | |

THE NEXT MORNING, after fitful sleep and no ghost sightings to report, we arose to steak and eggs and tortillas frying on the grill. All the guns—the semiautomatic, two shotguns, and the pistol Santiago had worn on his belt—lay on the table next to where we would be eating. After another expert meal, Santiago urged us outside, brought out the guns, and showed how to click off the safety and pull the trigger. They were already loaded.

"Aim above the trees over across the river and fire," he said in Spanish.

"Over into Mexico?"

"*No hay problema*," he replied. "Nothing's over there. Just aim over the tree line." Hope and I shot rounds from all of the guns and Santiago joined us, chuckling a little each time. "*Mas!*" he kept urging. We blasted away, shooting the pistol, semiautomatic rifle, and one of the shotguns, firing at nothing in particular. The rapid fire of the rifle and the sharp staccato reports from the 9 mm were both surprisingly smooth; so little kick, so easy to handle.

After locking up the guns and holstering the pistol back on his belt, Santiago drove us in his truck to the lone chimney standing in the field near the river and said, "This was where I saw a man disappear into thin air. He was standing there by the chimney and as I went toward him he evaporated. I was shaking all over as I searched for him around behind the chimney, but he was nowhere." I didn't bring up the Holy Ghost discussion from the night before, but appreciated that Santiago had waited until daytime to tell us.

He led us from the chimney down a short path to the river he had cut with his grass trimmer the previous day. We stood at the steep bank and gazed across the narrow channel into Mexico. Tall and thick marsh grass waved in the morning breeze as dark storm clouds gathered to our south and began to head our way from Mexico. There was no fence at all at Palmito, and no border marker but the river—just water, river plants, and then dry-land vegetation as far as the eye could see.

I asked Santiago if he had seen anyone coming across the river there. He answered, "Sometimes migrants swim the river and pass through here on foot at night. I don't see as many as I used to. Boats pass by sometimes. Border Patrol boats, maybe drug runners do, too. But I don't get involved. I just keep working. I'm just the *ranchero*."

# NINE

# Border Guards

BORDER PATROL STATION, TEXAS STATE ROUTE 4

AFTER SAYING GOOD-BYE TO SANTIAGO, WE RETRACED OUR tracks along the ranch road, returned to the Route 4 pavement, and headed toward Brownsville. The clouds to the south darkened and the winds picked up, and a few drops of rain fell just as we neared the easternmost Border Patrol station in the United States. There had been no one checking eastbound traffic the night before, but

A Border Patrol truck drives away after checking the photographer's identity at Friendship Park near San Diego, California.

that morning plenty of signs warned westbound drivers to prepare to stop ahead. A small mobile office was situated alongside the road in the middle of sand and low-growing bushes. A large round cage fan was blowing air onto the area where the officers usually stand to inspect cars. The traffic that morning was so sparse that the two officers on duty were inside their small air-conditioned outbuilding when we pulled up to the huge stop signs and the yellow line. Since ours was likely the first westbound vehicle to approach the station that morning, no one was outside, and with rain coming, I thought we might get a wave-through.

I was wrong. As we slowed, a tall, heavyset man in his early thirties, dressed in a dark green uniform and a shiny and heavy black gun belt, stepped out of the building and walked toward our car. He said good morning and asked where we were headed. "To Brownsville," we both replied. Bending down and looking in the car window at both of us and into our back seat, he asked, "Are you U.S. citizens?" and we each answered "yes." He stepped back to wave us on. But knowing no one was behind us, I decided to ask him a few questions about his work before driving off.

His nametag said Johnson. He said he had come from the Midwest and hadn't worked on the border long. He told us he rarely saw people trying to sneak across where they were located. But migrants could wade or swim or cross by boat and then catch a ride with someone on the U.S. side and head toward Brownsville, he said. Or maybe there could be a drug run down the river during the night. I wanted to ask him how often that happened, but just then a bolt of lightning flashed as rain began to fall in huge sporadic drops and a gust of wind hit the side of our car. "Have a safe trip!" he said, running toward the building. Less than a minute later, rain fell so hard we could barely see the road.

Creeping along westward with the windshield wipers not keeping up, I bumped the dashboard with the heel of my hand. "Why didn't I ask to photograph him while we were talking?" I had realized then that I couldn't talk about our trip along the border without including the Border Patrol front and center. I knew it would be the first of many encounters, and so I wanted to start documenting them right away.

One of the first things to know about today's Border Patrol is that it is now under the auspices of Homeland Security, the anti-terrorist agency created after 9/11, and is no longer charged with merely controlling U.S./Mexico interchange. According to the U.S. Customs and Border Protection (CBP) website, the Border Patrol is on the front lines of the government's "War on Terror." That meant a huge change, but it was not the first revamping. Looking back over the last century, it is possible to trace our nation's history of deepest concerns by learning about the Border Patrol's different phases.

Back when they started patrolling in 1905, the border guards were a group of seventy-five watchmen under the auspices of U.S. Immigration Services. They operated out of El Paso and were charged with protecting the entire border—on horseback. In 1915, during the middle of the Mexican Revolution, Congress funded a separate entity known alternatively as the Mounted Guards or Mounted Inspectors. Their main charge was to track down migrants trying to come through Mexico, particularly Chinese people trying to get around the U.S. Chinese Exclusion Act—a law that blatantly tried to prevent Chinese people from immigrating to the United States. The Border Patrol's short website history doesn't even mention catching Mexican immigrants during those years—it wasn't a priority. The Chinese were the main target instead.

When Prohibition began in 1919, the patrol's focus changed to cracking down on illegal liquor being trafficked across the border for sale to dry Americans. The Prohibition-era recruits made $1,680 a year but had to furnish their horses and saddles out of their salary. By 1935 they had started using motorized vehicles. During the World War II years of 1941–1945, the force increased to over fourteen hundred officers. By then the Chinese were off the radar, and the Border Patrol was charged with searching for "Axis saboteurs"—namely the Germans, Italians, and Japanese.

It wasn't until around 1950 that "illegal immigrants" from Mexico began to be the explicit target, when some fifty-two thousand Mexicans were deported back to Mexico. That repatriation program known as

"Operation Wetback" occurred, perhaps not by chance, in the middle of the Bracero program's two decades. Coincidentally, that was also the beginning of the McCarthy era, when the misguided search for Communists commenced. It was during this time that the Border Patrol gained authority to search vehicles anywhere in the United States and law allowed the agents to arrest anyone traveling in the country without documentation. That was likely the first time officers began looking into cars and asking about citizenship.

With the passage of several fence-building bills in the mid-1990s, Including Operations "Gatekeeper" and "Hold the Line," which coincided with the passage of the North American Free Trade Agreement in 1994, the Border Patrol got another boost as their numbers were increased to over ten thousand.

I realized that the five men who came to my farm during the 1980s were part of the group the Border Patrol website said were "a tremendous influx of illegal immigration to America." I knew firsthand that some of their targeted population had come to fill jobs in poultry plants by invitation. I'd seen a photograph of a billboard in Oaxaca advertising the jobs. And the workers had told me as much. They weren't "illegals" to me; they had names, families, and jobs—and it was clear we had needed them, and asked them to come.

September 11 changed everything for America. Afterward, we began to fear a different enemy: a stateless and sinister group of terrorists with dirty bombs and an ideology of hate. But when the economy took a nosedive in the Bush years, fears of terrorism mixed with anxieties about losing our jobs and services to "illegals." New venom spewed on talk radio and TV. New vigilante groups sprang up. We began holding the line even more, and the Border Patrol numbers shot up to twenty thousand, which included new recruits like Officer Johnson stationed on Route 4.

Boca Chica wasn't the first place where I had been stopped by Border Patrol officers. I'd gone through numerous roadblocks while driving in Arizona in previous summers, often with groups of students in a BorderLinks van. I'd never felt comfortable with the exchanges, particularly with young people involved. The premise that the officers were there to keep us safe never comforted me either. I was especially bothered when some members of our diverse student group, particularly Latinos and Asians, were subjected to further questioning than the others. It was embarrassing to see them profiled, as their passports were taken in for inspection and held longer while all of us waited. At least the wait gave us time to think and talk about border policies.

Amidst the small talk and joking that went on in the van while officers took the passports inside and checked them by computer, I sometimes used the opportunity to ask what the students thought of it all. Once I told them about my connection to Checkpoint Charlie, the infamous Berlin gate into no-man's-land surrounded by barbed wire, brick walls, and barricades. My Uncle Bill had been stationed in Berlin during the Cold War. He brought back his stories and slides of that infamous barrier, and I had taken a special interest in it since he told us about it in the 1960s. Another time I asked two Korean students, one with a passport and the other, a student visa, about the Korean DMZ. It wasn't a happy comparison to have to make, but it resonated. One time as we drove away from an Arizona checkpoint, we tried to think of all the places in the world where walls like ours had been built and border guards were common, such as Northern Ireland and the West Bank or between Kuwait and Iraq, Botswana and Zimbabwe, Spain and Morocco, for example. None of these barriers had been encouraging places in the world, we concluded. The discussions were never lighthearted, but I believed it necessary to have them. I was in the business of helping educate citizens after all. Of course, we need police to protect us, and everyone can agree on that, but I believe it's okay for us to ask questions about how we are policed. Americans always have.

|   |   |   |   |

BORDER GUARDING HAD BEEN one of the few bright spots on the U.S. employment front during the Great Recession, and one of the few government jobs that representatives of both political parties champion. Tens of thousands of young people from their early twenties up to forty with "an ability to learn Spanish" had trained for and taken the jobs in the last twenty years. The patrol had hired men and women, Hispanic and white for the most part. Some new recruits had never seen the border before their training; some, like Officer Johnson, were rural people from the Midwest. Some were from the Southeast, as a training center had opened in South Carolina and in other locations far away from the border. The pay was good, with the advertised salary in 2010 ranging from $40,000 to over $70,000. The Border Patrol had been a veritable federal jobs stimulus plan, bringing a significant boost to the economy in this region that has lost its tourism. Sales of four-wheel-drive vehicles and motion detection and satellite technologies to find migrants had boomed as well.

For the applicants, the Border Patrol website advertised the work as follows:

> Customs and Border Protection employees protect our Nations [*sic*] borders from terrorism, human and drug smuggling and illegal entrance into the United States while simultaneously facilitating the flow of legitimate travel and trade. Border Patrol Agents play a vital role in preventing terrorists and terrorist weapons from entering the United States. Border Patrol Agents rescue individuals who fall into dangerous conditions traversing our borders.

The site said that 9/11 had changed their purview: "Since the terrorist attacks of September 11, 2001, the focus of the Border Patrol has changed to detection, apprehension and/or deterrence of terrorists and terrorist weapons." Of course we know the terrorists of 9/11 came through Canada by plane and with legal documents, but the Mexican border had been getting the most attention.

So many themes like that came up with the students in the van while we waited for the guards to return. "Are border checks effective?" I asked.

"Do you think the measures they're using are the best way to catch the bad guys?" One replied, "Wouldn't the worst of them be sophisticated enough to find other routes?" We knew from experience that the guards detain a lot of different people, as we were seeing at that very moment at the roadblock, and we, just a university group, were among them. I also brought up the drones at the border, and more discussion about surveillance and civil liberties ensued. Students who had traveled internationally, or who had lived elsewhere in places like Korea or Israel, were always good to bring in comparative perspectives.

We talked of other topics like U.S.-made guns, night-vision goggles, and body armor going south into Mexico, falling into the hands of the drug cartels, and allowing them to terrorize citizens there. In 2010 the *Miami Herald* reported that 253,000 U.S. guns are smuggled to Mexico annually. In other words, we are arming the cartels, and as Secretary of State Hillary Clinton said in Mexico in 2009, they are using our guns to shoot our guards and other U.S. citizens. And then there is the little-known tragedy of Border Patrol agents who have committed suicide— twenty of them in the two years prior to Hope's and my sojourn. There was never a shortage of topics to discuss with the students, even if the answers weren't always forthcoming.

|   |   |   |   |

MY UNCLE BILL'S assignment as a military vehicle driver had been to support the team guarding the East/West German border and to keep Checkpoint Charlie safe. I thought of two white men from rural areas fifty years apart in age: one named Thompson, the other Johnson. Two assignments: one at an urban checkpoint in the largest city in Germany in the Cold War, and the other at a little hut on a dead-end road in south Texas post 9/11. The former was a guard stationed by a massive wall only recently erected to try to contain communism and subsequently torn down— casting doubt on the reason for its construction. The latter was part of a newly militarized zone lined with walls, guards, and roadblocks that was still being expanded, and that now groaned under not only the weight of the past but also all that we live with now, and all that is yet to come.

As we neared Brownsville, I thought of Santiago. Sometime after the storm passed, I knew he would be heading back to his home in Brownsville and driving through the same border checkpoint we had just crossed. I could only imagine the exchange Santiago might have with Officer Johnson. I hoped it would be a conversation between peers, one newly arrived guard protecting today's border, perhaps learning something from a seasoned former palace guard from Mexico who had lived the border all his life. That's what I hoped for, but I feared something else.

# TEN

# Brownsville Raids

DOWNTOWN BROWNSVILLE, TEXAS

BY THE TIME WE REACHED BROWNSVILLE, THE STREETS WERE running like rivers, some low spots rushing two or three feet deep, and the winds were blowing at gale force. With trees bending over and ready to break in half, we knew we needed to seek cover fast. We spotted a sturdy brick drive-through behind a local restaurant on Route 4 and drove under it to wait. The women working inside knew what we were up to. They acknowledged us with a wave and didn't ask us to move. We waved back, mouthing a "thank you" for the favor. We waited under the shelter for over twenty minutes.

When the wind and rain began to slacken, we followed signs toward the Historic Brownsville Museum a few blocks away, careful not to drive into the lower dips where water pooled and a few cars had stalled out. We had seen the sign for the museum as we drove into town and hoped we could find more information about Fort Brown there, or even something of the soul of the city itself. As with so many American places, there was little to distinguish Brownsville at first glance. There was only the typical jumble of plastic colors and fast-food logos in a strip. Somehow the small, plain museum sign had stood out in all of this.

We found the stately brick museum, parked on the highest ground nearby, put on our rain jackets, and waded through water flooding over the sidewalks. We entered the building to find the floors inside also flooded. The staff people were mopping up when we entered, but they said we could wait inside the gift shop to keep safe. After fifteen minutes or so, they had the worst of the water puddles cleaned up and allowed us to pay our admission fee and enter the driest room first.

The border wall with a new road, lights, and a Border Patrol truck near Douglas, Arizona.

Inside we read panels about the Last Battle of the Civil War and Bagdad and looked at early photographs. After we had seen that room, we got permission to tiptoe around the puddles to visit the others. The next room contained hand-carved furniture that had once belonged to the Celaya family. Simon Celaya had been the president of the Rio Grande Railway, whose headquarters had been in the museum building back in its heyday. There was also some memorabilia in the room about the famous King Ranch in Texas. The owner, Richard King, had amassed his wealth by hauling troops and supplies during the Mexican-American War. Using those fortunes, he started buying land in the new state of Texas soon after the war ended. He owned 614,000 acres by the time of his death. His partner in the Rio Grande shipping business, Mifflin Kenedy, also bought over 600,000 acres, calling his expanse La Parra Ranch.

All of the museum exhibits were educational, but arriving back at the gift shop, I still hadn't seen anything about Fort Brown. I asked the hosts who had literally given us shelter in a storm, "Do you know where Fort Brown is?" None did. One of the young docents behind the counter mentioned that Texas Southmost College might have information in their library. But all agreed there was no other site to visit as far as they knew.

I'd read before the trip that Fort Brown had been a key border stronghold and that there had been a painful racial incident there, one eventually requiring a presidential pardon. I had wanted to see it or at least go to an exhibit about it, but as we walked out the door of the best museum around, I realized I would have to dig into the history of the place on my own. I began a quest that would lead me back into the past some two centuries.

The ghosts were unavoidable there. When I searched the web for Fort Brown, several sites came up that mentioned a military graveyard where thirty-eight hundred soldiers were buried and an infirmary where amputations and deaths were common. One site concerning Texas ghosts zeroed in on Fort Brown's graveyard. Graves had been exhumed and removed from the site, and now ghosts were said to roam there. I also learned that Fort Brown and its former graveyard are now part of the Memorial Golf Course at Texas Southmost College. Photographs show that a few remaining berms—remnants of old earthworks—make it clear this is no ordinary golf course. As with most private courses, the Fort Brown course is off-limits to nonmembers. One travel blogger got a few photos, but police had sent him packing after that.

An official Texas government site showed that the last remaining buildings were decommissioned in 1948 and deeded to the college—the same one where Professor Zavaleta teaches. I found little more online than that. Even the Texas government's site mentioned the fort only in passing, calling it "small and relatively unknown." Though there is a building called "Fort Brown Memorial Center" on the University of Texas–Brownville and Texas Southmost College (UTB/TSC) campus, the college site I read concentrated only on the characteristics of the auditorium it houses, not its layered history.

So I began reading deeper, heading back to 1803—the year the United States bought the Louisiana Territory from France and pushed the U.S. boundary westward to the edge of Coahuila y Tejas, Mexico. By starting then, I began to understand why Fort Brown mattered so much, and learned in the process that while traveling to a place is essential for understanding it, contrary to the words of Steinbeck, one simply cannot rely only on what one witnesses by going somewhere. One also has to dig into invisible layers of history that underlie places in order to find their true significance. Palmito Ranch and its ghosts had already shown me that once. Now in searching for an invisible fort, the lesson really hit home.

| | | |

THE POPULATION in the Mexican province of Tejas had been sparse at the turn of the nineteenth century. But a decade after Thomas Jefferson's famous purchase—with Texas now safely closer to the United States—this began to change dramatically. Illegal immigration increased, flowing south toward Mexico. There were no border markers then, no guards, just open land that seemed free for the taking. To U.S. horse and cattle ranchers searching for fresh grazing land and slave-owning southern cotton planters eager to expand their fields and numbers of slaves, open territory seemed a godsend, even if it existed south of an international border.

In 1810, with the Mexican population of Tejas at only two thousand inhabitants, the most aggressive settlers had started crossing the line to stake claims. Meeting little opposition from Mexico, they kept going farther south and west. The open territory became a haven not just for the white settlers and their slaves but also for freed blacks looking for a new start, as well as runaway slaves and mixed-race people hiding from night riders and vigilante groups based in the United States. Indians and outlaws also found hiding places south of the border.

As we have seen, the Mexican response to the newcomers—though they were forced to react in the middle of their war of independence from Spain—was to offer land grants to Mexican settlers as incentives to encourage them to move northward to occupy the land for Mexico. But too few took advantage and much of Tejas remained unclaimed. The Anglos kept coming, and soon they outnumbered the Mexican citizens. Resistant to Mexican oversight from the beginning, they began to spurn any governance from Mexico at all once they gained the majority.

By 1820, the Mexican government had tried a new strategy: to embrace the Anglos and win their loyalty by offering them *empresario* land grants, which were large tracts given to settlers with the understanding that they would in turn encourage other families to settle the vacant land around them and thereby establish population centers that would support the Mexican government. Mexico hoped the new settlers would also provide a buffer against Comanche and Apache war parties raiding to Mexico's south. The scheme worked to bring in even more settlers, with such noted newcomers as Stephen Austin and his father, Moses, becoming early *empresarios*. But unfortunately for Mexico, the land giveaway failed to buy the new settlers' allegiance.

By the late 1820s, there were over twenty-five thousand American immigrants, including the free blacks and slaves, living in Texas. They outnumbered Mexican citizens in the region tenfold, and they continued to ignore Mexican laws and customs and even began making their own. Most contentious of their common laws was their declaration that settlers could continue to buy and sell slaves, a practice forbidden in all of Mexico. Such moves created tension not only between Tejas and the Mexican government, but also internally between the recently arrived free blacks and the plantation owners. Mexican laborers struggling to find work on the new plantations were now made to compete with unpaid laborers, which added to the tension.

In 1829, Mexico tried again to stem the tide of migration from the United States, this time by executive decree as Mexico's second president, the revolutionary leader Vicente Guerrero, moved to abolish all slave ownership throughout Mexico. The immigrant slaveholders were the main violators and thus the targets. But instead of heeding Guerrero's decree, the slaveholding Tejanos began to ramp up their organized talks of seccession and threatened violent resistance. The weak and beleaguered Mexican government backed down a month later and retracted the abolition of slavery law, but only in Tejas, and only for one year.

The following year, the Mexican Congress voted to prohibit the importation of slaves into Mexico for good. They also levied more customs duties on imports and exports to the state from those already selling their products in the eastern United States or Europe. Open protests against these and other restrictions to commerce began in 1832. Some Mexican Texans, as they started to call themselves, fought by filing lawsuits in Mexico City. Others began making guerrilla attacks on Mexican customs houses. All the while, more settlers continued flowing into Mexico to stake new land claims. While some of the Anglos converted their slaves into indentured servants in order to comply with the law, a sizable number continued to keep African Americans as unpaid, permanent chattel.

At first, Mexico refrained from intervening militarily, as they were likely afraid that the powerful U.S. Army would come to the settlers' aid. This hesitation further emboldened the Texans, and they declared conditional independence from Mexico in 1835.[1] Mexico had had enough. That year, newly elected Mexican President Antonio López de Santa Anna sent four thousand troops to quell the rebellion. They met the Texans near present-day Houston, and a series of battles raged from Houston back to the Rio Grande. These encounters ultimately led to the ten-day standoff in 1836 at the San Antonio mission where 187 Texan defenders met their deaths.

The Walt Disney movie version of the Alamo story I saw as a child on television was the same one shown at the actual Alamo, where we took our son in 1996. It is a tale of gallantry and heroism, one so heart-wrenching that our seven-year-old son burst into tears upon seeing it, sobbed audibly for fifteen minutes, and couldn't be consoled. Colonel William

---

1. Matt S. Meier and Feliciano Ribera, *Mexican Americans/American Mexicans: From Conquistadors to Chicanos*, 56–58.

Travis, Congressman Davy Crockett, James Bowie, and others died that day in March 1836 and instantly became martyrs. No one at the Alamo mentioned, however, that their rebellion exploded from racially charged anger against Mexico for trying to enforce its own antislavery laws, exert control over its own territory, and squelch an unpatriotic uprising by immigrants. It was about freedom, but whose freedom?

The reckoning by the Texans is legendary. Texan reinforcements routed the Mexican army at San Jacinto near present-day Houston, inadvertently capturing Santa Anna, who had posed as an enlisted man as he tried to escape. Santa Anna bargained for his release by offering an empty promise of Texas's independence. Emboldened by the trickery, the new immigrants declared openly that Texas was now a free and separate republic. Meanwhile, Mexico's position was that the Texas fighters were insurrectionists and that their uprising should be squelched. So the fighting continued. Whether one believes those staging the revolt were freedom fighters or traitors, it is revealing that one of Texas's first acts as a "free" republic was to legalize slavery.

After winning a series of victories, the Anglo Texans chose to request annexation by the United States. Remaining free for too long, they reasoned, would make them vulnerable to recapture by Mexico. But slavery presented a major stumbling block as Texas's entry into the Union would create an imbalance between free and slave states. Slave state supporters lobbied for Texas's admission, but free-soil advocates worked against them. The first vote came in 1840, just four years after Texas's victory at San Jacinto. It failed the first time, but the Texans refused to give up.

By that time, antislavery movements had begun to take shape in the United States, with Abraham Lincoln, then a young Illinois legislator, weighing in on the issue as a free-soil proponent. Refraining from calling for outright abolition, the free-soil legislators sought to maintain the status quo by refusing to give up new ground to slaveholders. They believed that with the numbers of slave and free states at a stalemate, they could maintain some semblance of equilibrium for the Union. The admission of a new slave territory, especially one as large as Texas, would tip the balance toward slaveholding and could start a march toward civil war. The question remained on the table in Congress for another five years. Meanwhile the Mexican government, denying Santa Anna's promise, continued sending its army across the Rio Grande to fight to keep their territory.

In 1845, with the backing of land-hungry lobbyists, the U.S. Congress voted by simple majority to annex Texas. Some voted yes because other southern states had threatened to pull out of the Union, crying "Texas or Disunion" if they didn't get their way. To support their argument, Texas supporters in Congress relied on the Missouri Compromise of 1820, claiming that north and south of that line, Texas could be divided into a balance of as many as four slave and free states. This would make possible Texas's admission while the slavery debates were ongoing. Giving lip service for balance in the Union, their proposal claimed the state(s) of Texas could choose slavery or not: stating they "shall be admitted into the Union, with or without slavery, as the people of each State, asking admission shall desire; and in such State or States as shall be formed out of said territory, north of said Missouri Compromise Line, slavery, or involuntary servitude (except for crime) shall be prohibited."[2]

It sounded good on paper. But with some of the most powerful Texans already owning slaves, and knowing they were well below the Missouri line, many had every intention of retaining their right to those slaves from the beginning. After the vote, Texas dealt a major blow to the Missouri Compromise and the Union by opening their entire territory to slaveholders as a single entity.

Mexico saw the whole thing as a brazen act of international power-grabbing and broke diplomatic ties to the United States. Unworried by the move, the U.S. government ignored Mexico's demands and instead President James Polk sent an envoy to offer, under threat of takeover if denied, $15 million for the purchase of both the territory of Texas and the broader region extending all the way to Alta California—that is, everything west of Louisiana and north of the Rio Grande that Mexico owned. The territory encompassed half of Mexico, with land stretching all the

---

2. "Annexation of Texas. Joint Resolution of the Congress of the United States, March 1, 1845."

way from the Rio Grande to the Baja Peninsula and northward to today's Oregon. Before he got an answer, Polk sent troops into Mexico, hoping to provoke a skirmish and hasten the acceptance of his one-sided offer.

He succeeded. As clashes ensued, Polk declared war, ordering General Zachary Taylor into Mexico to occupy Matamoros, across the river from present-day Brownsville. There, Taylor's army routed Santa Anna's fatigued troops, sending them retreating toward Mexico City. Though both sides somehow claimed victory, only the U.S. Army remained on site to occupy the territory. Continued skirmishes over the ensuing months led to further weakening of Mexican forces even as the United States sent renewed battalions to their new southern border. The Mexican government's only options were to take the $15 million for everything north of the Rio or continue to receive the wrath of the United States. It was then that Fort Brown became a central stronghold at the contested line.

Fort Brown, built on the north side of the Rio Grande and named Fort Texas in 1846, was later renamed for the commanding officer, Colonel Jacob Brown, who died fighting there. From Fort Brown, General Zachary Taylor staged his attacks on Mexican strongholds, including Matamoros. Colonel Robert E. Lee, years later the revered Confederate commander of the Army of Northern Virginia, would command the fort for two years. Under cannon fire from Mexico, a green Ulysses S. Grant, the same soldier who would later accept Lee's surrender at Appomattox, would wait out Mexican bombardment bunkered inside Fort Brown. Shell-shocked, he would end up questioning his entire military service. He wrote in his memoirs, "For myself, a young second lieutenant who had never heard a hostile gun before, I felt very sorry that I had enlisted."[3] Ultimately Lee and Grant lived, and the fort held and ended up on the U.S. side of the border, to be fought over at Palmito Ranch and elsewhere by two opposing sides during the American Civil War.

Nearly two years after the construction of the fort, the two countries signed the Treaty of Guadalupe Hidalgo, with Mexico reluctantly ceding

---

3. *Personal Memoirs of U.S. Grant,* chap. 7, online edition (Bartleby.com Inc., 2000), http://www.bartleby.com/1011/7.html.

all of Texas along with much of the land that now makes up the western United States. Following the treaty, inhabitants of Texas had a year to declare their allegiance to the United States or to move back across the Rio. To sweeten the deal for those who were undecided, the treaty also said those who had been property owners under Mexican law—including valid Spanish land grants—could retain full ownership of their land. Not all of those who counted on this land grant received it, however, which led to continued land conflicts for decades to come.

Reflecting the finest in hypocritical diplomacy, the treaty opened as follows:

> The United States of America and the United Mexican States animated
> by a sincere desire to put an end to the calamities of the war which
> unhappily exists between the two Republics and to establish upon
> a solid basis relations of peace and friendship, which shall confer re-
> ciprocal benefits upon the citizens of both, and assure the concord,
> harmony, and mutual confidence wherein the two people should live,
> as good neighbors have for that purpose appointed their respective
> plenipotentiaries.

Nice words, but with one party to the treaty being forced into signing by military threat, "harmony" and "neighbors" was surely an exaggeration. The border's forced cut into the landscape would never quite heal.

Though unstated in the treaty, perhaps the greatest ideological conflict remaining afterward was how to treat people who worked in agriculture. As Mexican citizens, African Americans by law were supposed to remain free. As Texas residents in their new American nation, they would become chattel. Beyond that, it remained to be seen how U.S. landowners in Texas would treat former Mexican laborers now in their employ. With over two hundred thousand slaves in Texas in 1860, this influx of forced labor left Latinos sitting on a powder keg of racial politics.

The keg exploded when Texas voted to secede from the Union in February 1861 and joined the Confederate States of America a month later, still a month prior to the Confederates firing on Fort Sumter in

Charleston, South Carolina. As the Civil War broke out, Colonel John "Rip" Ford of the Confederacy—who earned his nickname for writing "R.I.P." on letters to the families of dead soldiers—became commander in the region and captured Fort Brown. His troops drove Union troops out of the territory for almost two years. Union soldiers recaptured the fort in 1863, but were routed again by Colonel Ford's cavalry in July 1864. The Confederates remained in control of the fort for almost a year after that, staying there after Appomattox and refusing to give up possession until shortly after they won the Battle of Palmito Ranch.

Reconstruction in Texas after the war was followed by the bloody and combative Jim Crow period when racial tensions led to yet another territorial war known as the Jaybird-Woodpecker War in the late 1890s. Afterward, a whole new Democratic Party wing, the Jaybird Democratic Organization—a party bent on disenfranchising blacks—was born near Houston. They used lynchings and other forms of violence to subjugate African Americans, ultimately pushing thousands of blacks out of the state. Many African American Texans were forced to join the Great Migration northward toward major cities like Chicago, Indianapolis, and Detroit.

In 1906, with racial tensions still at their height, U.S. military commanders decided to assign the Twenty-Fifth Colored Troops to Fort Brown. By then, the Indian Wars in which the Buffalo Troops had made a name for themselves had subsided, and the U.S. commanders believed the black soldiers could be used more effectively to guard against the northward flow of possible unrest from Mexico, which was by then brewing its own internal revolution.[4] The brigade's orders were to help protect the border, but the assignment would lead to even more trouble for them on the U.S. side. Ordering blacks to police the borderline put there only a generation earlier, in part by slaveholders, may have been honorable in its intent, but the plan was destined for failure.

The Twenty-Fifth Colored Troops brigade had been formed from Union veterans and other recruits immediately after the Civil War in

---

4. http://www.nps.gov/history/seac/brownsville/english/index-3.htm#confederates, accessed August 2013.

1866. By 1906 the brigade had fought the Indian Wars on the western frontier for decades. They also had served under Teddy Roosevelt at San Juan Hill and were among the first to reach the summit as depicted by the famous lithograph entitled "Charge of the 24th and 25th Colored Infantry," though this claim was not without controversy. One version of what happened says a white officer took the flag from the hands of the first black soldier to arrive at the summit and claimed the distinction for himself. Some claimed the white troops beat the black troops in the famous charge, though there were eyewitnesses who said that the black soldiers were faster to the top. Regardless, the Colored Troops arrived at Fort Brown with a strong reputation as brave and disciplined soldiers.

They received no hero's welcome. Local residents were outraged from the outset and members of the statewide racist organizations took it as an affront. Some Texas whites feared that the blacks could form alliances with the Mexican American community and upset the carefully constructed racial balance the whites had built, albeit with violence and intimidation, since Reconstruction. In protest, members of the white community sent letters to Washington asking for the soldiers' removal, but found no sympathy there. Then they banned the soldiers from the local saloon and other establishments in town. Tensions continued to mount.

Everything exploded on the evening of August 14, 1906, when a shooting occurred in Brownsville that left a local bartender dead and a policeman wounded. Residents immediately seized on the incident and blamed the black soldiers, with some claiming they had witnessed them firing their guns and others saying they had heard soldiers' voices during the skirmish. Though no one confessed and the white commanding officer swore that all of the soldiers were accounted for inside the barracks at the time of the shooting, the town authorities found twelve members of the Twenty-Fifth guilty based solely on the townspeople's allegations. There were no trials, no due process.

The army sent investigators after the fact. None of the soldiers they interviewed ever admitted to any knowledge of the violence—even under threat of court martial. Despite this, the investigators sided with the white townspeople and treated the denial of involvement as insubordination. Finding all the accused soldiers guilty, the army discharged the twelve accused along with the rest of the 155 black soldiers stationed in Brownsville. Many of the dishonored had been close to retirement when they lost their affiliation with the military. Most had been multiple enlistees. Six were Medal of Honor recipients. "Discharged without honor," unlike "dishonorable discharge," required no trial but only a simple maneuver carried out by the commanding officer. The soldiers lost their back pay and their pensions.

Though the white commanding officer, a number of subordinates, and the clergy associated with the brigade pleaded for leniency all the way to the White House, President Theodore Roosevelt, who had fought with many of the Twenty-Fifth in both Puerto Rico and Cuba, refused to intervene for them. He waited until after his reelection to announce his decision. Many black Americans and their allies were outraged, though only one white senator, Joseph Foraker, took up their cause at the time, and Roosevelt considered him an enemy for it. It was not until 1972—two years after John D. Weaver's 1970 groundbreaking book, *The Brownsville Raid*, was published—that President Richard Nixon pardoned the entire battalion.[5] Sixty-six years after the Brownsville Affair, all 155 of them received an honorable discharge. Only one member survived to receive the small sum of $25,000 offered as recompense. Reeling from what has since been called "The Brownsville Affair," the military abandoned the fort in 1906, leaving only empty buildings with livestock grazing on the grounds.

Five years later, when Porfirio Díaz was deposed after ruling for thirty-one years and various factions began fighting to control Mexico—including revolutionary forces led by Pancho Villa in the north of the country—the United States reactivated its most storied border fort. By 1913, when the U.S. consul in Matamoros reported pillaging in Mexico's streets, American troops, this time all white, were stationed at the fort again.

The military deemed them defensive forces in the beginning. Even-

---

5. John D. Weaver, *The Brownsville Raid*.

tually, however, the U.S. forces became more active, rekindling long-standing tensions with Mexico in the process. One instance was in 1915 when two signal corps officers took off in a small airplane in April from the Fort Brown Cavalry Drill Field and crossed the border by air to spy on Mexican forces. Their specific mission was to report on the movements of Pancho Villa's army. Though the pilots claimed that they never crossed into Mexican territory, Villa's soldiers shot at the plane with a primitive machine gun and small arms and almost brought it down—an unlikely feat if the plane had remained in U.S. airspace.

When the lucky pilots made it back to Fort Brown, they earned the dubious distinction of flying the first U.S. military plane ever fired upon, while getting the U.S. military even more mixed up in the Mexican conflict than before. But President Woodrow Wilson had wanted more action anyway. Well before Pancho Villa staged his infamous attack on U.S. soil, Wilson had itched to intervene in the Mexican struggle. When the attack did occur, Wilson deployed troops under the command of General John J. Pershing to pursue Villa. This move pushed Fort Brown back into the center of a new U.S. military theatre.

Following his failed chase of Villa into Mexico, Pershing was redeployed to Europe as commander of the American Expeditionary Force in World War I. Fort Brown remained in commission through both world wars, though it was mostly symbolic, especially because Mexico became a wartime ally and collaborated in the war effort through the Bracero program and other means. At the end of World War II the fort was decommissioned and the grounds given to Texas Southmost College.

| | | |

Thus Fort Brown had pulled me deep into border history and revealed some hard truths about our nation's racial past. In the process, I had found a clear link between the border and American slavery in the region. I'd also found links to the Buffalo Soldiers and to many of our most prominent wars. I realized why Fort Brown is not exactly a point of pride to be celebrated, and I could understand that it wasn't front and center on tourist brochures. At the same time, I now knew it was an essential part of the border story.

We decided to follow the Brownsville Museum's recommendation to swing by the University of Texas–Brownville and Texas Southmost College on our way out of town to meet Bill Rovira, a media contact Sarah Boone had found for us. I stopped for a minute to take a photograph of the modest sign for the college and to look for something on it about Fort Brown. Nothing. What I didn't know then was that inside the gates were some old Fort Brown buildings and a few berms still visible. But there were no signs, no historical markers, or monuments to lead me to them. So I got out at the gate not a hundred yards from the Mexican border entrance and took a picture of just the college sign and the flags flying around it, not knowing how close I was to the ghosts of Fort Brown.

"One day I'd really like to go back when Tony is here to guide us," I said to Hope as I got back into the car. I had no idea quite then about all the connections Tony could make with the fort. I was only talking then about the college itself.

I've learned since that phantoms are said to roam the halls of the old administrative buildings. There have been reports of mysterious noises in the hallways and unidentified faces peering out of windows. Maybe they had something to do with the amputations and the exhumed cemetery that was once near the oxbow lake on the campus. Definitely there had occurred some amputations of history that were yet to be reconciled.

Just south of the campus lake is the Fort Brown Memorial Golf Course—still in the United States and thus north of the Rio, but south of the wall. The company that manages the golf course rents the land from the college. To play there, golfers drive through the campus and pass through a gate in the border fence. The course is so close to Mexico at hole 16 that it is possible to drive a ball into Matamoros from the tee. I called the golf pro to ask about this. He told me that such a shot is possible, but is prohibited by law. He said the police would slap any violator with a hefty fine. I wish like anything I had driven through that gate.

# ELEVEN

# Rio Grande Guardians

SAN PEDRO AND LA PALOMA, TEXAS

WHEN I FIRST CALLED BILL ROVIRA, THE LEAD REPORTER FOR the Internet-based periodical *Rio Grande Guardian*, he had agreed immediately to meet us and to set up appointments on the Mexican side with several of his best contacts. First, we would meet with a local businessman who served as the chamber of commerce president for Progreso. The plan was to talk with him about border economics.

Though we had lost time in the storm and the detour by

A gap in the border wall at Los Indios near Progreso, Texas.

the college, I argued for sticking with our original plan to take the roads that hug the border, in this case, Texas Route 281, the Military Highway. Hope agreed—as long as I let Bill know. After some wrong turns and backtracking, we finally found the two-lane and in a minute or so it seemed we were in Mexico—the houses, cars, and people all looked the part—except that the border wall was to our south, cutting through the backyards of the houses on our left as we headed west. It was made of upright metal posts perhaps five inches in diameter and fifteen feet in height. The spaces between them were presumably too small for a human head to fit through. Not altogether unattractive, the fence in that area allowed the southern light to shine through, and we could see to the other side when looking straight on. Viewed from an angle, however, the posts ran together, the light closed off, and the wall appeared to solidify, an optical illusion. The fence seemed to undulate as light through the posts came and went. We would learn that the fence along the border had many different designs.

As we drove along, I could see fields between the wall and the meandering and now swollen river. Periodically there were dirt or gravel roads that turned left off 281 and headed south leading to those agricultural fields. There were no signs or barricades at the openings—just a road leading to the other side, all clearly north of the river. Trying to make sense of the scene, I asked Hope, "Isn't that Mexico on the other side of the wall?"

"I assume so, why else would there be a wall?"

"But that's north of the river. I have to go see!" I started looking for the next turnoff. Seeing one ahead, I gave a quick signal and cut into the gravel road that led straight through the wall. "I'll just get a picture of this opening and then we'll go."

There was no sign of any kind, but still I felt sheepish about driving through, so I stopped a hundred feet or so from the gap and walked with my camera up the dirt road to the soggy ground near the fence and framed the shot. The angle wasn't quite right. I looked around to make sure no one was looking and then stepped through the gap, trying to capture a particular curvature in the wall with just the right light.

Just as I pressed the shutter release, I caught sight of the fast-approaching green and white truck out of the corner of my right eye. The truck was traveling from the west on a dirt road paralleling the south side of the wall. I stepped back through the wall toward the car and made sure to act as if I was doing nothing wrong. Remember, I told myself, nothing told you to keep out. You're still in the United States. Smile and be friendly.

The female agent in the truck smiled back at me, said hello, and asked what I was up to. I replied, "Just taking some pictures of the border wall and the opening here. I'm just seeing it for the first time." She didn't seem worried, and I turned to go. Then suddenly another white and green truck came rushing toward the gap from the east. The driver parked next to the other, now blocking the opening as if I might make a run for Mexico. The second officer was male and did not smile. The female officer spoke with him out of my hearing, presumably telling him what I had said. I waved and headed back toward the car. They watched as I opened the rear car door. They just wanted me to leave, and that's what I was doing.

Then I thought for a second, got out two of my business cards, picked up the camera again, and walked back toward the two trucks, shutting the door. "What are you doing?" Hope asked just as the door closed.

I opened the driver's door. "I need to ask some questions. I'll be right back."

I approached the foreboding male agent's truck and addressed him. He looked pissed off. I said, "I just wanted to know whether I was doing anything wrong."

The agents remained in their vehicles. I walked up closer to their trucks to hear the answer. He did all of the talking. "You are not permitted to go through the fence," he barked. I guess that was supposed to be self-explanatory, but there was nothing saying not to go through, I pointed out. Then he asked my name. I handed each of them a business card and said, "I'm studying immigration and border policy. I wanted to see firsthand and take pictures of what our government is up to here so that I can show my students and write about the experience."

He looked scornful and said: "You came all the way down here from North Carolina just to see this?"

"I believe it's my duty as a citizen to know about the border," I answered, trying to act professional.

"I'm going tell my commanding officer about you. You'll be hearing from him about this."

I didn't take the bait. "That's fine. I'd like to talk with him." I thanked him, turned, and walked toward the car again, feeling the hardness of his stare on my back. I took my time putting away my camera, and we drove away. "I'm glad I went back," I said to Hope.

As we drove west, a verse from Woody Guthrie's "This Land Is Your Land"—the one about a no trespassing sign—came to me, as it had started to regularly on the trip. It wasn't so much that I wanted to sing it; it just wouldn't go away. I'd once heard a recording on the radio of Woody Guthrie's unmistakable voice singing it and had remembered these words, ones that they usually leave out of songbooks: "There was a big high wall there that tried to stop me. / The sign was painted, said 'Private Property.' / But on the backside, it didn't say nothing. / This land was made for you and me." Though there had not been any signs, I thought, the message got delivered anyway, that the land between the wall and border, still squarely in America as far as the river boundary goes, was definitely not made for you and me.

# TWELVE

# Progress?

PROGRESO, TEXAS, AND PROGRESO,
TAMAULIPAS

WE WERE ALMOST AT PROGRESO WHEN WE CALLED BILL AGAIN.
He was waiting in the parking lot off to the right of the bridge,
a protected parking area made for day visitors. We pulled in a
few minutes after the call and found him standing beside his car,
phone in hand, and ready to cross the bridge on foot. He was
easy to spot—he was the only person in sight besides the parking attendant. He approached our car and was ready to walk
across the bridge the second we got out. I apologized again and
told him what we had just been through.

He understood and said as we walked briskly toward the gate,
"We'll have no problem going into Mexico. No one will ever
check your passports going in, so hopefully we'll be on time. I
really think you'll find this guy interesting and I didn't want to
lose our minutes with him." We were some of the few on foot,
very different from what he had experienced in the past, he said.

"This used to be a busy spot for Winter Texans to come to
buy their prescriptions and eyeglasses. But it's dead now." As
we walked across the empty river bridge, I looked down on the
swollen waters and asked him why the river is called Bravo in
Mexico and Grande in the United States. He replied with the

adage, "*Grande para ellos, bravo para nosotros; bravo para nadar!*"—Big for [the U.S], but menacing for [the Mexicans]; menacing to swim!

Of course none of us wanted to keep Progreso's most prominent businessman waiting, but luckily we got to the restaurant where we were to meet a half hour before him. I was relieved my forays had not required further apologies. We had just gotten our drinks when a tall, attractive, and neatly dressed man of about forty walked into the restaurant, greeted us with a big smile, and insisted on buying us lunch. He spoke to us in Spanish: "My name is Alfonso Treviño Salinas, welcome to Progreso!"

Then he talked about the town, the construction company he owned on the Mexican side, and his work with the Chamber of Commerce. While we waited for our food, we asked Señor Treviño about the challenges of conducting business on the border. His points were lecture-ready.

"Tourism and economic interchange have plunged in recent years," he said. He cited four main

*Papel picado* flags and the military outpost south of the border crossing at Progreso.

reasons why: first, the new restrictions requiring passports for everyone crossing from Mexico into the United States, including U.S. citizens; second, the security issues that make Americans skittish about going to Mexico; third, the outbreak of swine flu—a disease that had been traced to a large American-owned hog facility in Mexico in 2009; and fourth, the international economic crisis, which had caused everyone to lessen their spending. I was writing it all down in my version of shorthand—Spanglish shorthand.

"Everything is very fragile economically," he said. "Though this small town is as tranquil as it ever was, business has declined drastically. Today all the services, eyeglasses, dentistry, a pharmacy, restaurants, and gift shops within four blocks of the borderline are open but empty. They're waiting for customers, but fear has driven the tourists away."

He acknowledged that drug trafficking in some areas had skyrocketed because of corruption and lack of law enforcement, but he didn't place all the responsibility on Mexico. "Of course we have to fight all of this," he said. "But we have to do it together. It affects both sides." He shifted to the root causes of border corruption: first there is poverty, caused not by culture, but by international politics and economics, he said. Macroeconomic strategies cause people at the microeconomic level to have to be creative to find jobs. All this leads to migration. And when people are neglected, they can turn to crime, which is encouraged by demand for illicit drugs. But the problem is bi-national, he said. "The U.S. sells Mexicans arms and the U.S. consumes the drugs. We're neighbors, and we have to work together."

I brought up the North American Free Trade Agreement, saying it looked to me as if the initiative had boosted trade for some but had displaced many workers on the Mexican side even as it caused Mexican farm commodity prices to plummet. I was pretty convinced, having heard that tale many times from farmworkers, but I wanted to hear a Mexican businessman's opinion. Mr. Treviño's reply was surprisingly succinct: NAFTA had helped the largest U.S.-based companies, but as far as he could tell, it had done nothing at all for his small town or any of the rural areas nearby.

Impressed with his candor, I asked about SB 1070, the law that had just passed the state legislature in Arizona that summer. News reports had said many Latinos were fleeing the state, damaging Arizona's reputation, at least among immigration reformers, and its economy as well. Still I didn't know how it would be viewed from the Mexico side. The answer came fast. "The law is a violation of civil and human rights," Mr. Treviño said. "We have a moral obligation to protest that law. It brings down the dignity of all human beings. Human rights must be a significant part of the free interchange of economic goods. Anything less would be immoral. We have to start with equality." I'm sure he didn't speak for every capitalist in Mexico, but his own business community had elected him as their spokesperson. I was struck by how different he sounded from the U.S. Chamber's neo-liberal perspective that holds the position that any barrier to trade has to come down even as they encourage the walls to prohibit human beings to go up.

Bill had interviewed Mr. Treviño for his online periodical, self-proclaimed as the "largest Internet-based paper on the South Texas border," a couple of times before, and they also had conversed on other occasions, becoming friends. They launched into several topics they had discussed before while Hope and I listened. One topic I asked both to clarify was the "*Tejanos de Invierno*"—Winter Texans. They said they are people who move to Texas seasonally for the climate, but also to take advantage of the lower Mexican prices for everything from food to pharmaceuticals. That interchange had been the economic lifeblood of Progreso, Treviño said.

After lunch, as we stood on the sidewalk shaking hands with Mr. Treviño and thanking him one last time, Bill pointed with his chin to an outdoor table at the neighboring restaurant directly behind me. "There are some Winter Texans now, why don't you ask them what they think?" I turned to see a foursome of white retirees—apparently two married couples—having lunch.

Their outdoor table was covered with the makings of fajitas. They were drinking margaritas and sharing a laugh when I approached with Bill and Hope walking behind me. They welcomed us and asked us what we were doing in town, and so I told them a little about our border trip. That got them started. They said they had been going to Progreso for years, that they loved the food and shopping there. They bought all their pharmaceuticals and their eyeglasses there, and even had their dental care done in town. The four, originally from Kansas, couldn't have been more quintessentially upper-middle-age, middle-class, white American in dress, mannerisms, and talk—the opposite of the bohemian types you see in some remote places. But they acknowledged they were some of the few heading to the border then, which made them seem like adventurous pioneers. "How could you get others to follow suit?" I asked. "Be good examples," they replied. "All we can do is keep on coming back here."

I looked southward as we prepared to go. Red, green, and yellow decorations, signs for tourists and patients in English, and professional dentists' and doctors' shingles were everywhere. One could still walk across the bridge without showing a passport, eat a good meal, get prescriptions filled without a wait, get one's eyes examined, and buy new frames all before the sun went down. There were no lines at all. The businesses were all ready for the hordes. But the four Midwesterners eating at the sidewalk café were it.

Looking back to the north, beneath the festive streamers perhaps left over from the "Day of the Tourist" the town had held back in March, I saw helmeted and flak-jacketed Mexican soldiers dressed in camouflage standing beside an armored truck with its large barrel aimed northward. The gunner's head peered over the hatch on top. I hadn't really thought about the military presence on the way in, but from the southern side they looked ready for an attack. I knew they were there to guarantee everything remained safe, but all I felt when I saw the tough young men in green was how far we were from a solution to our border problems.

How twisted it had all become, except when it wasn't. In a narrow focus, margarita glasses still sweated on the sidewalk café tables and the tortilla chips and salsa still were limitless for the few who were brave enough to go. The service was still attentive and the food cheap. The piñatas and flags still swayed in the wind at the stores. You could still buy all the legal drugs and best dental care and eyeglasses that Mexico has to offer, and everyone there needs you to. In a wider focus, tourists and armored vehicles and machine guns don't seem to mix so well.

We started walking northward, waving good-bye again to the four Kansans still enjoying their meal, and headed back across the bridge. We passed through the empty gate and exchanged greetings with the American officials. The customs agent on duty scanned our passports. When we told him we had nothing to declare, he said, "Thank you" and let us pass. We reentered the United States almost without breaking stride.

# THIRTEEN

# World's Most Honest Man

HIDALGO, TEXAS, AND REYNOSA, MEXICO

DRIVING OUR CAR, WE FOLLOWED BILL TO THE NEXT BORDER crossing, at Reynosa and Hidalgo, where we parked. We then rode with Bill into Mexico, crossing the international bridge some six miles south of McAllen, Texas. Reynosa is known as a major site for the export of illegal drugs and for human trafficking, both controlled by the Gulf Cartel, a situation that has led its inhabitants (unlike those in Progreso) to give up their tourist trade almost entirely. No one, it seemed, wanted to cross there unless they had to.

Despite this lack of small-scale human interchange, the trade of aboveboard goods moved in lines of tractor-trailers that clipped along over the Free Trade International Bridge in both directions. It was

Pedestrians crossing the Laredo/Nuevo Laredo Bridge.

easy for us to see that Reynosa is a key point of entry for NAFTA goods and on some level had benefited from the *intercambio* that averaged a billion dollars a day or more. At the same time, everything about the town looked poor. None of the money going by in trucks stayed here. But I knew there had to be more going on than met the eye.

Bill knew the border crossing well, having crossed it almost daily for years as part of his reporting job. Some of the ICE (Immigration Control and Enforcement, changed from the INS after 9/11) agents knew him by sight. We were on our way to visit Thomas and Yirit Koblecky, a couple who lived with their children in a Reynosa subdivision near the border. Bill had written a human-interest piece about the family just a few weeks before and he knew we would want to hear them tell their story in person.

Again we cleared customs quickly and turned down a street that ran alongside the south side of the border wall. Spotting some graffiti on one section of the metal fence, I asked if Bill could stop so I could jump out and get a picture of it. Bill said no, we'd better not. "That place is known for *narco* activity and the graffiti includes a gang sign. Someone just got murdered on this curve earlier this year, so you don't want to get out of the car here." Then he pointed out the initials for Cartel de Golfo. Though we could see no one nearby, Bill explained that informants were everywhere. Even beggars work for the cartels. They have to in order to survive. I thanked him, sat back in the seat, put the camera away, and breathed out slowly, as if I had just dodged a bullet.

Thomas and Yirit's neighborhood was just a few miles from the border. They lived in one of many streets lined with identical white concrete houses built quickly during the last twenty years. Every house had a black cistern on top for water. The cisterns filled up at night while water demand was down and allowed for gravity-flow usage by day. Most houses had concrete driveways and some had cars or trucks parked out front. There was no life on the outside; the neighborhood served only as a bedroom community for border workers, the very design saying people weren't comfortable outdoors.

All the houses had bars on the windows. There was no open space for kids to play. No basketball or soccer goals. No parks. This was also a barrio for people with no leisure hours on their hands. Their time, you could tell, belonged mostly to companies they worked for, and their lives consisted of working, driving to and from work, sleeping, and eating. Nothing on the exteriors distinguished any house from dozens of other houses around it as far as I could tell. Not a shrub, dog, tricycle, or anything else was outside. Likely there is a safety advantage in this kind of anonymity, and that was the only redeeming quality I could think of. But luckily Bill knew right where to go as he counted the houses and parked the car next to the curb. We walked up the concrete drive. Thomas Koblecky met us at the door before we knocked.

Thomas, a tall, thin, white American man in his late twenties, invited us inside and introduced us to his family. Yirit, a diminutive, dark-skinned Mexican woman with shiny jet-black hair, greeted us from the couch. She had been watching television while feeding their new daughter a bottle of formula. Their three-year-old son played on the floor in front of the couch. Yirit spoke to us in broken English, but switched to Spanish when she realized we could understand her. Then we realized that Thomas couldn't understand her Spanish, at least not entirely, and so we talked with him in English.

Thomas ushered us to the kitchen table and offered us a soft drink. Bill had already told him about our trip and our goals, so Thomas began to talk almost as soon as we sat down, even before I asked a question. Yirit looked on from the other room and added details. They had an immigration crisis on their hands and they didn't beat around the bush. I scribbled fast and pulled out my small video recorder to capture some of his words. Thomas opened a folder and read from a written statement he had sent to ICE: "I feel I have been victimized by the broad strokes of immigration law that has caught good people in its grasp." Then he and Yirit gave us more background on their situation.

Yirit had entered the United States without papers in the late 1990s. She came from a poor family. Her father had diabetes and couldn't work. Intent on sending money back to her parents, Yirit crossed the border to work in the agricultural fields. She had gone back to Mexico twice, carrying cash to give to her parents. When she reentered the United States a third time, still promising to help her struggling parents, she found a job stacking shelves at a Home Depot in a small town in Illinois. Thomas, who hailed from Illinois, also worked there. They met in the store. The unlikely couple, he a lanky, rural American unable to speak a word of Spanish, and she a new U.S. immigrant with no English, tried to communicate across linguistic lines. They fell in love despite the challenges and married in 2004. At that time, Thomas believed that his new wife should have full rights of citizenship. He didn't want to live with her in the shadows. After all, he had been born a citizen and they were now husband and wife.

"I didn't like the fact that she was illegal, had a false I.D. and so on," Thomas said. But Yirit, having already lived as an undocumented person in the United States for some time, was convinced no one was going to help them. No one she knew, no matter how law-abiding and smart, had ever been legalized. There was too much red tape, too many costs, and she had already been in the country working without papers. She knew they would have to pay thousands of dollars to hire an immigration lawyer. Most Mexican people waited more than fifteen years, perhaps thirty, for a green card, even if they applied while in Mexico. She warned Thomas that it would be impossible to get her papers from inside the United States, particularly if they told that she had entered the country before they were married. But he wanted to be married in the open and believed he had nothing to hide. He wrote out the full story and prepared to send it to ICE.

"I didn't have the money for a lawyer," Thomas admitted, "So I filed the application myself." A friend had told him to go to Catholic Charities to seek financial aid, but the nonprofit organization couldn't help with legal fees. He believed that if he answered honestly and straightforwardly on the application about Yirit and her father's illness, everything could be rectified. If he could only get the story to the right people, they would be fine. He asked for a green card for her, a pathway to citizenship. He thought her being married to a U.S. citizen was enough.

The written reply they received hit him like a fist in the gut. Not only had they been denied, but now ICE also possessed Yirit's story in writing, signed by her husband. The letter landed a second punch: she would have to return to Mexico or be deported. It added, in government legalese, that perhaps after some years out of the country (likely three to ten) she could petition for reentry and thereby receive the requested work permit—her green card. Thomas and Yirit tried sending letters of appeal, first to President Bush and then to President Obama. Then he sought legal aid with what little money they could raise, but lawyers said they couldn't help because he had already admitted she was in the United States before their marriage. Could they have gone to Mexico and mailed a letter requesting a visa from there? We'll never know.

Thomas had always been a law-abiding citizen. He also believed strongly that he should be with and provide for his wife and future children. When the family began packing to leave the country, their second child was already on the way. He couldn't in good conscience send them to wait in Mexico while he lived apart. He couldn't stand the thought of her having to go it alone without him, particularly with her parents in dire straits. So they both moved to Reynosa to live there together. According to law, as a U.S. citizen Thomas may work in his home country no matter where he lives. He found a job driving a beer truck close to the border. Leaving home every day before sunup, he crossed the border with his American passport, drove to the bottling company, and made his rounds in the truck, returning home to Mexico late at night. We know that thousands cross into the United States to work each day, leaving their families behind. Many live south of the line and work north of it, but few who do so look and sound like Thomas.

Thomas continued to hope that justice will allow a hardworking young couple a chance at life in the United States. In the meantime, he was doing the right thing by the woman he loves. Yirit has always been honest too, not greedy, not taking welfare, just working to shelve boxes in a store in Illinois for minimum wage, a job few others wanted. Their son was born in the United States before they left and therefore is a U.S. citizen. Their baby girl was born in Mexico, but is entitled to apply for citizenship because of her father. Their mother, however, can only raise them in Mexico; thus their home in Reynosa.

|    |    |    |    |

WE DROVE BACK THROUGH Reynosa's broken neighborhoods, overcrowded with stories of hardship, both close to and yet so far from prosperity. We backtracked to the curve of the drug cartel killing and Bill changed the subject to the drug gangs.

"They're known as La Mafia, *mañosos*, *narcotraficantes*, or simply as *narcos*," he said. "But you've got to understand drugs aren't just about them, but they're about both sides of the border, and nothing's simple." He brought up Jack Nicholson's character Charlie Smith in the 1982 movie *The Border*. In the movie, Nicholson plays a U.S. border guard who starts selling drugs. Movie reviewer Vincent Canby of the *New York Times* wrote the following about the movie the week it was released: "At night, the Rio Grande, which forms the U.S.-Mexican border at El Paso, teems with poor, desperate, illiterate Mexicans seeking entrance into the land of milk, honey, bigotry and exploitation."[1] The reviewer seemed to blame the Mexicans, who he thought were unskilled and ignorant about the country they are entering. Thomas and Yirit are only some who prove otherwise.

Bill also brought up the collusion of drug kingpins with big business and government. "None of this could happen without the military," Bill said, meaning that the cartels work in collusion with the military in Mexico —and the United States is giving military aid to Mexico. Since the signing of the Merida Initiative in 2007 and 2011, the U.S. government has funded $1.8 billion worth of training and equipment for Mexico's military.[2] So we work together in some sense, but not at all as one might hope.

---

1. Vincent Canby, "The Border (1982): Jack Nicholson in 'The Border,'" *New York Times*, January 29, 1982.

2. Ioan Grillo, "NGOS to Washington: Cut Military Aid to Mexico," *Global Post*, November 10, 2011.

He then added another important fact: it is legal to possess and use small amounts of heroin, LSD, cocaine, and pot in Mexico—one of the means Mexico used to fight its war on drugs was to remove the prohibition and thus reduce the profit margin. The law passed both houses of the Mexican Congress in 2006, but after the Bush administration protested, Mexico's President Felipe Calderón refused to sign the bill into law. Slowly and quietly it became law in 2009 anyway. That means the demand and big profits have been pushed northward.

The war on drugs in the United States has done little to stop drugs from crossing the border from Mexico. Everyone seems to know that despite our drug laws, and perhaps because of them, the Mexican cartels are mopping up billions in illegal profits. I asked Bill what would stop it. Only taking the profits out of the equation, he said. Profits breed competition and violence, and as long as there is profit, the cartels will compete down to the last man. Killings, like the one at the curve we had just rounded, will continue. As far as Mexico goes, he said, "Until one person is in charge of all the drugs, they're going to keep killing each other." He was quoting a sheriff he had heard on National Public Radio: Every drug lord wants to be at the top of his pyramid, and to topple the pyramids of his competitors.

| | | |

WE DROVE TO MISSION, where Bill joined us for a brief meal with a former student of mine named Jean Abreu. The daughter of Cuban immigrants and fluent in Spanish, Jean had won a Cesar Chavez Fellowship with the National Farmworker Center of the United Farm Workers and was living near Mission for the year. I was happy to see her working for justice at the border, but worried about her isolation and vulnerability. She was so young and alone. Her job was to tutor twenty-five kids whose mothers live with them in the United States but have fathers who are migrant workers and sleep apart from them in Reynosa. They go to school in Pharr, she told us, a little U.S. town of fifteen thousand. She helped with dropout prevention, homework, and academic enrichment. She seemed exhausted.

She told us about her day. That morning Jean had had to answer questions from some of her pupils' parents about a written notice the kids had taken home from school. The note mentioned the possibility of federal raids in their apartment complex and warned that parents could be apprehended. It reported that children could be left alone—particularly those children born in the United States—if the parents were taken. The notice, written by a school official, used the word "alien," Jean said, and the kids were incensed not just about the threat of deportation, but the word itself. "That means we're aliens!" They thought it meant they were being called freaks from other planets. Of course our Constitution says children born in the United States aren't "aliens" after all—only their parents have to live like extraterrestrials.

Bill asked, "How could a child concentrate on getting ahead in school when at any moment a raid could destroy his life?" Jean only nodded and frowned. It disturbed me to see a young person stripped of some of her optimism, but I could offer no magical words of encouragement. All we could do was try to get her to talk about the challenges and to give her some nourishing food. After seeing us for just an hour, Jean had to go back to her organization again. They had called an emergency meeting with the parents. We convinced her, with some urging on Hope's part, to at least finish her salad before heading back.

After Jean left for work, we had a few minutes to talk with Bill about his own personal border saga. His wife is Salvadoran and can't live in the United States or even visit Bill while they are petitioning for her visa, so they await the results of her appeal for citizenship while living apart. If she crossed the border without papers, she could be deported and never allowed to return, he explained. So when possible, Bill would travel to meet his wife in Mexico at some halfway point.

The rest of his time he spent driving along the border in search of stories, amplifying the voices of those like Thomas and Yirit. He talked with his wife by Skype at night. The border, he said, had given him a vocation, but it had also cut through the middle of his marriage.

# FOURTEEN

# Cowboy Priests

MISSION, TEXAS

JUST BEFORE WE STOPPED FOR DINNER, BILL TOOK US BY THE border region's first American Catholic mission, from which the town gets its name. The picturesque little chapel named La Lomita, literally the little hill, was completed in 1849, only one year after the Mexican-American War ended. After the signing of the Treaty of Guadalupe Hidalgo, the fathers of the Oblate Order rode horseback out to remote Texas villages to minister to those who had become, whether they knew and accepted it or not, new Americans. Like cowboys, they slept on the ground and prepared their own food on campfires. But instead of herding cattle, they rounded up souls.

The Texas Oblates earned the nicknames "cowboy priests," the "mounted posse," and the "Cavalry of Christ." They wore cowboy hats, chaps, and their clerical collars. They became legendary both for their work with the poor and their frontier skills. According to a pamphlet we picked up in the back of the chapel, one of the original priests, Father F. Bugnard, "never opened a fence," but took all of them jumping. The original mission site had a small house where the priests stayed and a livestock stable where they fed and took care of their horses. Today

only the little chapel remains, situated between the old railroad bed and the Rio Grande. Not exactly a rails-to-trails tourist spot, the railroad bed today serves mostly the Border Patrol officers hoping to catch sight of migrants wet from swimming across.

The statue of Jesus overlooking pictures of members of Our Lady of Guadalupe Catholic Church in Mission, Texas, who have served in the military (including those who died during their service).

The river is deep there, but it looked as though a moderate swimmer could cross it in a few minutes. People say, however, that invisible currents run under the surface, and many migrants can't swim.

The church is open for any pilgrims to visit, including those who make it across wet. We sat in one of the pews for a few minutes and then went toward the altar, where we could see that the hands of the Virgin of Guadalupe icon in the back corner showed wear from being touched countless times by people who have prayed to her. Votive candles with various imprints of saints on the glass had been placed at her feet, and freestanding candles left with prayers had long since burned into puddles of wax on the floor.

We exited through the side door and walked toward the front so I could take a picture. As I focused on the church, trucks stopped on the road above us; first one, then two, then a third green and white Border Patrol vehicle came. The officers said nothing, but just waited on the road above us as I photographed. When they cruised away, the three of us walked down the hill toward the river to see Pepe's on the River Bar and Grill. Father Roy, one of the modern-day Oblate priests we met briefly earlier in the day, had recommended we eat dinner there. It's a spot where locals drink beer and eat comfort food while sitting on the outdoor deck overlooking the Rio Grande. The deck was drenched with the afternoon sun, and the temperature was perfect for sitting out, but it was closed on Mondays. We sat at a table for a moment anyway and watched the river flow by. Near our table was a large banner advertising Lone Star beer that welcomed "Winter Texans."

| | | |

LATER BILL DROPPED us off at Our Lady of Guadalupe Catholic Church where we were to stay at the invitation of Father Roy Snipes. Meeting us in the front room, Father Roy, a large and bespectacled Texan, talked to us first about his favorite topic: his dogs. They were impossible to miss: the three huge, loving, and somewhat decrepit black labs were glued to him, watching his every move and listening intently to his voice. The oldest, probably weighing over a hundred pounds, climbed nearly into his lap. The two others lay at his feet, one with his head propped on Father Roy's boot.

Father Roy, an early riser, was ready to turn in for the night soon after we arrived around nine, but before he left us, he made sure to tell us where we could find the Lone Star beer in the refrigerator. He loved beer, Texas A&M, and animals, he said, as he talked with us for a few minutes about his menagerie of livestock in the stables out back. It was like the stable in Bethlehem, he said, before ducking into his office "to finish a few chores." Closing the door, he said he would talk with us about his work on the border in the morning. Knowing it was a big topic, we both wanted to save it. I couldn't wait to hear more about the animals as well.

As we headed to the guest quarters, we looked at the clippings and posters plastering the hallway walls: political cartoons about the border, Aggies sports paraphernalia, fishing pictures, and cowboy and Lone Star posters all hung interspersed among religious imagery. One poster stood out: a brown-skinned Virgin of Guadalupe in a prayerful pose over a mounted cowboy. The images spoke of the outsized personality of a man who loved south Texas and all it stands for. They also made it clear that Father Roy loves migrants who cross the border from Mexico into Texas. His courage and love showed through in the newspaper photographs on the walls. The pictures caught his laughing eyes as he talked about his border ministry. His dogs seemed to be in every photo.

We climbed the stairs to the spotless and cool simple bedroom furnished with four single beds. As we turned out the light and started to talk of monasteries and border politics before drifting off to sleep, a donkey brayed outside our window. I went to sleep thinking about cowboy priests riding their horses along the border while green trucks chased men and women running and plunging into the water. One cartoon I'd seen downstairs played into it all. The drawing showed Joseph and Mary on their donkey trying to get across the U.S. border. Baby Jesus was in his mother's arms.

|  |  |  |  |

BEFORE THERE WERE AMERICAN conquistadors who defeated Santa Anna and his army in the 1840s, there were Spaniards who brought their swords and guns to conquer the worlds once controlled by the Aztecs, Mixtecs, and the Maya. Catholicism began in Mexico when the Spaniards led by Hernán Cortés and his soldiers first landed on a Gulf of Mexico beach in 1519, planted a cross-shaped sword in the sand, and knelt to give thanks to his God for delivering them. After praying, Cortés ordered his men to burn their ships and head on horseback and foot to the city of Tenochtitlan. Through a series of military maneuvers, along with trickery that entailed bribing rivals of the Aztecs, Cortés's small detail of soldiers overtook the powerful Montezuma and his legions of soldiers.

Then Cortés killed the Aztec king, declared victory, and claimed Mexico for the King of Spain in 1521. He did all this as a faithful Catholic.

Conquest and Catholicism continued to operate hand-in-hand for centuries to come, as the church took land from the indigenous as willfully as the soldiers did. But that is not the whole story of Mexican Catholicism. One notable exception was the Spanish Dominican friar named Bartolomé de Las Casas, who wrote the famous treatise against harming the indigenous population of Latin America entitled *A Short Account of the Destruction of the Indies and in Defense of the Indians*.[1] In his book he pleaded to the Spanish king for fair treatment of those in New Spain. In every era since, despite the centuries of genocide and the theft of cultures, histories, languages, wealth, and belief systems from the native populations, there have been solid examples of Catholic benevolence.

The Oblates seem to have been some of the good cowboys for God. Their order began in France in 1816, only three decades prior to their arrival in Texas. Eugène de Mazenod, a former nobleman who refused to serve in the traditional priestly role, was the inspiration behind the brotherhood. Having been troubled from an early age by the living conditions of poor people, he chose a ministry with farm laborers, preaching the message of God's love in the hinterlands of France instead of in churches. His example led to the founding of the Oblates of Mary Immaculate, an order dedicated to ministering to the poor in nontraditional church settings.

When they arrived at the Mexico border, the Oblates met up with the Mexican Virgin Mary of Guadalupe. The *café-con-leche*-skinned, beatific Virgin, wearing a green and gold robe surrounded by roses and borne by cherubs, is the most important symbol of Mexican church history, and has been proclaimed the national symbol of the whole country as well. "Guadalupe" and, of course, "Maria" have been the namesakes for countless girls born in Mexico, as well as for towns and hundreds of churches

---

1. Bartolomé de Las Casas, *A Short Account of the Destruction of the Indies*.

in Mexico and beyond, including the Catholic Church in Mission where Father Roy and his fellow priests serve.

| | | |

WE AWOKE THE FOLLOWING morning and headed downstairs to a breakfast with Father Roy. He was already at the kitchen table surrounded by his fellow Oblates, Father Jim, Father Philion, and their dogs. Father Jim held a Chihuahua cuddled near his neck as he read his section of the newspaper with one hand. The three priests were discussing the day's news when we got to the table. One particular event had captured Father Roy's attention—a robbery at gunpoint by members of a drug cartel on nearby Falcon Reservoir, an impoundment of the Rio Grande where he likes to take his fishing boat. In fact, he had said just the night before: "I'd like to take us fishing in my boat if we had more time." The mugging hit close to home for Father Roy.

This led directly to my asking him about the border. "It's more complex than a parish priest is going to find out!" he answered. Instead of dwelling on the border violence, he went immediately to his anger about immigrant bashing, as he called it, calling out former Colorado Congressman Tom Tancredo by name. "What does he really have to be afraid of? We should make it possible for people to come and work. They're the best people we'll meet. They're willing to work. It's *crime* that is our enemy, not the workers. The *drug cartel* is our enemy. But you can't jump a man who wants to feed his own family. They call them 'illegals,' but what kind of legality is that? They're making something black and white that's not at all black and white. Glenn Beck sucks in people telling them there's a clear good and evil. But it's not that simple."

He turned to the role of the priests. "The Oblates got here and there was barely a border at all. Back then there was even a different border, and you couldn't draw a line between one side and the other. Now the Minutemen and groups like them are preaching against people trying to come to work. Their daddies fought against Hitler, now spiritually they're taking Hitler's side." He called the attitude "group think and fear."

"They don't know the border personally," he said.

> I grew up with some prejudice, but this is some kind of mean-hearted hostility. Here at the border, we don't take a hostile attitude toward an alien being, but we think of him as a neighbor. In my ministry I take a "don't ask, don't tell" policy about immigration. There was a man beaten up and dumped in a cane field at the river. He made his way here by the sound of the church bells, and we ministered to him. Then there was the rancher who was run off his land by the drug cartel. We minister to him here.

In other words, there was no borderline in any sense at Father Roy's church. Anyone can receive blessings, he said: "Whosoever thirsts let him come. The way we 'Border Texans' look at it is worlds apart from Tancredo and those guys."

After breakfast, the Father took us to see his animal stables. He and his Latino helper named Davíd snapped leads onto halters and led the llama, two donkeys, and all the dogs as a group over to the church for photographs with Father Jim and the Chihuahua. He lined the animals up in loose formation and asked, "What do the Oblates have to offer the world?" He answered his own question: "We're the old cowboy priests; we're from the stable of Bethlehem. We come from the rancho." After photos, we walked into the church with Father Roy and the dogs while Davíd waited outside with the larger animals.

Capturing my attention inside was a table filled with photographs of veterans in uniform. A large statue of the Virgin stood with her hands outstretched over all of them. There were more than a hundred different people in the photos, men and women, all of whom looked Latino. They glowed with the light shining through the stained-glass windows above them. Father Roy came over to point out which were photos of soldiers who had fought and died in Europe and Vietnam, and there were other more recent ones who had died in Afghanistan and Iraq. "They're all Catholic war veterans from this church. Many were born in Mexico, and we received them and then they went to war for this country. It shows that loving this country has nothing to do with being anti-immigrant."

Then Father Roy led us to the altar for more photographs with his dogs. Father Jim and his Chihuahua joined us. The dogs go to every service, they said. On the altar is a lifelike statue dedicated to the memory of their most beloved Labrador retriever. "They're all part of the ministry too," said Father Roy. Even the ones that had passed on still had a role.

Nativity scenes everywhere include the animals that attended the birth a child belonging to a family of refugees who slept in a stable. The newborn undocumented immigrant's first bed was a hay manger. He was born in a foreign town where his two migrant parents had paused in their flight from violence. Jesus would grow up in a different land and go on to say that he, the "son of man," had no place to call home. He blessed the poor and the immigrant in his Sermon on the Mount. He and his mother would cross many other borders after that, appearing in a variety of forms globally. In Mexico, Mary appeared first to a *campesino* (farmworker) named Juan Diego and told him, presumably in his indigenous language, to take a message to the bishop. And her skin was the color of his.

# FIFTEEN

# The Hand-Drawn Ferry

LOS EBANOS, TEXAS, AND GUSTAVO DÍAZ ORDAZ,
TAMAULIPAS

A HALF-HOUR'S DRIVE WEST OF OUR LADY OF GUADALUPE
Church on Route 48 is the only hand-drawn ferry linking the
United States and Mexico. It was a must-see according to Sarah.
Father Roy told us how to get there. There are no state signs, no
markers indicating where to turn. You just go left at the sign for
Los Ebanos, Texas, a little hamlet of a few hundred people, and
follow the narrow road south for several miles. We went toward
the lowest and southernmost point in town and suddenly we
were there.

There was a little hut with warning signs and instructions for
customs declarations but nothing foreboding, and no signs that
said to keep out. In contrast to the militarized locations with
tanks and flak-jacketed guards, here there were only picnic tables, shade trees, and a state historical marker. A low metal cable
stretched across the road with a sign that simply said "closed."
We guessed it was because of the high water from the storms.
We stepped over the cable and walked in.

The morning was sunny and perfectly calm, but no one was
there, not even a watchman. We passed the guardhouse and
headed down the hill toward the river. The boat, named *El*

*Chalán* ("Horse Trader"), was tied off with cables fastened to the bank, just far enough from shore so that no one would get any ideas about using it, but close enough to avoid getting washed away by high water.

When the ferry is running, six men, all of them related, pull the ferry back and forth by hand, using ropes connected between Los Ebanos, Texas, and Gustavo Díaz Ordaz, Tamaulipas, the Mexican sister town. Díaz Ordaz's streets began only fifteen car lengths or so away from Texas on this high water day—likely half that during a drought. The men charged ten pesos (one dollar) for pulling a pedestrian across the water and thirty-five pesos (three and one-half dollars) for pulling a car. The ferry began in Los Ebanos in 1950 and has operated there since. *El Chalán* is the second vessel to be used there, as the original ferry was destroyed in a flood in 1980.

We sat on the picnic table under a large eucalyptus tree towering over the historical marker and talked of the billions of dollars already spent and of the additional funds allocated to enforcing the border with new

The hand-drawn Rio Grande ferry named *El Chalán* ("Horse Trader") at Los Ebanos, Texas.

Border Patrol members, National Guard soldiers, high walls, and electronic surveillance equipment recently purchased with taxpayer money. I had been accosted only a few days earlier for taking pictures, so I was wary. But nothing happened; no one showed up.

Being at the Los Ebanos ferry was like being in another country, in another era. It easily could have been 1950 on a river somewhere in rural Mexico where farmers needed to get their carts across to do their work. But even that bucolic place had been affected by the drug violence. According to a feature by Damien Cave about the ferry in the *New York Times Magazine*, people from Díaz Ordaz who live in the United States are afraid to go back across on the ferry these days because they fear the cartels.[1] That fear led to an opportunity for the ferrymen, who go across multiple times every day when the water allows. Some former residents entrust the boatmen with their house keys and pay them to look after their homes.

Almost everyone using the ferry is a Mexican citizen who must continue to navigate life on both sides of the river. For them, *El Chalán* continues to be the best option for getting across. While they continue to negotiate the realities of violence and all that makes the border what it is, they also step onto an old handmade ferry that uses no gas, no electricity, only the power of human strength, and ride across as people have done for more than a half-century. Momentarily they float between two worlds.

Though standing on land, we seemed to float there, too, in a land somewhere long ago. Then we got into our car and drove away. No one stopped us. No one asked questions. No one was there to care.

---

1. Damien Cave, "Whatever Floats Your Boat," *New York Times Magazine*, March 4, 2011.

# SIXTEEN

# Prohibition Bar

LAREDO, TEXAS, AND NUEVO LAREDO,
TAMAULIPAS

SARAH BOONE HAD CALLED JAY CASTRO, THE OWNER OF THE
Villa Del Rio Bed & Breakfast, right after hearing from us the
first time. I learned later that he had helped Sarah think of
many of the contacts on the list. He also invited us to stay at
his place in Laredo, Texas. When we decided to take him up on
his offer, we didn't realize he would be giving up his own bed
and sleeping on his couch. We finally spoke with Jay in person
shortly after leaving Los Ebanos.

He agreed to meet us at his apartment in the converted hotel on
the Laredo border at five o'clock
that afternoon.

Border Patrol vehicles parked
below the train tracks heading
into Nuevo Laredo, Mexico,
from Laredo, Texas.

We arrived in Laredo early enough to explore the Mexican side. We walked over the busy international bridge where thousands of pedestrians cross each day between Laredo and Nuevo Laredo. We looked down on the vehicle entrance as we headed up the sidewalk bounded by chain-link fencing high enough to prevent jumping off and curved outward to prevent any climbing up. Then we passed over the river and the Border Patrol vehicles parked underneath the bridge. A railroad bridge was just upstream from there. A train was slowly moving across it.

When we were just above the borderline and looking down from the bridge, a Border Patrol boat sped down the river and a helicopter hovered over the water in support. The pedestrians seemed oblivious to the many forms of policing and didn't even look over at the dozens of Border Patrol SUVs and vans sitting with their engines running and their occupants looking toward Mexico. But I was mesmerized. It was like being in a war zone without any visible enemies anywhere.

In the other direction, toward the skyline in Mexico, flew the largest flag I've ever seen, as big as a city block and so heavy a typical desert breeze couldn't lift it. It only undulated as if dozing. When finally a strong gust did take hold of it and the red, white, and green flag jumped to attention for a second, it commanded a huge part of the skyline over Nuevo Laredo, and then quickly drifted back to its slumber.

Back in Nuevo Laredo's heyday, thousands of Americans crossed the bridge to take advantage of the food, the beer and tequila, and the shopping there. Hope grew up going there as a child with her family, traveling from San Antonio in the back of their Impala station wagon. The family never thought much about border safety in the sixties and taking children there was no problem. When we crossed over forty years later, no other gringos of any age were anywhere in sight. There were no tourists at all as far as I could tell, just thousands of Mexican citizens going both directions to work or to buy things like electronics that you can get cheaper in the United States.

It was easy to tell, even from the bridge, that Nuevo Laredo's economy wasn't going well. Despite all the vehicle traffic we could see idling in lines below us as we started over the bridge, which had to mean commerce, the money didn't seem to be benefiting the city businesses south of the line in any visible way. Back in the sixties and seventies the peso had been on the rise as Mexican oil wells gushed out new profits, but then came the global oil glut of the 1980s and Mexico's economy began to dry up. The government intervened to save it by slashing the value of the peso, which dropped to a tenth of its former value overnight. Mexico's economy hasn't fully recovered since. As we walked down the ramp into Nuevo Laredo we could see the streets were dirtier, nearly everyone looked poorer, the storefronts were shabbier, and the merchandise was of lower quality than its Texas counterpart just a few hundred yards away. There is no disparity quite like that anywhere else in the world.

The United States boasts an economy fifty times larger than Mexico's. Yet, seeing the thousands going back and forth on that single bridge, it was clear that many Mexicans are helping the U.S. economy hum. It was impossible to believe that somehow we did it on our own in America, or that Mexicans are less industrious or care less than we do about getting ahead. Of course, walking that one span didn't readily tell the story of free trade agreements, laborers who work for low wages, U.S. companies moving to Mexico, or what is going on with the black market in drugs and guns. But the results of all these forces were so stark that in walking that span, it served as a refresher in international trade and politics.

We meandered through a few streets to get our bearings as Hope talked of childhood memories. Her parents let the three kids wander through the open market and gave them small change to buy things on their own. Now our quick walk through the first lines of shops revealed no trinket that grabbed our attention, much to the disappointment of the anxious vendors who had been waiting for who knows how long for a tourist. Probably we were the only gringos all day, and for that reason nearly everyone called out to us. Some even came out to offer deals that dipped by half with every step or two we moved away. Any glance seemed to encourage them more. It was maddening and heartbreaking at the same time. But our main purpose was not to browse anyway. We were headed to the

Cadillac Bar. It had been on Hope's list since we first started planning in March. Even if it was only three o'clock in the afternoon, we had to visit.

Growing up in San Antonio, Hope had been immersed—mostly because of her mother's foresight—in the culture and language of the Texas borderlands, and therefore enjoyed a very different childhood from most of her white suburban peers. She learned Spanish as a kindergartner, gained firsthand experience with the language from interacting with Mexican housekeepers who lived part time with her family, and rode every month or two with her family to take in the sights and sounds of Mexico. Nuevo Laredo was one of the family favorites. Back then, no one thought about checking for drugs and guns. Even their undocumented housekeeper made the trip without worrying much. Hope knows because she traveled home with her once.

Every time the family visited Nuevo Laredo, they ate at the Cadillac Bar. The place had loads of character, excellent food and service, and great Mexican drinks. Hope's father preferred Bohemia. Her mother enjoyed a tequila sour. The children got to drink Mexican Cokes, which always tasted better there. Well-trained waiters always doted on the kids. Hope recalled live mariachi music, photographs and memorabilia that hung on the restaurant's walls, and, most vividly, one of Pancho Villa's saddles on display.

The Cadillac Bar's heyday began during Prohibition in the United States when American demand for alcohol needed international assistance. According to its website, the bar had first started in New Orleans in the early 1920s, but "Prohibition caused the original owner to pack up everything and move to Nuevo Laredo, Mexico in 1926." With alcohol outlawed in America between 1919 and 1933, heading to Mexico became a brilliant move. With good tequila and beer available there every day, countless thousands of people began crossing the border to drink safely and legally at the Cadillac. Mexican people also went there, and the bar thrived for the rest of the twentieth century. Though Mexican specialties like *cabrito* (grilled goat) became favorite items, the menu always retained a flavor of New Orleans, serving jambalaya and andouille sausage as well.

The Cadillac was open but empty when we walked in. The waiters and the bartender were standing around talking, not expecting anyone. The local Mexican clientele wouldn't be there for hours and as far as we could tell, international visitors had stopped going altogether. We chatted some with the staff, who said business had dropped off drastically in recent years. Things did not look good, they said. When Hope told them of her childhood experiences, they let us stay as long as we wanted. It was too early to eat, but we ordered beers and walked around to look at the place while sipping from our frosted mugs. Every wall was filled with images that bespoke Mexico's love of family, place, music, dance, and everything stereotypically *ranchero*, just what one would expect on the border, and done tastefully.

But Pancho's saddle was gone and the staff didn't have a clue where it went. Most had never heard it was there. Other details had changed too, but the employees' attitudes toward guests had not. We felt as if we were their most important customers ever, even though we ate nothing. We bought a few shot glasses as gifts and then headed back outside and walked toward the bridge.

It was only a few months later, after we were already back in North Carolina, that we heard on NPR about the bar's demise. John Burnett, a regular reporter for *All Things Considered*, had featured a number of the border's Prohibition bars in the context of the changes that violence has wrought in the border economy. The piece included the following: "A sign taped to the door of the famed Cadillac Bar, which opened in Nuevo Laredo in 1926, says it is 'temporarily closed' as of August 1. Nuevo Laredo—across from Laredo, Texas—has experienced a new spasm of violence between the Zetas gang and the Gulf Cartel. A few months ago, someone tossed a hand grenade into the U.S. consulate. A parking lot attendant on the corner says he'll be surprised if the Cadillac reopens. 'There's no future now,' he says."[1] Burnett also reported that in contrast to

---

1. John Burnett, "Mexico's Drug War Hits Historic Border Cantina," *All Things Considered*, August 16, 2010.

the Cadillac, the cartels in Ciudad Juarez had kept certain bars open by providing them protection. The radio piece left me questioning whether the violence was really the only cause of the financial loss, or whether fear brought on by reporting about violence also played a role. Regardless, we were some of the last Americans to visit the Cadillac. I wish we had bought more souvenir shot glasses.

|  |  |  |  |

THE CADILLAC'S SUCCESS south of the border is only one side of the Prohibition story. Alcohol sales north of the border during Prohibition were the dark underbelly, all too similar to the soaring drug sales fueling the traffickers today. Huge illicit networks formed in the 1920s. Poisonous alcohol flowed into back alleys in the inner cities. Networks of sales stretched across state lines and gave rise to the Mafia. Federal forces began to crack down, but history shows that Prohibition was a miserable failure as it boosted the profits of crime syndicates and did almost nothing to curtail alcohol consumption. Lawmen were never able to defeat their Prohibition foes. Only legislation turned the tide when the Twenty-First Amendment repealed Prohibition. Obviously our nearly century-old War on Drugs, which incidentally began during Prohibition, has not worked either.

Many U.S. citizens today have gone public with their opposition to drug prohibition. One organization with a major public presence on this issue is LEAP (Law Enforcement Against Prohibition). With a list of nearly fifty thousand e-mail members that includes judges, police chiefs, and other officers, its website states that its members "believe that to save lives and lower the rates of disease, crime and addiction, as well as to conserve tax dollars, we must end drug prohibition." Regarding the drug war and the border, they are clear:

Just as we put alcohol traffickers out of business and ended their violence by ending alcohol prohibition, we can do the same with today's prohibited drugs. Putting the drug gangs and cartels out of business, while spending less time endlessly chasing drug users, will free up our time and resources to protect our country from other threats. The alarming rise of violence in Mexico and Central America must be stopped, and as those of us who have worked the border know, ending drug prohibition is the only way to do it. We need to stop empowering criminals and protect our citizens instead.[2]

The prohibition of alcohol in the United States had put the Cadillac Bar on the map to begin with. Could ending a second de facto prohibition on drugs bring it back?

2. www.leap.cc.

# SEVENTEEN

# Border Walker

LAREDO, TEXAS

WE CALLED JAY FROM THE U.S SIDE OF THE BRIDGE WHEN CELL reception magically reappeared. He told us he would meet us at the big round hotel within sight of the main crossing. When we pulled up at the entrance, Jay was outside to meet us. In his early sixties, Jay was tanned and wore his graying wiry hair over his collar. He had on a Hawaiian shirt and jeans. He seemed in a hurry to get our bags inside and without stopping for chit-chat started pulling Hope's luggage to the lobby before I had mine out of the trunk. It was obvious early on that he didn't dally around, and soon we found he was always on duty with his work as well.

Maybe back in the sixties, perhaps when Hope's family had toured the area in their wood-paneled Impala station wagon, the Rio Grande River Hotel

A few of the ICE Detention Center identification bracelets made into a chain left at the shrine to the Virgin Mary at the Casa del Migrante in Ciudad Juarez, Chihuahua.

had drawn tourists. Sometime since then, however, the multistory circular building had been converted into apartments and allowed to deteriorate. The pool outside was no longer in use. Stained shag carpet and broken fountains greeted us in the lobby, and the elevators made me wonder if we would make it to the eighth floor where Jay lived.

Jay explained that the place provided an inexpensive means for him to live and work on the border, and once inside, his place seemed pleasant enough and had a great view of the Rio. Jay rented two connected rooms. He insisted that we take his bedroom, saying he would stay on the couch in his office. Dismissing our protests, he closed the door and gave us some time to shower and rest up before dinner.

Right away we went to the large window that overlooks Nuevo Laredo, where we had a bird's-eye view of half a dozen Border Patrol vehicles parked down at the river bridge. We could also see, and hear faintly, a few ATVs buzzing around and a Border Patrol boat speeding up the river yet again. Were these real emergencies, perhaps someone swimming across, a drug trafficking threat? It seemed highly unlikely in broad daylight with so many patrollers present. But for whatever reason, they sped about, leaving and returning, then sitting idling in their vehicles, all of them ready for action all the time. To me, from high above, all the commotion looked like the work of highly motorized ants traveling to and fro.

For dinner, Jay suggested we eat at a little Tex-Mex diner in downtown Laredo within walking distance. He talked the entire way and I scribbled notes, sometimes stopping to write a sentence and then trotting to catch up. He never stopped talking throughout our dinner either. He was full of information about border justice and environmental sustainability, and made all of it connect to government conspiracies. I had never met anyone more consumed with border politics, the wall, detention, and environmental degradation, and for Jay, everything fit together into one grand nefarious scheme. His analysis seemed paralyzing to us, but somehow finding the interconnections gave him more energy to fight, even if he were the last man standing.

Jay had started an organization as a direct response to Congress's passage of the Secure Fence Act of 2006, the act that had made possible the construction of seven hundred miles of wall. Jay's first action as director of Border Ambassadors was to organize a series of protest walks. His initial walk along the border was from Laredo to Brownsville, and it took fifteen days. He received financial support and accompaniment from the ACLU, the Audubon Society, independent ranchers, Native American leaders, and others. The walk helped form a coalition of people championing humanitarian, environmental, and legal change in border policies. We learned Sarah had included some of those on the list she made.

Jay talked in a cadence as we ate, as though we were still walking. At one point he brought up Pat Nixon's dedication of Friendship Park in San Diego. She had stood before a crowd at the border and said, "May there never be a wall between these two great nations, only friendship." I wrote down the quote, knowing I would likely spend time at the park if it still existed. "How far down we've sunk since that day," Jay said.

After completing the walk in 2006, he organized another in 2007, calling it "Hands Across el Rio." And then he did it again with "Spring Break Walk" in 2008. A variety of flash points pushed him along, from the debate between Hillary Clinton and Barack Obama in 2008 on CNN to the proposal to put the wall through the University of Texas at Brownsville and Texas Southmost College—the one at the golf course. He had been there to protest them all. And he connected militarization and harm to migrants with environmental damage, as with the deliberate defoliation of the Rio's banks. He also went "up against the Border Patrol" before the national media, he said.

The most gripping of his concerns was what he called the "concentration camps" run by Immigration Control and Enforcement and outsourced to private companies such as the Corrections Corporation of America. One he kept mentioning was the T. Don Hutto Residential Center in Taylor, Texas, north of Austin. It was only one of the private detention centers paid for by taxpayers, Jay said. Others had been built and run by Boeing, Raytheon, and other military industrial companies, all with ties to the Bush administration and particularly to Vice President Dick Cheney, he said. And they were still at it after leaving the White House.

"Concentration camps?" I repeated when I found an opening. That set him off. He told horror stories about women and children kept in private prisons without representation, without media scrutiny—hundreds, likely thousands, of them are there, he said. The conditions were deplorable according to witnesses who have gotten away: cold temperatures, no blankets, lights on twenty-fours a day, maggots in food, spoiled milk, and worse. "They're maltreated with impunity," Jay said of the detainees.

"CCA operates other detention centers, including one in Raymondville north of Harlingen, Texas; one in Bayview, east of Harlingen; Los Fresnos near Brownsville; and the Florence and Eloy sites in Arizona. The CCA erects big circus-style Kevlar tents where they house two hundred people per tent." I was chagrined that these centers had not been on our itinerary. "There have been 450,000 immigrants detained in the previous year with prisoners from fifty different countries!" he said. His figures checked out on the Detention Watch Network's website when I looked later. I also found other figures from the American Civil Liberties Union: in 2011 alone more than 429,000 immigrants were detained. In protest, Jay had organized a fourth walk, calling it "Citizens Walk for Human Dignity."

Back in 1994, Jay had started and become the executive director of the Rio Grande International Studies Center, an environmental and cultural organization whose purpose is to preserve and foster respect for the river and those who live along it. The environmental group had evolved as Jay had discovered more about human rights violations. He realized his work was about more than water shortages, and that the 355,000 square miles of watershed for the Rio Grande in the United States connected to the Corrections Corporation of America's detention facilities and the rest of the border security complex. His current project was to learn about Operation Endgame, the plan begun in 2003 by the Office of Detention and Removal Operations of the U.S. Department of Homeland Security's Bureau of Immigration and Customs Enforcement to detain and deport all "removable aliens" and "suspected terrorists" currently living in the United States by 2012.

It didn't have to be that way, he said. "The border is the confluence of the Americas. Here, you get it," he said. "You know these crazy laws can't be enforced in such a place. And on top of that, there's corruption and bribery, even as the military complex is making billions of dollars. There are twenty-five thousand Border Patrol agents and they're working on bringing ten thousand more, and still human trafficking occurs."

Michael Chertoff, a secretary of the Department of Homeland Security under the Bush administration, had been one of the worst violators of our civil rights, he said. As head of the department, Chertoff was given power by Congress to override and waive laws that he deemed interfered with national security. "He waived thirty-six federal laws and environmental protections to build the border wall," Jay reported.

Jay continued piling on the facts, all of which I later read in other places. He said that the Women's Refugee Commission has uncovered, mostly through the work of independent researcher Amy Thompson, abuses of huge numbers of children under the age of eighteen caught crossing the border. "When CCA detains a migrant, it makes $7,000 a day in taxpayer money, and, when they no longer can hold them, they bus them back to the border and let them go—too often to wander on their own. Used to be 'catch and release,' but it has now been turned into 'detain and deport.' Detention equals profit! But the government keeps it secret. This is why we do the protest walks."

As we walked back to the hotel for the night, my head was spinning with details. What energy the man had! I looked toward the river from the Laredo streets where we could see huge Border Patrol spotlights run by generators. You could feel the tension in the air. As he looked over toward Mexico, Jay released another barrage of words. "These countries should be symbiotic. We should be neighbors. Why do we want to piss these people off? We're treating them like they're the invading force. Xenophobia! Racism!" He trailed off.

A year after our visit with Jay, PBS's *Frontline* aired an exposé entitled "Lost in Detention" that detailed the stories of men and women caught in the web of deportation.[1] It said the federal government claims it is

---

1. "Lost in Detention," *Frontline*, October 18, 2011.

deporting only those with criminal records, but in fact mothers and fathers whose only offense is a simple traffic violation, and others with no violations other than working in this country without papers, have been detained and deported. At least four hundred thousand deportations a year have occurred since President Obama took office, all of them mandated by Congress. Only about a third of those deported have had criminal records, *Frontline* reported, and many of the convicted have only committed minor traffic violations. The detained and deported include minors, some perhaps born elsewhere and brought to the United States by their parents as very young children, even infants. Even as the Obama administration has deferred action on the deportation of children brought into the country by their parents, no one in government seems to be talking about the detention centers. And the only mention of the border wall is about enforcement, seemingly always the beginning point of the debate.

|   |   |   |   |

THE NEXT MORNING Jay took us to his office to meet Wendy Morales of Univision TV in Laredo. It was my turn to be interviewed as Hope and Jay watched. Wendy did a story in Spanish about our trip, saying afterward how glad she was that someone had taken an interest. Afterward, Wendy told us about several other border advocates in Laredo. One of her heroes was Catholic Sister Rosemary, who started and ran a shelter for women migrants called *"Casa Misericordia"*(Mercy) in one of the low-income barrios. The shelter helps female migrants who have just arrived in Laredo with no place to sleep and no money to buy food. "Some have children; some *are* children traveling alone," Wendy said, and "sadly, too many have been raped or attacked by thugs while traveling." As undocumented immigrants, they have no rights in the United States, thereby making the nongovernmental organizations like Sister Rosemary's indispensable to them. But she can only go so far. Wendy said that when the cartels operate in the sister's neighborhood in Mexico, she has to pretend that they are invisible and look the other way.

| | | |

LEAVING RIO GRANDE International Study Center, we drove down the nearby hill toward the border and by the Border Patrol station at the railroad tracks. A cargo train had stopped above the station. Jay had mentioned in passing that while the officers patrol the riverbanks closely for pedestrians, there are twelve hundred to fifteen hundred railcars and perhaps fifteen thousand trucks crossing the border daily in Laredo that get too little attention. I stopped to take a photograph of the train and the little station beside it.

Stopping at the edge of the public right-of-way at the inspection station, I framed a few wide shots of the train with Border Patrol vehicles in the foreground. No one came out of any building, no one pulled up in a vehicle, and no one said anything. Still I hurried with the camera, thinking I would be approached at any minute. I got the shot and jumped back into the car, and we drove away fast. Then I realized that I'd begun policing myself, already acting as if I'd been doing something wrong by stopping on a public road and taking a picture.

Frightened by my own timidity, I asked Hope, "Is this how fascism works? Does fear make you second-guess yourself and you stop doing what you think could be suspect? Do citizens do the work by policing themselves?" Hope retold me the story of her visit to Spain as a student during the waning years of the Franco regime.

"You remember what happened with my camera, don't you?" she asked. While taking an innocent photograph of some ships in a harbor, she had been detained by two police officers and made to open her camera and expose the film inside while they watched. In Franco's world, no one could photograph any government structure, even a bridge or port. After 9/11, I remembered that a few amateur photographers had been arrested for similar offenses. Police suspected they might use the photos to study how to place bombs in public places. I had not heard of arrests for taking shots of Border Patrol cars and headquarters, but I wasn't sure it had not happened.

We rounded a curve near the Laredo Community College and passed a row of twelve-foot metal posts planted some six inches apart alongside the road. Uphill hundreds of feet from the river, maybe a quarter of a mile, the wall was out of place. We surmised that building it so far away from the line prevented having to police a steep bank on an unpopulated hillside. But when Homeland Security chose to put the fence there, they had created a space where nature had started subtly taking back the landscape. Apparently they hadn't sprayed any defoliant there yet.

I braked, backed up, and reached for my camera. A few paces behind the car I found a perfect wild sunflower peeking between the bars and bending eastward toward the early morning sun. I peered through the viewfinder, breathed deeply, and tried not to care as a truck approached from behind.

| | | |

AS WE LEFT LAREDO, a friend of ours called to say she had just heard on the radio about a daytime shooting on the border near El Paso. She said to Hope, "I just wanted to make sure you're okay." We were nowhere near Juarez, but we were shaken by the news. A Border Patrol officer had shot and killed a youth accused of throwing rocks at the officer from the Mexico side. The fifteen-year old was unarmed. Right away videos were posted on YouTube showing the whole incident. Mexican citizens were outraged, and protests had begun at the border by the time we received the call. The boy's name was Sergio Adrián Hernández. People who knew him said that he had been taking college classes in El Paso. The *Huffington Post* reported that the president of the union of Border Patrol officers said that rock throwing can cause serious injury, and that one "deadly force encounter" justifies another.

"We're fine," Hope reported to our friend. "We're just leaving Laredo. But how horrible!" We mourned as we drove on. We later learned that Sergio Adrián Hernández was the seventeenth person killed or wounded by U.S. immigration authorities in 2010, already eight more than the previous year, and it was only June.

# EIGHTEEN

# The Road to Eagle Pass

FARM TO MARKET ROAD, TEXAS

ROUGH CALCULATIONS BY MAP SHOWED EAGLE PASS TO BE just over a hundred miles away. We were to eat lunch there at noon with Mayor Chad Foster. I wanted to take the back road. Hope wanted to stick to the interstate so we could be on time. I knew she was right about the speed we could travel, but I argued that when there is a clearly marked road to follow along the border, we should take it and not just go the easy route. "Besides, we *can* make it on time," I said. "See, here's the route. One hundred miles and we have just over two hours." She looked, but sensing something wasn't right, Hope said, "It was your idea for this trip in the first place," leaned back in her seat, and pretended to take a nap.

Finding the back road wasn't easy. I pulled off an exit and went inside a convenience store to ask directions. The attendant gave me some idea of where we were, which had to be close, but he had never heard of getting to Eagle Pass by any route except the interstate. That should have been a warning.

From the store, I turned onto a service road and began winding through a surprising maze of warehouses and parking lots, where hundreds, perhaps thousands, of transfer trailers were

parked, all of them waiting for some task of hauling. I kept making my way through them and then suddenly there it was, a four-lane road

A wild sunflower stretches toward the morning sun at the border wall in Laredo, Texas.

exactly where I had hoped the border road would be. It was called alternately Farm to Market Road, El Indio Highway, Las Minas Road, and Eagle Pass Road on the map. This had to be it, though it had looked small on the map. I gloated a little to Hope, "See there's the road, and look, it's much bigger than we thought." Her eyes remained closed.

The road was lined with warehouses with official-sounding trade names like International Commerce Center, Las Minas Industrial Park, Pan-American Business Park, International Trade Center, International Distribution Park, and Pelegrino Industrial Park. I was amazed at all the activity, but suddenly it all began to make sense. I couldn't believe how many trucks there were. Hope couldn't help but look when I said, "We've just run into one of the big conduits of trade between Mexico and the U.S.!" Located where most motorists, even local convenience-store clerks, would never go was a major artery that pumped truckload after truckload of goods from Latin America into the United States.

I later checked the satellite image. It showed a major road from Mexico just two to three miles west of the Laredo population center. It was called the *Commercio Mundial* and cut across the border by way of the *Puente Internacional*, also known as the World Trade Bridge. All of it, the satellite image shows, eventually connects to Interstate 35. Zooming in, one can tell that it is where the thousands of trucks cross. They carry newly manufactured goods assembled in the many maquiladora plants built south of the border—all made possible by NAFTA.

Admittedly, when Jay mentioned that fifteen thousand trucks crossed at Laredo every day, I had been skeptical. I wondered how even a hundred trucks could make it through that bottleneck at Nuevo Laredo. But this hidden highway made me a believer. Seeing all of it without the benefit of the satellite image, I reasoned that the little road on our map had been widened due to NAFTA commerce and that our map was outdated. All we would have to do is follow the big new route right here in front of us. It would be as good as driving the interstate.

I zoomed along on the road, making good time for some ten miles, then reached a crossroads and encountered another four-lane, numbered Route 255. It cut back to the east at a right angle. "It's amazing how many roads they're building through here," I said, but then I noticed all the truck traffic was turning right and caught a glimpse of I-35 on the horizon where they were headed. I didn't say anything to Hope about that as she had gone back to napping.

As I stayed straight on the Eagle Pass Road, I noticed there was only one other vehicle going our way, an SUV. As the roads diverged, the median ended. Our road immediately narrowed to two lanes, and there was a Border Patrol barricade placed there. As we approached, a German shepherd pulled hard on the patrolwoman's leash as it circled the SUV in front of us sniffing for drugs. Then it was our turn. The dog circled our car fast and we were on our way.

The two-lane blacktop that lay ahead of us looked solid and far more interesting than the interstate. We cruised along at sixty, even seventy going downhill, and I grew more confident by the mile that we would make our lunch with ease. Then we topped a hill and the pavement ended. I slowed down some, but the gravel road was still fairly smooth. It lured me onward. If the road didn't get any worse, then I could do it. I was used to driving on gravel.

We had gone some thirty miles when the gravel also stopped. The road had turned to unimproved dirt with potholes, which due to the recent rains were large and sometimes filled with mud so deep I wondered if we could make it through. Hope sat up as the car fishtailed through a number of them. "We need to go back," she said. Convinced we had covered a lot more ground than she knew while she slept, I assured her we had to be close to Eagle Pass.

It was just past eleven. Now our average speed couldn't have been more than thirty. We came upon a Border Patrol vehicle parked at the top of a rise and stopped to ask if we were on the right road. They said, "You can get there from here but it's still pretty far away." I hated for Hope to hear that. We drove on and the car's clock reached noon, our meeting time, and we had not had phone reception for the last hour.

We passed a few four-wheel-drive vehicles and dump trucks going the other direction, and their drivers looked at us as if they'd never seen a car out there. I'm pretty sure they hadn't. The road got so bad that I started to think we would never make it, but Hope mercifully said nothing. At least our low-slung Chevy was holding steady, I thought, but then we hit a large sharp rock hidden underwater in a mud hole and bent the rim of a wheel. By the time we were on the other side of that mire, the tire was flat. I slowed the car to a crawl until we came to a level and dry spot where I could get out and change the tire. In the trunk I found only one of the toy tires meant for getting you to the nearest suburban service station. Hope, now feeling sorry for me, stepped out to lend her moral support as I jacked up the car and changed the tire as fast as I could. There was still no phone reception. We topped the next rise with the three and a half tires and there was pavement. A sign there said Eagle Pass was another twenty miles.

The paved road was there because of the Kickapoo Lucky Eagle

Casino on the Kickapoo Indian Reservation. A sign there said that it "overlooked the scenic Rio Grande River." I now realized why one of the names was "El Indio Road." Then suddenly we had reception too, and I called Mayor Foster with profuse apologies. "Oh, you came on the Minas Road," he replied, with what sounded like a little chuckle. "Not too many take that." If I had been on time, I would have felt proud to be among the few, but as we were now late by over an hour and still not there, I could only say I was sorry. I apologized to Hope as well.

The Eagle Pass Road once had been slated for improvement, but one ranch family named Treviño had held it up, Mayor Foster explained. They had a lot of control and wanted to keep the road as it is. I could see their point. Having mud holes sure keeps traffic down and makes it safer for cattle and other animals to cross the road, and maybe even keeps illegal trafficking at bay. But at least some grading and gravel couldn't hurt.

Even with the mishaps, deep down I felt satisfied that I had stuck to the original route. Even if we had seen only roadrunners and scrub brush, I had proved it could be done. Actually, all I proved was that one has to be a little crazy to drive the 114 miles of the jeep trail in a rental sedan, but at least we could say we had been where one of the world's most developed international trade highways meets one of the worst roads in the United States. I'm sure Hope wouldn't claim that as a triumph, but she forgave me nonetheless.

# NINETEEN

# Border Ambassador

EAGLE PASS, TEXAS, AND PIEDRAS NEGRAS,
COAHUILA

CHAD FOSTER COULDN'T HAVE BEEN CAST BETTER FOR HIS part if this had been a Hollywood movie about the border. Mustachioed and with a big white hat he referred to as his "Texas toupee," this tall gregarious man in his late sixties greeted us with hospitality that wouldn't stop. We were relieved to find out our original message about lunch hadn't reached him or perhaps he had chosen to forget it, and so he had eaten by the time we arrived. We weren't about to bring up the fact that we hadn't had a bite as he ushered us into his real estate office.

Mayor Chad Foster of Eagle Pass, Texas, shows off his signed copy of the Jeff Parker cartoon that reads, "They say they're building a wall because too many of us enter illegally and won't learn their language or assimilate into their culture."

The walls inside were filled with dozens of portraits of political gatherings and posters. We sat with him at his conference table as he puffed away on cigarettes. "I hope you don't mind if I smoke," he said, having already lit up. There was no way that either of us would have objected. He launched into his soliloquy about the border almost without prompting. I was taping the interview. "The border is the most misunderstood place in the country. We have lived here together for generations and I'm all for keeping that kind of relationship going. The wall is not the answer. Those people in Washington who are trying to legislate divisions between us and are down here building the fence just don't understand this place. They need to come down here to learn about the border from those who live it."

If he seemed to be performing, it was because just after we arrived, a documentary film crew doing a story on the town of Eagle Pass had come into his office to film his every word. One of them stood behind me with a video camera as I asked my questions. Their goal was to film him in cinema verité style. They fudged a little on their "fly-on-the-wall" technique by using my interview to get part of their story. I didn't mind the extra focus or the performance.

Mayor Foster was eloquent and photogenic—the perfect Texas border ambassador, a politician who exuded confidence without condescension. No wonder he had been elected for multiple terms. Though he confided that he would be stepping down come November, he made clear that he would never stop working to promote the towns on both sides of the border. He had kind words for Mexicans, both for the laborers who cross to work the fields—"they're the best workers in the world"—and for the politicians he worked with on cross-border economic development projects, some of his best friends—"They always treat me as a special guest when I go there." Dozens of photos on his office walls showed him with those Mexican leaders at meetings and ribbon-cutting ceremonies, his broad smile, white hat, and western suits common to every shot.

At one point, he took down a framed political cartoon from his wall and showed it to us. The artist Jeff Parker had given him a signed copy.

The illustration published in *Florida Today* depicts a group of stern Native Americans standing by a large palisade of logs after having prohibited a boatload of bewildered Pilgrims from entering. One pilgrim sitting in a boat says to another as they look longingly at the shore, "They say they're building a wall because too many of us enter illegally and won't learn their language or assimilate into their culture."

The mayor's life had been an antithesis to the sentiment of the cartoon. He had learned Spanish as a boy, participated in Mexican culture ever since, and now considered himself a resident of Eagle Pass's sister town of Piedras Negras nearly as much as his own. He was proud to be part of both.

When there was a break in the interview, we told Mayor Foster about the flat tire. He jumped on the problem immediately, shouting into the adjacent office, "Shirley, get me Pedro on the phone." While she made the call, I stepped outside to survey the damage, hoping I might slip across the road and buy a snack before going back in. Just as I reached the car, a Latino man in dusty work clothes pulled up in a beat-up Toyota truck and asked if he could help me. Thinking Shirley was just making the call, I said no thanks and told him that we already were getting help. The driver looked puzzled and said, "Mayor Foster called me, he said someone needed help with a flat."

"Oh, I'm so sorry," I said sheepishly. "That *was* me who needed help. You came so fast that I didn't think it could be possible you'd be the one he'd called." It had been less than five minutes since we told the mayor. He got out and introduced himself. "Pedro," he said, extending his hand. I shook it, then opened the trunk and showed him the bent rim. After examining it for a few seconds, he said he needed to go get his sledgehammer and drove off as quickly as he had arrived. He was back by the time I could walk across the street to buy a couple of packs of crackers.

We lifted the dusty tire out of the trunk and he rolled it out to an open spot, laid it down, took aim, reared back with the big hammer, and came down on the bent rim with a clang. He hit the dent dead-on and bent it halfway back to its original position with one swing. With four softer blows he had bent the rim back into place. He then took the tire to have it pumped with air, saying he would change it when he returned. I entered Mayor Foster's office, saying, "I don't know what we'd have done without you!" He lit another cigarette and said, "Y'all still have time to go down to Piedras Negras?"

"We'd love to go," we said, grabbing our things. We climbed into his luxury F350 Ford pickup and he drove south out of his parking lot and through downtown. Almost everyone we passed seemed to recognize the truck. Most waved, including all of the local law enforcement officers. Mayor Foster slowed to shout greetings to a few of them. You could tell downtown Eagle Pass was suffering economically, though a few businesses held on. A few had reinvented themselves, changing from department stores to used furniture and clothing and junk. Regardless of the decline, the mayor continued as head cheerleader. At the river we passed a nine-hole golf course along the north bank of the Rio, but the green and white Border Patrol vehicles parked nearby indicated tourism wasn't so popular there anymore.

Mayor Foster veered onto a dirt road paralleling the river and drove up a ravine to a flat hill above it. At the top of the rise was a children's playground. "See those Border Patrol vehicle tracks up on that hill? They've started using our park as their lookout. It's ruining the grass and kids can't play there anymore." Then he turned and pointed to a hillside down below. "They're also building a wall right through there. This used to be where families would come with their children to picnic. Now it's all torn up. No one wants to come out here anymore." No one was playing on the golf course either.

The presence of so many federal agents prowling his town and along the river he had grown up fishing and swimming in as a boy made him angry. He complained that many of the agents were unfamiliar with border culture: "They just send them down here and they don't have any idea where they are." He complained about their cultural insensitivity. I decided to tell him about the Border Patrol officers who had questioned us. He was incensed. "If they give you a hard time, you just tell them,

"Kiss my grits! They have no right doing that." I wished at that moment we could travel the rest of the way with Mayor Foster—in his truck.

He acted almost as if he were honorary mayor on the Mexican side, too. As we passed through the ICE checkpoint, Mayor Foster shouted hello to the border guards, shifted to flawless Spanish, and shared a joke with the Mexican police. He showed us examples of recent industrial development he had helped promote; the most prominent among them was Grupo Modelo's huge Corona Beer bottling plant. It seemed to be his very own pride and joy. Already Corona was the world's most popular Mexican beer, with sales at one billion dollars annually in the United States alone. This plant would make distribution into the U.S. even easier. The mayor also did a turn through the parking lot of the new arts center, a project he had helped start. It was obvious that the Mexican side was growing faster than its U.S. counterpart.

"You know what Piedras Negras means, don't you?"

"Black rocks?"

"It refers to coal," he said. "It was named that because of the coal mines in Piedras." Forged in the decades of coal mining, the town had boomed, and the interrelationship with its northern neighbor had been ongoing since. The mines are dormant now, but the beer sales are skyrocketing.

The tour had to be quick because of both of our schedules. As he drove back toward the United States, he pulled up some photographs on his smart phone. He showed us his family and pointed out the son who would be celebrating his birthday that evening, one reason he had to rush the tour, he said. Then, like a kid showing his toys, he smiled and said, "Here's my tequila collection." He scrolled through the photos and we marveled at the dozens of different shapes and sizes of bottles from probably every distiller large or small in Mexico—just one more reason he loved the country. No one even glanced at his documents as he drove back into Eagle Pass cracking more jokes with the guards he knew on a first-name basis.

When we arrived back at the mayor's office, we found the original tire back on the car and could see it was holding up. We insisted on leaving money for Pedro, but the mayor refused, saying, "He's already getting paid by the hour working for me!" He had just spent his afternoon with us after our late arrival and now had paid money to help us out of a pinch. He was a border ambassador you don't read much about in the news. Unfortunately, stories about good border people like Mayor Foster travel like a rental car taking the muddy pothole-filled Minas Road, getting a flat and arriving late. Meanwhile, the hyperbole about the worst of Mexico speeds unchecked on Global Commerce Highway in bumper-to-bumper semi-truckloads, heading straight to the heart of America, poisoning both what we believe about our country and dividing us from our southern neighbors.

# TWENTY

# The Last Stay at Del Rio

DEL RIO, TEXAS, AND CIUDAD ACUÑA,
COAHUILA

LEAVING TOWN, WE STOPPED AT A GAS STATION TO MAKE
doubly sure our tire wasn't losing air, and at that moment Sarah
Boone called. All along the way, Sarah had been our guardian
angel, our tour guide by phone, even our surrogate mother, and
now we were late getting to her place, too. Of course she called
as any guardian would. "I just wanted to make sure you're safe,"
Sarah said, as we explained the whole mess. "And please do try
to get to Del Rio right away so I can show you some of the sights
before dark." Luckily we were only an hour away, and 277, the
two-lane road connecting the two towns, was a major highway
in comparison to the roadrunner path we had taken into Eagle
Pass. Hope and the car were much relieved.

Following Sarah's directions into the heart of Del Rio and
through an old neighborhood, we drove up to a stately but weath-
ered manor in a surprisingly humid forest. Formerly a single-
family dwelling in an old neighborhood of elegant homes, the
villa sat on the edge of a swampy oasis where grass is lush and
the trees tall—nothing at all like the parched desert with low-
growing mesquite and cacti extending from Del Rio in every
direction. There were no other cars in the driveway besides

Sarah's, and the house was in need of some paint and upkeep. We soon learned why.

Creative Options is but one defunct business along the border. The rainbow on the sign appears to arch over the border wall near Jacumba, California.

We walked into the side door, meeting Sarah face-to-face for the first time. On the phone her voice was so large and exuberant and her personality so outgoing that I expected someone much taller. I also expected her enthusiasm to continue in person. But Sarah, who is not much over five feet tall, seemed subdued, perhaps a little sad, in person.

As she reached up to hug us like old friends, she told us we would be the villa's last guests. We were some of the few people she had been able to talk with about the closing. She would begin the process of shutting the inn down as soon as we checked out the next day. A few packed boxes in the corner showed she had already started. "You'll stay in our best room named for the border lawman, Judge Roy Bean. His frontier courtroom was nearby and it's still a tourist site," she said with a bittersweet smile.

We could guess why the B&B was suffering, but we needed to talk about it anyway. "Bad news from the border has taken away our Winter Texans," Sarah said, "and the tourists don't want to come here anymore either." The villa's website had claimed it was "the closest Mexico border destination to visit Old Mexico for most Texans," but that honor had lost its sheen. The most recent visitors to sign the guest book had stayed there over a week before us.

We dropped our bags in the Roy Bean room and left immediately to make the most of the remaining daylight. Sarah drove, first to the crossing at Ciudad Acuña, where she stopped short of going through the gate. "There's nothing I want to show you there right now," Sarah said. She had wanted to take us to a restaurant named Crosby's on the other side, but when she had called, it was closed, we all assumed just for the day. "They are great people," Sarah said. "I love taking guests there and introducing them to the owners. It blows a lot of stereotypes for people. I'm so sad you won't get to meet them." What she didn't know was that the restaurant had closed for good that very week. Businesses on both sides of the border were failing.

We drove back toward the springs and looked down from the car windows at the cool water flowing alongside the road in a series of cascading pools surrounded by big oak, pine, and cypress trees. "That water put the town on the map," Sarah said.

The natural springs had given life to indigenous peoples and wildlife for thousands of years. Spanish missionaries settled there in 1635, naming their mission and town "San Felipe Del Rio," which was later shortened to simply Del Rio. Around 1869, ranchers living near the mission channeled the springs into concrete irrigation ditches and directed the waters to their parched desert pastures. Soon the surrounding area became known for its livestock production. Many of the old water channels remain to this day, though seepage around them has created marshes and, unfortunately, mosquitoes—not exactly a tourist draw.

A century or more ago, of course, people didn't have the luxury to make travel choices based on mosquito control. Water was everything, particularly in the parched ground of South Texas. Stopping to refill water barrels at the springs was a must for travelers along the dusty Lower Immigrant Road, later renamed the San Antonio El Paso Trail. The trail through Del Rio was a main route used by settlers, livestock drivers, and soldiers from 1849 to the 1880s. Hotels sprang up along it. With the newly arrived Buffalo Soldiers and other cavalry patrols fending off Apache attacks—which had become more common as pressures on their land increased—the town grew further. Starting in 1883, the springs were used to supply water for the new steam trains of the Southern Transcontinental Railroad. They pumped some ninety million gallons into the locomotive boilers annually, thereby helping the Southern run, tying the region to the rest of the nation and creating new business opportunities in Del Rio.

The railroad and the new growth surrounding it would have been impossible without the 1853 Gadsden Purchase, an acquisition of 29,670 square miles for only $10 million brokered by and later named for Ambassador James Gadsden. The purchase provided the crucial flat land for linking the Pacific Ocean and the Gulf of Mexico by rail, something Gadsden had personally dreamed about for decades.

James Gadsden was a Yale-educated South Carolinian with the dubious distinction of writing while in public office that slavery was a "social blessing." After graduating from college in 1806, he entered the military and served under General Andrew Jackson in the War of 1812 as well as the war against the Indians of Florida in 1819.[1] After completing his service in the army, and while a planter, slave owner, and legislator in Florida, Gadsden was appointed in 1823 as Florida's commissioner in charge of the removal of the Seminoles first to southern Florida and eventually to Oklahoma along what became known as the Trail of Tears. He had no qualms doing that job because he believed firmly in the doctrine of Manifest Destiny.

Journal editor John L. O'Sullivan was the first to put the term in print,

---

1. Leonard L. Richards, *The California Gold Rush and the Coming of the Civil War*, 153.

including it in his article in *The United States Democratic Review* in 1839, fourteen years before Gadsden began his work on the land purchase that would be named after him. O'Sullivan wrote that Americans possessed the "right of our manifest destiny to overspread and to possess the whole continent which providence has given us for the development of the great experiment of liberty and federated self-government."[2] Leaders like Gadsden who subscribed to this doctrine thought that God would help them promote commerce, along with liberty and democracy, even as they pushed others off their land and onto reservations where they had neither history nor experience. He believed the land purchase would be one tangible way that America could solidify its rightful ownership of land all the way to the Pacific.

After his decorated career in war and Indian removal, Gadsden turned to railroads. By 1840 he had become president of the South Carolina Railroad and started planning a southern route from the Atlantic to the Pacific in the territory north of what was then Mexico. He encountered three major obstacles. First, the Treaty of Guadalupe Hidalgo—written following the Mexican-American War in 1848—had left the borderline vaguely defined and politically insecure, particularly in western Texas and beyond, and thus a dangerous place to run a railroad. Second, exiled Comanche and Apache nations originally in Mexico had moved into the ungoverned and ill-defined region of west Texas and southern Arizona, making it their stronghold for raiding in both Mexico and the United States. Third, the region above the border line in west Texas and Arizona was mostly mountainous and unsuited to rail lines.

Dreaming that he might overcome these barriers if he could get the right backing, Gadsden and his company introduced specific railroad plans in 1851 just after California became a state following the Hidalgo treaty. Central to Gadsden's proposal was that the southern half of California be formed into a slave state, thereby making all of the southern U.S. stretching between the Atlantic and Pacific suitable for trading

---

2. Julius Pratt, "The Origin of 'Manifest Destiny.'"

slaves along with other goods. Gadsden believed the railroad magnates could, in turn, use slaves to build the railroad. Though Gadsden's proposal never made it out of committee in Congress, his star continued to rise nonetheless.

Regardless of where railroad owners stood on the question of slavery, they knew the southern route needed to swing deeper into what was then Mexican territory in order to miss several mountain ranges. There could be no compromising on that. Hearing the pleas made by the railroad magnates, the administration of President Franklin Pierce—strongly influenced by Secretary of War Jefferson Davis, who later became president of the Confederacy—moved to acquire the Mexican territory in question. Conveniently, Pierce appointed Gadsden as minister to Mexico in 1853, only two years after the rejection of Gadsden's California proposal.

Though a questionable statesman, Gadsden had proved himself good at leveraging land from a weaker foe. He was the perfect choice for wresting land from Mexico. He relied on strong-arm tactics again in negotiations with a hesitant Mexico, procuring nearly thirty thousand square miles by the end of his first year in office. He paid only $10 million for it, just a fraction of its value even then.

Even after acquiring the land to build the southern rail line, the institution he considered the "social blessing" derailed Gadsden's hopes for the newly acquired territory. He would never capitalize on the results of his own diplomacy. By the mid-1850s national discord surrounding slavery had killed any progress toward the southern line until well after the Civil War. In contrast, even as the war ground on for four years between 1861 and 1865, the Lincoln administration pushed ahead with the construction of the northern Transcontinental Railroad. The U.S. Congress approved funding in 1862, and construction began on the rail connection between San Francisco and Council Bluffs, Iowa, in 1863. Irish and Chinese immigrant workers provided much of the labor—well before the Chinese Exclusion Act of 1882. Following the Civil War, veterans from both sides along with freed African Americans helped complete the northern route, finally driving the last spike in 1869. Only after Lincoln's armed forces restored Texas and other rebel states to the Union did rail-road magnates begin constructing the route that would link California's coast with the Atlantic shipping lines and pass southward through New Orleans and other ports.

The southern route would put Del Rio on the map, but not until 1883, fourteen years after the northern route's completion. When trains finally did arrive in Del Rio to take on water, stockmen from both sides of the border began to use the rails for shipping their wool and mohair to the eastern textile plants. This earned the town two nicknames: Queen City of the Rio Grande and the Mohair Capital of the World.

| | | |

AS WE DROVE FROM the springs back out to the main road, Sarah showed us a few less-than-touristy landmarks, including several houses she had heard were owned by drug lords. The ones I saw were large, sur-rounded by walls, and otherwise nondescript. Bill Rovira had shown us similar showplaces in Progreso, Texas. From our small and unscientific sampling, it appeared that shootouts, murders, disappearances, and sales across the border had provided financing for nice places where the boss-es could live peacefully north of the border. I assumed they needed a safe place to raise their kids.

The border at Del Rio also once gave rise to XERF, the AM radio sta-tion known for its unregulated super power that could blast all of the United States when the station began its broadcasts in 1931. A Kansan named Dr. John Brinkley, a quack who believed he had found a way to boost male virility with a tincture made from goat gonads, owned the station. He used radio commercials to hawk his wares all over the U.S. until the Mexican government shut those ads down. In the 1960s the sta-tion came to life again as the "Border Blaster" featuring Wolfman Jack. With no airspace or wattage limitations in Mexico, the station reached millions of American listeners by stepping all over U.S. stations around the country.

Also in Del Rio is the Laughlin Air Force Base from where U-2 spy planes involved in the Cuban Missile Crisis of the 1960s flew southward across Mexican airspace, raising controversies in the process. Today things are much quieter with Cuba, but the fifteen hundred military personnel who work and fly out of the base still are Del Rio's best economic assurance. Apparently, however, few of their family members stay at bed and breakfasts.

We took Sarah out to dinner in downtown Del Rio. After ordering our food, we laid out our maps to plan our next leg of the journey. "I'm afraid I'm going to have to get you up early," she announced, apologizing. "But we'll have you a big breakfast and I'll pack your lunch." The early schedule would be necessary for all of us. She had dozens of errands to run the next day, including going to the bank to arrange the villa's closing. To make the morning tour at the Seminole Canyon State Historic Site, we would need to be out the door by 8 a.m. as well. So the following morning, Sarah fed us well, handed us our lunch bags, and ushered us out. We said our good-byes at the doorstep, voicing our deepest gratitude, and we each gave Sarah a big hug for all she had done. She would be heading back to Alabama soon, she said, to be closer to her grandkids. Then she waved and closed the door behind us, and Villa Del Rio was no more.

# TWENTY-ONE

# Seminole Canyon

COMSTOCK, TEXAS

ABOUT TWELVE MILES NORTH OF DEL RIO ON THE TEXAS Pecos Trail we reached the bridge over the Rio Grande impoundment named Lake Amistad. The Amistad Dam project had resulted from a cooperative undertaking by the American and Mexican branches of the International Boundary and Water Commission a half-century earlier. It began when U.S. President Dwight Eisenhower and Mexican President Adolfo López Mateos signed the initial agreement in Ciudad Acuña in 1960. A few years later, Presidents Lyndon Johnson and Gustavo Díaz Ordaz stood on the Inter-

*Maker of Peace*, a bronze sculpture by Bill Worrell, stands in the Seminole Canyon Texas State Park.

national Bridge nearby to inaugurate the project. Presidents Richard Nixon and Díaz Ordaz dedicated the completed Amistad Dam in 1969. The impoundment created a lake that extends well beyond the international boundary on both sides today.

As we drove across the bridge, Hope and I talked about how ironic the word "Amistad"—friendship—now seemed. The shared waters, once a diplomatic act of good faith, had become a policing problem, and Homeland Security viewed the open lake with no fence across it as a challenge because it has been used for drug trafficking by boat and thus armed police boats must patrol it. No one hears "Amistad" used to refer to any U.S./Mexico projects today. The wall, of course, is unilateral. No presidents stood together to inaugurate its beginning. The only thing most U.S. politicians say about it now is that they want more miles of it, more technology, and to make it higher. Forget Amistad. Mexican politicians aren't even asked to participate.

| | | |

ROUTE 90 FOLLOWS more or less the "Old Spanish Trail" used for hundreds of years as an Indian trading path and then followed by the first European explorers. The modern road, first built in 1915, was touted as the shortest driving route between the Atlantic in Florida and the Pacific in California. We drove westward along it some twenty miles from the lake before turning south into the Seminole Canyon Historic Site entrance. Arriving at the small museum headquarters, we paid for our tickets and found Ranger Tanya Patruney preparing to lead the morning's only tour.

Shortly thereafter she led our small group of seven out the back door. Passing through a small cactus garden outside, we stopped at the striking bronze sculpture by artist Bill Worrell of a tall human/animal figure called *Maker of Peace*. Ranger Patruney explained that we would see human figures with deer heads like this in the cave paintings below us. The statue holds in one hand an Aztec atlatl and a long spear, and in the other a staff from which a large bird, maybe a raven or hawk, takes wing.

Down inside the canyon, we walked to the edge of a small stream where we talked about the importance of water and food grown from it by the first inhabitants. "They farmed corn and beans to supplement their hunting," lectured Ms. Patruney, who then demonstrated how to use an atlatl to launch a spear. After a few practice tosses she threw the spear forcefully well over a hundred feet in the air. It could have taken down a deer at that distance.

We climbed the rock ledge from the creek up to the massive stone overhang known today as Fate Bell Shelter. People had lived there perhaps twelve thousand years ago, she said. Red paintings dating back six thousand years or more were all over the back wall. Particularly striking were the human figures with antlers painted with upstretched arms as if in ecstasy—the ones Worrell had gotten his inspiration from. There were also ancient red handprints on the back wall, looking as if they had just been made. Outside the cave was a boulder scarred by generations who butchered meat and ground seeds and herbs on it.

Early hunters bearing their rock-tipped throwing spears and atlatls traveled the region tracking mastodons and eventually bison. Though the arid landscape is quite harsh for humans or large animals to survive in today, the prehistoric place was dramatically different. Rain was plentiful then and the canyon was green with grasses and trees. As the climate changed to the arid conditions familiar today, the inhabitants continued to grow corn along the creek, which helped them sustain their small communities in the same location for centuries.

Humans first moved into the canyon well after the stream had carved out the shelter in the rock. The overhang afforded a safe place to sleep, cook, and store food inside. The winter sunlight stretching to the back wall warmed their quarters, which faced southeast. Their designs on the ceilings and back walls of their rock dwellings are known today as Pecos River–style paintings. No one knows exactly why they painted; perhaps as high praise to powerful gods, perhaps to document their history, or maybe they were just artistic musings or graffiti. Regardless, the illustrations show just how imaginative these canyon dwellers were. Paintings in the nearby Panther Cave have been carbon dated to approximately seven thousand years ago. Archaeologists have discovered over two hundred other pictograph caves in the same style, all showing that ancient people living there shared a multifaceted life in this small canyon known today as "Seminole."

| | | |

THE NAME GAVE ME pause at first, as I was sure it had nothing to do with the people who made the art. "Seminole" was a name given to Native Americans originally from Florida and later exiled to Oklahoma by Colonel Gadsden and others, and I knew they were not related by kinship to any indigenous group in the Southwest. But I was wrong about the name being unrelated to the history of the canyon.

The Seminoles had gone there after all, but only in relatively recent history. It turns out that Seminole Canyon is named for U.S. Army Seminole-Negro Indian scouts stationed at Fort Clark, a garrison once near present-day Brackettville on Route 90 east of Del Rio. Their work was to make military forays to fight Apaches in the place the park occupies today.

A photo and short description of the Black Seminole scouts feature in the Seminole Canyon Historical Park brochure. The brief write-up portrays them as protectors of the west Texas frontier—fighters against marauding Apache and Comanche bands between the years 1872 and 1914. The scouts, it says, were "known for their exceptional cunning and toughness." None of them was "ever wounded or killed in combat, and four earned the prestigious Medal of Honor." The brochure left out, however, the fact that the scouts' years of service spanned both Reconstruction and the worst years of the segregated period known as Jim Crow.

The brochure also could have mentioned that the Black Seminoles had indigenous ancestors who had intermarried with African Americans after slaves escaped and found refuge with the Indians. Although the soldiers may have appeared phenotypically black and spoke a Creole similar to Caribbean dialects, they were also Native American and likely spoke Seminole as well. Thus when they were transferred from

Fort Clark in Brackettville to track and fight against the Apaches and Comanches, they were engaging populations in some ways similar to their own ancestors, many of whom had been transferred to Oklahoma from Florida by Gadsden.

The peoples the Black Seminoles fought against were equally complex. Although some histories of the border region encourage us to think of the Apaches and Comanches entirely as outlaws, a deeper reading into their past shows that their raids were a survival tactic used by a landless group in a region of scarce resources. It helps to know they were not just warriors but whole communities of people made up of children, women, and men, old and young. Think of family groups huddled together in back canyons hiding from columns of well-armed U.S. Cavalry troops guided by Seminole scouts. It is true that the Apaches and Comanches raided civilians in Mexico and the United States, stealing food and supplies and sometimes killing to get them. But there are other facets to that story. The Apache's version of American history is something else entirely, and it starts with their having been there first, long before Manifest Destiny had been invented.

As the tour ended, I stood on the ledge of the canyon near the present border in Seminole Canyon where an indigenous community once fed itself by farming, hunting, and gathering and thought of modern indigenous peoples from rural Mexico and Central America who had recently been making their way across the border to help feed their families—and us. I realized anew that migrations and the conflicts surrounding them are as present today as ever in human history. As we turned back toward the park office, the prayer-maker statue at the back door of the visitors' center greeted us again—an eons-old symbol of upstretched hands reaching upward asking for help and giving thanks at the same time.

|   |   |   |

LEAVING THE SEMINOLE Canyon Park, we took a short detour off Route 90 to the overlook at the Pecos River. The side road ended at a high cliff near where the highway crosses the highest bridge in the State of Texas, a structure rising 273 feet above the Pecos where it runs through a 2,180-foot canyon. Pulling off at an overlook, we peered straight down to the river and also gazed upstream at the replacement for the Southern Pacific Railroad's Pecos High Bridge built in 1892. The older bridge, now gone, had been an award-winning engineering marvel in continual use until 1944. Near that point in 1883, railroad company representatives drove their silver spike into the last railroad tie, completing the final link in the southern transcontinental railroad. The southern rail line was nicknamed the "Sunset Route."

Gadsden never realized his dream of building a slave railroad. Instead it was Collis Huntington who built the bridge and owned most of the line linking the southern borderlands to New Orleans and California, and who brought high hopes to the south Texas region and profits to his own bank account—all this after slavery ended. Though the original bridge is gone and the trains no longer pass through Del Rio as they once did, the abutments are still visible from certain points within Seminole Canyon today. They are down inside the canyon by the muddy Pecos, abandoned.

# TWENTY-TWO

# Braceros in Murder City

EL PASO, TEXAS, AND CIUDAD JUAREZ,
CHIHUAHUA

WE HAD FIRST MET PONCHO SEVERAL YEARS BEFORE AT A
conference at the University of Barcelona. I'd been invited there
to show *The Guestworker,* a documentary film I directed with
Cynthia Hill about a sixty-six-year-old Mexican farmworker
who made an annual trip from Mexico to North Carolina to
work in farm fields as part of the guest worker program known
as H2A. After the screening, Poncho, the only Mexican citizen
in the audience, was the first to stand and respond. With tears
streaming down his face, he spoke about the film's resonance
with the ex-Bracero workers he had worked with. He told the
audience that he had interviewed people in their eighties and
nineties, learning about their border crossings, the harsh conditions of their labor, and their struggle to get the retirement
benefits they had earned. Their stories linked directly with
the film, he said, even though they had been in the U.S. fields
two generations earlier. Afterward we sat together at dinner to
talk about collaborations. He invited me to work with him in
Mexico.

Poncho, whose full name is Luis Alfonso Herrera Robles,
grew up in Ciudad Juarez, worked in maquiladora factories as

a teenager, and eventually climbed from low-paid jobs to higher education. He completed his Ph.D. at the University of Barcelona and was reuniting with his grad school colleagues at the conference when I met him. Despite his success, Poncho had remained devoted to his Juarez family and the workers he had come to know in his hometown—returning to teach there even when he had other opportunities. His research focuses on labor, mostly in Juarez. In a book he wrote about the city titled *La Sociedad Del Abandono* (The Abandoned Society), he uses the term "societal abandonment" regarding the condition of the poor and working class. In contrast, his work has been to reach out and work with them.

Ex-Braceros gathered in Benito Juarez Park in Ciudad Juarez, Chihuahua, for their weekly demonstration for retirement benefits.

Poncho had been present with the Braceros of Juarez every Sunday he was in town, joining them at the Benito Juarez Park and often bringing his students to help draw attention to the cause. Their plea was simple: give us the retirement benefits we earned when we went as replacement workers for GIs who left farms during World War II. As Poncho's mentor,

Professor Manuel Robles, explained, the Braceros know they may not receive payment in their lifetimes, but they demonstrate in the park every week to make a statement, not only for themselves but also on behalf of present-day workers who have not received their due.

|   |   |   |   |

HOPE AND I DROVE north more than a hundred miles from Seminole Canyon on Route 295, turned west onto Interstate 10, and headed toward Juarez. We were to meet Poncho at his university, where he wanted me to show my film at a conference. We were jumping past some of the border locations in order to make the scheduled date. We would return to the missed parts a few days later.

We had been on the interstate only a short distance when we noticed the traffic beginning to back up ahead of us and concrete barricades funneling vehicles into a Border Patrol inspection area. We could see dozens of Border Patrol vehicles parked along both sides of the highway. We inched ahead, knowing the drill.

As we neared the checkpoint, we caught sight of Border Patrol officers escorting five scared white college-age kids, male and female, toward the temporary patrol headquarters. The youths, who had been traveling along the interstate several hours from the border, were already in plastic handcuffs, their hands restrained behind their backs. Officers had each one by the arm as they guided them along. Drug possession was our guess. But of course they weren't at all the stereotypical *narco-trafficantes* we've heard so much about, the implied targets of so many billions of tax dollars; they were nothing like the sinister drug lords from the Medellin Cartel. If they were, in fact, being taken in for drugs, their arrest revealed the great paradox of the "drug war."

We go after the bad guys, we say, while so much of the demand for drugs comes from white middle-class America. Though Americans typically think "other" when we think drug trafficking, the enemy is also us. We intend to target the ones who sell the contraband to the kids, who bring it across the line by the tractor-trailer load: the drug sellers from the border who look like Hollywood's version of crooks. Say "drug trafficking" and chances are some could picture Latinos or stereotypical low-income inner-city black neighborhoods as depicted in the HBO series *The Wire*.

White suburban kids may play around with drugs, but typically they finish college and get jobs. Their communities protest if the police get too aggressive around where they live. So the inner-city black and brown youth are the ones arrested, and their records build, and they bear the brunt of the domestic side of the drug war as our society abandons them. At the border we pump billions into the wall and into traffic stops as well. Yet on that day the system caught five middle-class white kids with no visible intent to cross the border. I felt sympathy for the frightened parents who would get the calls and soon head to a detention center to post bond, but I guessed from the kids' car and clothing that the parents had money to hire good lawyers.

| | | |

A FEW CAR LENGTHS beyond the office, we pulled up to a covered shelter where a Border Patrol agent asked to see my driver's license and registration. "How are you, sir?" he said, as he looked over the documents. We exchanged the usual niceties. Then he asked, "Where are you headed today?"

I didn't answer, but in my friendliest voice I asked a question in return. "I'm curious, sir, how much information am I required to give you at these stops? I mean, what does the law say that I have to answer when you ask where I'm going?" Without showing any emotion or surprise, he replied, "We're just trying to make conversation and any information people give us is by mutual consent." He said no more, but dropped the questioning, and after looking over my license for a second more, stepped back to wave us through. "Thank you and have a good afternoon!" I'd just experienced white privilege and I knew it.

Then we drove on toward Murder City, one of the world's capitals of drug and human trafficking, where only a few days before a fifteen-year-old boy had lost his life for allegedly throwing rocks. Meanwhile, I could push back with such a question from an officer. I knew that wasn't possible for everyone. Still, I knew it wasn't smart to reveal we were headed to Juarez. Better to let that fact lie.

|   |   |   |   |

WE ENTERED THE El Paso city limits and turned southward toward the city center. Arriving early, but not really wanting to go into Juarez without getting our bearings, we parked the car and walked awhile in the deserted Saturday downtown, with no particular destination in mind. After going a few blocks we found ourselves in the spacious pedestrian area called Pioneer Square staring up at the fourteen-foot statue of Fray García de San Francisco. Without planning to, we had stumbled upon the marker for the route by which religious evangelization came to the Southwest: El Camino Real, or "the royal highway."

The plaque below the García statue explained that the Spanish friar had arrived in El Paso in 1659 by traveling the camino from central Mexico. Hernán Cortés himself had traveled the first section of the road, from today's Vera Cruz to Tenochtitlan, or Mexico City, in 1521. After the discovery of silver in the Zacatecas Mountains, Spaniards extended a second leg northward. In 1595, Juan de Oñate, conquistador, silver baron, and husband of Cortés's granddaughter, received authority from King Philip of Spain to extend the Camino Real for a third leg: beyond the Zacatecas Mountains through the Chihuahua Desert and into what is today part of the United States.

Oñate and his men rode their horses across the Rio Grande near today's El Paso and became the first Spaniards to see the area.[1] Near the river they came in contact with the Manso and Suma peoples whose ancestors had lived at the site for thousands of years. Oñate then followed

---

1. "El Paso del Norte," http://www.tshaonline.org/handbook/online/articles/hdelu.

one of the Manso/Suma trading paths farther north and west. By 1598, some three years after his arrival, Oñate had claimed all of what is now western Texas and New Mexico for Spain. Soon afterward, the king appointed him as the new province's governor.

Sixty-one years later, in 1659, Fray Garcia, the missionary depicted in the statue, traveled the same road to the river, where he established the Manso Indian Mission of Our Lady of Guadalupe. According to the plaque in the square, his permanent mission at the Pass to the North led to the founding of the twin international cities of El Paso, Texas, and Cuidad Juarez, Chihuahua. Measured by Manso history, he was a latecomer, but the monument deemed him the founder.

The sculpture also depicts García building the mission single-handedly. His right arm is wrapped around the lintel beam bearing the mission's name and the year it was founded. The name is intertwined with grapevines—a symbol, says the plaque, of his introduction of European agriculture to the region. It doesn't mention the Manso crops alongside the river. It doesn't mention that European agriculturists depended on indigenous seeds and labor for their survival. It also leaves out the likelihood that the Manso or Suma people were probably the ones who lifted the lintel and the rest of the materials to build the mission. I had now started questioning every bit of history I read and searching for the lost and the erased under every stated fact.

For decades to come, many Catholic fathers traveled northward through El Paso on their way to establish missions in all of New Spain. Many of their picturesque missions in Mexico and what is now the U.S. Southwest remain intact today, including the first mission that the Fray had built in Juarez. El Paso, the name the Spaniards gave the place, lives on despite the fact that the river is but a trickle and the ford across it long ago fell from use. Of course, calling the border city where today a major wall separates two countries "El Paso" is full of irony. *El Muro*, the wall, is more like it.

|   |   |   |   |

IN 2007 JUAN DE OÑATE, the conquistador of El Paso, made national news. A major historical controversy had arisen when the city commissioned sculptor John Sherrill Houser to create a statue of Oñate at the airport—thereby making the conqueror a symbol of today's city. It was to be the largest bronze equestrian statue ever made. Agreeing to the deal, Houser began referring publicly to his work-in-progress as the "last conquistador." When indigenous leaders began to get wind of the work, they protested. The Pueblo Indians took the lead. Their fight intensified when they realized the statue would be of a mounted rider rearing triumphantly on his horse as though celebrating his victory.

Native American peoples, they argued, had been using the pass across the Rio for millennia before Oñate's arrival. But even more grievous was that Oñate's men had killed and tortured many of the Pueblos' ancestors. Shortly after their arrival in Acoma, Oñate's mutinous soldiers began to prey upon the community, raping Pueblo women and enslaving and stealing from the tribe. In retaliation, the Indians rebelled and killed eleven Spanish soldiers, including Oñate's nephew. Gregory Rodriguez, a *Los Angeles Times* reporter, wrote in 2007, "Onate's response was swift and harsh, wiping out their village, killing hundreds of men, women and children and famously severing one foot of each adult male survivor."[2] The massacre was so horrific that the governor of Mexico punished Oñate, a rarity for its time. Oñate received a fine, was banished from Mexico City for four years, and exiled from the territory known as New Mexico for life.

Given this outrageous past, Native American activists and their supporters demanded that Oñate's name be withdrawn from the statue. They picketed at the statue's site, some of them holding signs reading, "Oñate? My foot!" Though the dedication of the statue continued as planned and the unveiling took place in August 2007, the city did finally remove Oñate's name, calling the horseman simply *The Equestrian.* Underneath the statue the city placed three explanatory panels that tell a more nuanced history of conquest that includes sympathy toward those

2. Gregory Rodriguez, "El Paso Confronts Its Messy Past," *Los Angeles Times*, March 25, 2007.

conquered. PBS's program *POV* later aired an episode called "The Last Conquistador" that chronicled the controversy, noting that without the recent fight, Oñate's atrocities would have remained buried.

Back at the central square, Fray García's statue seemed resolute and oblivious to all the problems that would come from his arrival. He stared upward toward heaven, his lintel in his grasp, his expression showing faith and confidence that his mission would be successful.

| | | |

THERE WERE A NUMBER of El Paso parking lots near the pedestrian bridge into Ciudad Juarez where attendants sit in little huts and charge a parking fee of five to eight dollars a day to guard the parked cars. After walking around downtown, we drove to within walking distance of the bridge and pulled into one of the lots where dozens of cars were parked. A Latino man about seventy years old got up from his card game at the little house and gave us a numbered ticket. He asked how long we would be gone and let us choose a spot. We got a few things out of the car and started walking across the bridge.

We joined throngs of people walking south. Most of them seemed to be heading back home after a day of work or shopping, as some carried bags from stores. We followed the sidewalk along chain-link fencing and toward the middle of the bridge. There we looked down at two concrete channels where, when there is water, the Rio Grande is divided into northern and southern branches. That day the northern canal held water, albeit a small stream hardly big enough to float a small canoe. The southern branch, the part that would have contained Mexico's water, was bone dry. There it was in full view: the United States was taking all that remained of the water of the Rio.

It was just a few minutes after four in the afternoon; we had arrived on time. Yet, as stepped into the streets of Juarez, we realized no one was there to meet us. We stood at the end of the bridge for a few minutes, trying not to be too obvious, though as the only gringos, we might as well have had on orange jumpsuits.

A Mexican young man around twenty-five years old dressed in jeans and T-shirt and with a ball cap pulled low over his eyes approached us. Another young guy who could have been an accomplice moved with him, staying back at a distance. I could feel adrenaline kicking in. Would they ask for money? Was this a more sophisticated trap that would end up taking us somewhere we didn't want to go? Did they want our luggage? We had been in Juarez for all of five minutes, and the violence we were warned about was already close. At least that is what my senses told me.

"Where are you trying to go?" he asked in Spanish. I didn't know whether to answer without giving away much or to ignore him and keep walking. I decided on the former.

"We're meeting a friend who lives here," I replied with my best Spanish accent, conveying as much confidence and control as I could muster, though another part of me wanted to grab Hope's hand and our bags, and turn and run like hell back toward El Paso.

"You're at the wrong bridge," he replied. "There's another one that pedestrians use just around the block. I'll take you there."

I'd seen that ploy used before. The deal is first to get somebody out of sight in an alley and rob him, or perhaps worse. But since no one was meeting us where we stood, we decided to believe him and walk, half following him, half as if under our own volition, keeping him in front of us. We held our luggage, particularly my camera bag, a little tighter. Then he slowed up to walk with us and began talking about himself, even as I kept watching for anyone else who might be coming at us from behind.

"The other bridge is just over there," he pointed out as we rounded a corner, assuring us that it was the place people meant when they said to meet at the bridge. We were in public after all, and the stories the young man told made him seem less threatening. He had always lived in Juarez, he said. He had been looking for work for some time. I began to drop my guard as we rounded the last turn. "There it is," he said, pointing. I breathed in with relief when I saw the much busier pedestrian crossing.

He had done us a favor. He didn't hold out his hand for money, but just to shake ours. He had already turned and was headed away when I called to him again, reached into my front pocket, handed him the loose twenty-peso note I had set aside. He thanked us, smiled, and disappeared into the masses of people.

Still no Poncho, so we decided to walk into a small pharmacy beside the bridge and call him. Our cellphones had become useless inside Mexico and Verizon was already sending us texts about expensive upgrade for international calls, but we declined. The pharmacist let us use the landline and even dialed the number for us. They handed Hope the receiver. No answer. We waited fifteen minutes and called again. Still nothing. I decided in my head that after waiting thirty more minutes we would head back. I knew the pharmacy would close eventually, and I felt we could not wait alone in Juarez past sunset.

Hope seemed less nervous. "Don't worry, it will work out," she said. Now I was the one anxious to get somewhere on time and she was telling me to relax. The half hour passed and I was ready to leave when Hope tried once more and Poncho answered. He explained that he had been delayed in taking his mother somewhere and his phone wasn't working in that part of the city. He was already on the way. So we waited in the *farmacia* where complete strangers had taken us in and treated us like guests, where business went on as usual all around us, and we were starting to feel, despite my overactive imagination, safe.

| | | |

PONCHO DROVE UP in his Nissan and soon we were navigating through traffic on the way to visit the Catholic service organization called Casa del Migrante. Traffic was heavy and we were moving slowly so I had my camera in my lap, occasionally taking random shots of sights in the city, particularly the cars and the overhead signs. Suddenly a black pickup whizzed out of its lane and cut in front of us not more than thirty feet away. In the back of the truck, supported by a rail welded onto the truck bed, eight federal police dressed in all black and wearing face-masks stood at the ready with automatic weapons. Almost by instinct, my hands moved to the camera and Poncho barked, "Keep the camera down!" Luckily I had not lifted it above the dash.

I had just learned all over again that the Mexican police were not there to protect and defend people. Many were corrupt and connected to gangs. Photographers had been killed in Mexico for taking photos of gang members. And the *federales* colluded with them in some locations. I thanked Poncho and sheepishly packed the camera away in my bag.

These men in black became numerous after President Felipe Calderón created a new drug police force as part of the war on drugs he declared in 2006. Most agree that these tough and militaristic police have done little but prey upon the citizenry, extorting money and even sending arms and trained converts to the cartels, which in turn have murdered tens of thousands. The police were always looking for reasons, like my photography, to make traffic stops so they could extort money. They had done worse, including helping create a new drug syndicate known as the Zetas, a gang that is one of the most powerful in Mexico today. The United States had backed Calderón financially and provided police training, which had helped create monsters. Taking pictures of them could have been disastrous.

"The men in green belong to the Mexican army," Poncho explained. "They're less corrupt than the federal police. The green-uniformed men might ask for bribes, but the ones in black would take your camera and might arrest you." A fine was the least of the options, he said. "People are afraid to go out of their houses when they're around. They even avoid driving at night. We all just stay in with our children." I learned quickly that drug gangs have their territories and you stay away from those, but the *federales* are everywhere.

We didn't have to be reminded that death casts a long shadow over Juarez. Even some of our Mexican friends told us to avoid the place. Most horrible was the rash of murders and disappearances of young women that became public in 1993. Their mutilated bodies turned up in ditches, empty lots, and dried-up riverbeds; some were buried in shallow graves. Between the time the story first broke and our visit, over eight hundred female bodies had been recovered in Juarez alone, with some of the victims as young as thirteen. Another three thousand women had disappeared. No group had claimed responsibility and most of the crimes remain unsolved.

Though there is disagreement about the causes of these deaths, it is irrefutable that the murders coincide with the rise of globalization and the high numbers of single women recruited for jobs in maquiladoras. Being single and childless are de facto requirements for many of the jobs. Having to travel there alone to work with no previous urban experience could be the beginning of the problem, leading to trafficking and forced prostitution as well. In 1994, as the number of NAFTA factories in Juarez rose to over four hundred, the murders increased. Most of the victims were from rural communities and had no family nearby.

Some writers caution against using the term "femicide," noting that sexualizing the murders could unfairly put blame on the women themselves for forsaking traditional roles. It is true that women have been targets, though many men from traditional and poor families have also died in Juarez. That both male and female victims have been dark-skinned also points to race as a possible factor. Almost certainly all of this is tied to drug activity and human trafficking, which know no gender boundaries.

Regardless of the causes, advocates concentrate on demanding that the murders stop. For that Mexico needs good police protection and investigation. But the police are part of the problem.

Poncho joins many who point out that the main problem in Juarez is that the Mexican government has reneged on its responsibility to protect its people. After numerous advocacy sessions, bi-national conferences, the rise of advocacy organizations, and countless news stories, the police have yet to solve the crimes. Indeed, as I had just been reminded, some of the police have become terrorists themselves.

In his book *La Sociedad del Abandono*, Poncho argues that whole communities lack support from the police and have no social services. Many do not have access to schools, water, or sewer systems either. On top of that, multinational companies prey upon those desperate for jobs while giving few protections in return. Many companies pay nothing toward building the infrastructure around them. Some call it neoliberalism, meaning among other things that companies are liberated to come and go as they please, and have no obligation to give back.

And "go" is what the maquiladoras have done. Many factories built in the 1990s had pulled out by 2010 and headed for Asia. As we drove through ramshackle neighborhoods in south Juarez, Poncho, speaking in Spanish sprinkled with English, showed us many factories that were already vacated. "There's an abandoned shell. See the neighborhoods over there, hardly anyone lives there anymore; the houses are abandoned, too." As he said the word "*abandonado*" or some form of the word probably twenty times over the hour, I started to understand its finality: that abandonment begets further loss and despair. I could feel it as we drove slowly by the empty buildings, each surrounded by small houses in rows—"company houses" as they once called them in the United States—whole streets vacant and deteriorating.

After the exodus, a relative few factories stand sadly amidst the carcasses of the others. They are left mostly to their own devices. Few if any environmental regulations govern them. No pay standards or protections are required for their remaining workers. Unions are demonized and people usually are afraid to fight for their rights. They have been forced to accept wages that averaged only eighty dollars a week in 2010 as the companies tried to undercut others in the globalized marketplace. They know their employers can also leave for places where wages are even lower.

I tried to imagine a young woman with no money arriving alone and vulnerable in a city collapsing under its own weight, where pay is barely enough to buy street food. Then I imagined her suddenly losing her job. How would she find another with factories closing nearby? Unemployment had shot up from virtually zero when the factories first moved to

The Virgin Mary draped with detention center bracelets left by deportees who have stayed at the Casa del Migrante in Ciudad Juarez.

Juarez in the 1990s to almost 20 percent by 2010. Desperate to find something to send home, would she try to go north across the great economic divide? Many such economic refugees are arrested trying to cross the border. Then they are sent back penniless. If they are lucky, they find help from a church or nongovernmental organization upon their return, maybe some guidance, some resources, and some sense of hope. But jobs are what they want. People sleep in shelters so they can do day labor for whatever people will pay.

|   |   |   |   |

WE PASSED A BEATIFIC statue of the Virgin as we drove through the gate of Casa del Migrante, a Catholic center for migrants. Most residents are deportees who have been recently held in U.S. detention centers, as our guide and Catholic priest, Fray Gerardo Árias, explained. They are dumped off at the border with no possessions or money. The Casa is all many have to turn to. When they arrive, some haven't even been in touch with their families. Father Gerardo was gentle but grave about the migrants' plight.

"In the U.S. they call them detention centers, but they're actually jails for punishing criminals," he said. "When Mexicans are deported from the U.S. as felons, they're seen as criminals here, too. In some places where they're deported there are no organizations to help. At least here in Juarez, we're prepared to help them. We don't have anyone at the border, but we're prepared here [a few miles away] with food, clothing, and shelter."

The inscription painted on the front of their building says, "*No era de aquí y tu me acogiste*." The passage is from the book of Matthew, "I was a stranger and you welcomed me." The logo painted above echoed a now familiar theme: a Mexican man in sandals, a poncho, and a broad-brimmed hat leading a donkey ridden by a woman holding her baby as they make their way through the desert.

The migrants are left off at the border on the U.S. side and they must walk southward into Mexico still wearing their prison IDs and holding their belongings in Homeland Security–issued plastic bags. Some of them are from Chiapas or Oaxaca, a thousand miles from home, and they have no one to meet them. Many have never seen Juarez before. When they get inside the country, the Mexican government allows them one call at the government migrant aid agency called Grupo Beta located just south of the entrance, but as most have no money to travel and the family is unlikely to have anything to send either, many have to stay and work to earn enough either to cross back into the United States or to go home. If they are lucky, Grupo Beta will tell them how to reach the Casa, where they can find a bed, shower, and hot meals for free. Sometimes they arrive in large groups of thirty or more, said Fray Gerardo. His organization shelters and feeds all the migrants they are able to.

None of the deportees were in their rooms in the middle of the afternoon when we arrived—every one of them had gone out in search of jobs. Still, Friar Gerardo showed us the guest rooms in their absence: large halls lined with beds, all of them clean and well made. There were separate rooms for men and women. They resembled army barracks except for the artwork adorning one of the walls—mostly pencil drawings, many striking in their artistry. I was drawn to two in particular: one showing Jesus as a migrant dressed in worker's clothing seeking a job in the United States, and a second showing Jesus in detention, alongside the beatitudes in Spanish, including, "Blessed are the poor for theirs is the kingdom of heaven."

We walked outside the dormitory to see the statue of the Virgin of Guadalupe up close. Made of concrete, she stood in a grotto of rocks, her hands folded in prayer. She stands about four feet tall, and the rocks around her depict her aura of light and form a protective cave simultaneously. Encircling the rocks and the statue was a long chain made from the plastic ID bracelets from U.S. detention centers. Upon arrival at the Casa, deportees removed their plastic identification tags bearing their names and photographs and reclasped them, interlocking each one. The chain encircled the rock structure and then draped over and around the Virgin's arms and hands. Every one of them bore an untold story of loss.

After the visit, Poncho drove us to the Ramada Hotel where he needed to get us checked in early so he could get back to his family before dark. After putting our things in our room, Hope and I had a meal beside the pool and chatted with the waiters. We sipped Bohemias with lime and watched two young children play in the water with their father. Two different weddings took place in the courtyard the same evening. Both were elaborate and long celebrations with live music, fancy clothing, mounds of food, and photography sessions outside by the pool. Inside the walls we watched as families displayed many of the best traits of Mexico: multigenerational celebrations, fiesta, food, music, and civility.

Meanwhile, outside the doors of the hotel, another world continued. While we slept in safety over two nights, the papers reported that twenty-four people died violent deaths in Juarez. We couldn't know how many others disappeared. We heard no gunshots. No sirens blared. I began to know why only that word *abandonado* would do.

| | | |

THE NEXT MORNING we rode with Poncho back across the bridge to El Paso to visit the decade-old *Centro de los Trabajadores Agrícolas Fronterizos* (The Border Farmworker Center). Poncho, along with the center's director, Carlos Marentes, had arranged a screening of my film,

*Brother Towns/Pueblos Hermanos*, for the workers housed there. When we arrived, Mr. Marentes gave us a tour of the impressive eight-thousand-square-foot El Paso center only a block north of the border. As we toured the center, dozens of workers began returning from their work in the fields. After showering, they congregated in the main meeting hall and prepared to watch the film on a large television. They would sleep that night on mats in the same room, Carlos told us. They would also eat there after the screening.

*Brother Towns/Pueblos Hermanos* is a bilingual film about indigenous Guatemalan day laborers in Jupiter, Florida. Over a hundred men watched as I stood looking on from the back of the room. A question-and-answer period followed. One man seemed to speak for the group when he told me the story of sacrifice that I had portrayed about indigenous people working in Florida was also their story. Though the film is about Guatemalans, he said, it is the story of Mexicans too. "All of us are struggling to find a living in the world," he said.

I couldn't help noticing that while they watched the film, the farmworkers sat under a banner that said, "*Paro General* (General Work Stoppage): A Day without Mexicans." The banner had been used during a May Day celebration in 2008 when Latinos and their supporters marched in the U.S. streets calling attention to their contributions to the U.S. economy. Some groups staged an action during which every worker walked out for a day. Of course the melon crops these men harvested that day would have rotted in the field without them. Everyone seems to know this, but we have a strange way of showing it.

As we drove away from the center and headed toward the bridge to Juarez, I turned back to photograph the scene of workers starting to line up outside for their evening meal. Most had harvested U.S. cantaloupes for twelve hours that day. They would do so again the next. Forced to choose work over freedom of movement, they ate donated meals in a shelter and slept on mats on a floor away from home, all provided by a low-budget NGO.

The two centers we had visited in two days had manifested two sides of the Mexican migrant reality: a shelter for U.S. deportees in Mexico and a shelter for workers still working in the U.S. fields, a few miles from each other, but they are worlds apart, though interconnected by the United States' fickle demand for undocumented laborers.

The next day I showed the same film to students at the University of Juarez and answered their in-depth questions about my fieldwork methodology as well as about U.S. immigration policy. It was a difficult discussion to have—particularly when it came to how to represent workers who must live in the shadows of the border wall. I struggled to explain this quandary to a group of young intellectuals who also lived its realities, and I sat mesmerized when they spoke of their lives and work at the border. I wanted to stop talking altogether and just listen. I realized I knew nothing of living on the *frontera* the way they did, but I was the one in the front of the room.

The next day was Sunday. We went to meet the Braceros in historic Benito Juarez Park for the first time. "We'll help my parents serve them coffee and *pan dulce*," Poncho promised. "Oh, and you should take your camera," he said.

# TWENTY-THREE

# Fort Davis and the Buffalo Soldiers

FORT DAVIS, TEXAS

FOUNDATIONS OF ADOBE BRICKS ARE ALL THAT REMAIN OF many of the buildings at the national landmark called Fort Davis, Texas, about two hundred miles northeast of Juarez. Despite its deterioration, of the ten forts where the Buffalo Soldiers served across the western frontier of the United States, Davis is the best preserved. Some whitewashed buildings, mostly officers' quarters and their family homes, remain, but most of the barracks where the enlisted men slept are gone. The surviving foundations stand at

These adobe foundations are the only remnants of some of the barracks of the Buffalo Soldiers who served at Fort Davis in Texas.

the base of craggy rock outcroppings in the foothills of the Davis Mountains, from where soldiers rode out to engage in innumerable battles of the Indian Wars.

| | | |

SOME SAY NATIVE AMERICANS coined the nickname "Buffalo Soldiers" because of African American soldiers' dark skin and hair. Others say it came about because they fought like wounded buffalo, never giving up. Still others point out they wore buffalo-hide coats in winter and argue that the nickname came from their garb. These and other stories continue to survive about the African Americans who made a name for themselves in the U.S. military.

Their story began when over 186,000 black soldiers who had fought as volunteers in the Civil War as the U.S. Colored Troops were transferred to the western frontier. Thirty-eight thousand of their comrades had given their lives during the Civil War. Many of those who remained were still ready to fight for America. The U.S. Army conscripted six African American units, two mounted cavalry units, and four infantry units in 1866. An additional fifty or so Black Seminole scouts served with the military beginning in 1870, with some of them stationed at Fort Davis.

The Fort Davis soldiers and their scouts patrolled throughout Comanche and Apache territory in what is now part of Texas and New Mexico. According to some reports, they received old horses and inferior supplies, but others say that post–Civil War units regardless of skin color were issued used Civil War equipment so that despite the prevalence of racism, the black troops appear to have fought with weapons and supplies similar to those given to white soldiers. That's not to say that the men themselves were treated as well as whites.

Regardless of their treatment, no military service units had better retention records than the black units, due both to their perseverance and the lack of other opportunities for blacks in post–Civil War America. Stories of the Buffalo Soldiers' bravery abound, but it would be patronizing to say they were braver than other soldiers. They also had no better rapport with the Apache and Comanche than did whites. But without a doubt, they were disciplined and loyal soldiers—417 African Americans who served as Buffalo Soldiers received Medals of Honor. That they accrued such stellar records of service during the Jim Crow period is extraordinary.

To its credit, the National Park Service has included some less self-congratulatory facets of the Buffalo Soldiers' story on its Fort Davis website and related literature. One example is the origin of the name of the fort. When first built in 1854, the fort was named after U.S. Secretary of War Jefferson Davis, the same man who seven years later would become the president of the Confederacy and who was already known for his promotion of slave ownership.

Months before Southerners fired on Fort Sumter to begin the Civil War, Davis, then a senator from Mississippi, stood in the U.S. Senate Chamber and argued in response to New York Senator William Seward that the Constitution should protect slaveholding. His words, addressed to the president of the Senate (Vice President John C. Breckinridge), are some of the clearest about why he believed in slavery:

> The condition of slavery with us is, in a word, Mr. President, nothing but the form of civil government instituted for a class of people not fit to govern themselves. It is exactly what in every State exists in some form or other. It is just that kind of control which is extended in every northern State over its convicts, its lunatics, its minors, its apprentices. It is but a form of civil government for those who by their nature are not fit to govern themselves. We recognize the fact of the inferiority stamped upon that race of men by the Creator, and from the cradle to the grave, our Government, as a civil institution, marks that inferiority.[1]

That Fort Davis, the outpost named for the same Davis who presided over the Confederate States of America that this mind-set gave rise to, would become an outpost for black soldiers is yet another border irony.

Fort Davis was first commissioned to protect the settlers traveling along

---

1. Jefferson Davis, *The Papers of Jefferson Davis*, vol. 6, *1856–1860*, 277–284.

the San Antonio/El Paso (then called Franklin) Road and the Chihuahua Trail. Nearly four hundred infantry were stationed there, making the fort one of the largest posts of its kind. No matter how well provisioned, however, the foot soldiers could only patrol so far. Mounted Apache, Comanche, and other tribes could raid the wagons heading west and disappear back into the hills before the foot soldiers could get there. Thus the first foot soldiers rarely encountered their enemy even as the settlers lost supplies, horses, guns, and at times their lives. For this reason, even while the raids were going on nearby, Second Lieutenant Zenas Bliss, the commanding officer, wrote that life at the fort was "exceedingly dull." Men took to gardening, fishing, and horse racing with the few animals they had.

One of Secretary Jeff Davis's ideas for transportation was to send camels from the Middle East to the fort in 1855. They were superior to mules and oxen in that they ate less, could haul more, and could survive extreme heat, but when the Civil War broke out, the experiment was forgotten. In fact, the entire fort was abandoned when Fort Davis soldiers were transferred to fight Confederates in 1861. This vacancy gave the Second Texas Mounted Rifles, the Texas sharpshooters fighting for the Confederacy, a chance to move in. They held the fort until Union forces retook it in 1862. When the rebels retreated, the fort remained empty for the remainder of the war.

In 1866, a year after the war ended, the Ninth Cavalry formed as part of the United States Colored Troops. Their first assignment was to escort and protect immigrants, stagecoaches, mail coaches, and others heading westward who continued to be hit hard by the Apaches and other mounted tribes. Fort Davis also became a temporary safe haven for thousands of settlers staking claims on farmlands, opening businesses, or heading to the California gold mines. Small detachments of the Buffalo Soldiers rode out from the fort to protect stagecoach stops, as other troops scouted and patrolled the vast Trans-Pecos region of western Texas.

Even then, whites who received protection from Buffalo Soldiers spoke down to them and resented their presence. Too many of the travelers believed that blacks should not wear the U.S. uniform. Unreformed and rebellious Confederates heading west into the territories were especially hostile. In San Angelo, Texas, a gambler shot a Buffalo Soldier and sympathetic townspeople helped the shooter escape. Black officers never got the chance to prove their leadership abilities in combat. Henry O. Flipper, the first black officer trained at West Point and stationed as a Buffalo Soldier in Texas, was never allowed to enter combat, but received a desk job instead. He was later charged with embezzlement and given a dishonorable discharge. The charge was bogus, but his conviction was not overturned until 1999, when Lieutenant Flipper received a posthumous honorable discharge from President Clinton.

| | | |

THE STORY OF THE Apache leader named Victorio helps fill in the other side of the history of the Indian Wars.[2] His people called him Beduiat. He rode with Geronimo and the famous Chiricahua Apaches before he and his people were forcibly relocated to the Ojo Caliente in their ancestral homelands. When the once-remote area began to be in demand for white settlement, Beduiat and his people were moved again.

Though some say he was one of the fiercest chiefs the U.S. soldiers ever confronted, by the time the Ninth Buffalo Soldiers arrived on the scene, Victorio and his people had been subdued, moved to the San Carlos Reservation in the Arizona Territory, and half starved. It was the late 1870s when the Buffalo Soldiers were moved in to act mostly as custodians of the captured tribe, keeping them from leaving, but also protecting the Apaches from cowboys who hunted them for sport. The going rate for Apache scalps in Mexico and even in some places in the United States was high: fifty dollars for a male scalp, twenty-five for a female, and ten for a child's.

After moving to their new location, Victorio's Apache clan had been prevented from transporting or even raising food there. Early on, the cavalry had permitted them to hunt with rifles, but when white settlers began

---

2. "Buffalo Soldiers & Indian Wars," last accessed 2013, http://www.buffalosoldier.net/
BuffaloSoldiers&ChiefVictorio.htm.

finding armed Indians in their midst, they protested. General Philip Sheridan, the commanding officer over the San Carlos reservation, was quick to oblige and had all their rifles confiscated. As food began to run out, however, the tribe had little choice but to steal horses and weapons and fight.

Victorio escaped with his and other tribal groups in late 1879, ambushed the Ninth, killing five men, and fled with nearly four dozen horses. This escape led to months of Apache raiding through New Mexico, including what became known as the Alma Massacre during which they killed forty-one white settlers, a small number compared to their own losses at the end of a gun, but scandalous to the U.S. government nonetheless. Victorio's people then escaped to Mexico with the Ninth Cavalry in pursuit. The Ninth laid ambushes on both sides of the border, but to no avail. Victorio was still free.

Then Mexico's army joined in, and with two national armies in pursuit and hundreds of well-equipped soldiers riding after them on both sides of the border, it was only a matter of time before Victorio and his people were subdued. Finally, the Mexican army spotted the Apaches' hiding place inside a canyon and closed in, informing the Ninth Cavalry they would no longer be needed. As the Mexican soldiers began to develop their plan of attack, the U.S. forces reluctantly went back to their side of the border to make sure none of Victorio's people crossed back into the United States alive.

On October 14, 1880, the Mexican army moved in at daybreak. By noon, Victorio and his sixty warriors lay dead. They had succumbed quickly to the stronger and better-armed Mexican military. Eighteen women and children died and were laid out alongside the warriors. Those who remained alive—sixty-eight women and children—were taken prisoner.

In the movies I saw as a child, the Indians always appeared to outnumber the soldiers. The settlers circled the wagons as what seemed like limitless numbers of warriors bore down on a brave and embattled handful of whites who always seemed to be running out of ammunition. Apache women were never killed in those scenes. Children weren't part of the story at all.

|  |  |  |  |

I HAD A HARD TIME throwing away my toy Fort Apache set complete with a faux log fort and dozens of soldiers and Indians in a variety of combat poses. I had spent hours as a child arranging them, each time making sure to position the figures in a setting as realistic as possible, sometimes with real dirt and vegetation brought in from outside. Many of the plastic figures were mounted, the cavalry in saddles, the Indians bareback. I knew every little face. Several of the Indians were in death throes, arms thrown back, having just been hit by bullets. Some were meant to be in camp and some on the attack. There were teepees, a supply station, wagons, barrels, totem poles, firewood, a well with bucket and crank, and plastic trees. I'd gotten the set for Christmas when I was about ten years old. I'd cherished it so much that I asked my parents to keep it in the basement after I left home for college.

In college I began to learn more about America's treatment of its native peoples, and gradually knew I didn't want to keep the fort. Throwing away a well-preserved toy set in its original box seemed wasteful, but I didn't want to give it away to a child either. Only now have I come to realize as I think back about Fort Apache that all my plastic cavalry soldiers were white guys. There were no Buffalo Soldiers in that make-believe world. I remember the fort hitting the bottom of the dumpster with a rattle, any hint of my lingering innocence landing heavily with it.

|  |  |  |  |

AFTER WALKING THROUGH Fort Davis and the accompanying museum staffed by a black park ranger, we drove into town, also called Fort Davis, which is the seat of Jeff Davis County. Though back in the late 1800s the white-owned establishments in the town had prevented the African American soldiers from entering their establishments, they made a profit by supplying them with goods. With that money and other profits from travelers protected by the soldiers, a small town grew, later bolstered by the arrival of cattlemen. The town erected its first courthouse in 1880. After the fort was abandoned in 1891, the town almost shut down too. Around 1910, local business owners began reviving Fort Davis, the town. Today some twelve hundred inhabitants live in the hamlet and tourism is their main source of revenue.

On the courthouse lawn in the center of town stands a bronze statue of a soldier about two feet tall and mounted on a stone pedestal. The soldier is depicted holding an automatic rifle and wearing a World War II helmet and uniform; the tarnished green patina on the bronze was fitting for the uniform of the era. A plaque explains that this statue was dedicated to the town's hero, Manuel Gonzalez, lauding him for his exploits as "Fort Davis's one man army" and describing the nearly superhuman feats this Latino man accomplished singlehandedly. Latinos and Native Americans like Gonzalez had signed up for the military in large numbers, giving added layers of meaning to the phrase "fighting to protect our homeland."

However, only in recent decades have these soldiers and their families begun to assert their hidden histories, insisting on their inclusion in the American story, though all too often it takes superhuman feats to accomplish their goal. Many heroes like Gonzalez and the Buffalo Soldier Henry Flipper have gained recognition only after death. Many once called "savage" and, as Jeff Davis said, "unfit to govern themselves" have had a long fight after the official battles ended. For too long they have been purged from history as well.

So the battle to preserve and correct our collective memory continues. Is Manuel Gonzalez's little bronze statue on Fort Davis's lawn a harbinger of the recollection to come? Will the Buffalo Soldiers one day have a statue in Jeff Davis County? Given that they made the town's founding possible and protected the first inhabitants, it might not be too much to ask. Given my time immersed in a white child's version of history known as Fort Apache, I believe I have an extra responsibility to say so, not out of guilt, but as a necessary correction to the history I had inherited and played with as if it were a fantasy.

# TWENTY-FOUR

# National Park on the Line

BIG BEND NATIONAL PARK AND CHIHUAHUAN
DESERT, MEXICO

THE BROCHURE PROVIDED BY THE RANGER STATION THAT WE
read on our drive southward into Big Bend National Park addressed the question, "Is it safe?" The Park Service must have
been getting that query regularly and decided to address it
head-on. The brochure assured the reader that as long as tourists practice safe driving and watch out for wildlife, they should
be free of danger. It warned, however, that buying goods from
Mexican people who sell crafts at the river is illegal. Purchase
souvenirs only at the designated official areas, the Park Service
warned.

Searching the web under Big Bend and the question "Is it
safe?" I found that a number of people seem to be afraid they
will meet up with drug gangs there. Those familiar with the area,
however, are quick to dismiss that fear. For one thing, they say,
just south of Big Bend there is the harmless town of Boquillas
and then beyond that "a whole lot of nothing." They reason that
if a drug gang wants to make trades with people, they would
do so where there are roads, or where there are people to buy
or carry the drugs. And those who ask about safety perhaps
haven't seen the height of the mountains or the depth of the

canyons there either. Foot travel across the border is nearly impossible at many points in the park.

There were signs of border fears from a previous era on the official website. A "Did you know?" blurb at the bottom said that in 1942, "soldiers from Fort Bliss installed a machine-gun emplacement along the Rio Grande pointed at Boquillas, Mexico." That was exactly the same year the federal government began bringing thousands of Bracero workers into U.S. fields to harvest our crops—right in the middle of World War II. As we have seen, the U.S. military wasn't afraid of a Mexican invasion then, but they were concerned that the Axis soldiers might invade from the south and arrive through Mexico. One gun pointed at Boquillas didn't seem enough somehow, but then again we've done lots of posturing within our border history. Some would argue that building a wall continues that legacy.

Our first destination in the park was Boquillas Canyon, a picturesque stretch of the Rio Grande where the river flows by rock faces pocked

*These painted walking sticks and small copper animals made by a Mexican family were laid along a path in the Big Bend National Park. The sign asks for contributions in exchange for the objects.*

with caves, the little *bocas* (mouths) in the sides of the canyon walls. Hope waited for me while I hiked alone through the intense afternoon heat, heading up over a rocky rise and then down a trail to the river. I never found the remnants of the big gun aimed toward the little hamlet below, but at the rise I did find green and red painted walking sticks and twisted copper-wire scorpions—for sale. There was a green soft-drink bottle with its top cut off and a message beside it saying, please leave money here if you would like to take one of the objects. No one was there hawking; it was just an honor-system jug. Thinking of the warning, I walked by without stopping.

The Rio was so low that I began to step easily on dry rocks making my way across without getting my feet wet, just to see how hard it would be to cross into Mexico. As I jumped along on the rounded rocks, I first noticed the two horses grazing nearby, and then a moment later a man emerged from the cottonwood thicket behind them. I shouted a greeting, "*Buenas tardes!*" while standing in the middle of the river and he waved and replied in kind. He carried himself with the posture of a humble man, his very stance seeming to offer an apology. "I live over there in Boquillas," he said, pointing. "I'm a farmer. Those are my horses." They were his transportation, and his beasts of burden with which he plowed his fields. But this was a difficult place and time to farm, I acknowledged. "Very dry," he shouted. The rains had not arrived even in the rainy season as they once did. There was a five-year drought. The crops had not germinated. The corn that had started growing was now drying up and the leaves were turning yellow.

I asked him if he was the person who left the copper scorpions and walking canes. He replied, "Yes, my family and I make those." He would go across the river after dark to retrieve his goods and any money left. "We used to go across without any problem. Now it's different." He didn't plead for money or mention the crafts again. We shouted back and forth a little more about his farming life; then I bid him good-bye and walked back to find Hope.

On the way over the rocks, I stopped at the makeshift sales area along the trail, looked around to make sure no one was watching, dropped a five-dollar bill into the otherwise empty bottle, and picked up a small intricately twisted copper scorpion. I gave it to Hope when I got back to the car. I told her that the proceeds from the gift were probably the only income a small farmer in Mexico had made that day, and that she now was in the possession of illegally traded goods.

|   |   |   |   |

THE NEXT DAY we had scheduled a trip with Big Bend River Tours through Santa Elena Canyon, a stretch of rock etched deeply through millions of years of the Rio's run. In 1992, the *Handbook of Texas* had bragged that Santa Elena Canyon was "for dedicated river runners" and featured a "swirling series of Class IV rapids that sling boats." When we launched the boats with our guide, right away they scraped along the mud and gravel, and things didn't improve much as we headed upriver. No rapids challenged us; hardly any water swirled at all. But we spent a delightful star-filled night camped at the base of majestic cliffs that lit up with pastel colors at sunset. As we strolled along the riverbank before dinner, a dramatic curtain of shadow drew across the rocks as the sun disappeared and the stars began to glow. We camped far enough uphill from the river to avoid the flash floods that our guide, Wayne, assured us could come any evening—but all night the water remained frighteningly shallow. Another week or two of dry weather and the River Tour companies would have to cancel even the route we were on.

What stood out most about the incredible scenery of the Big Bend canyon is how both towering rock faces of the canyon are required to make the whole of the park. There would be no way to have this park without Mexico. In fact, while in Santa Elena we camped in Mexico. No one checked our papers; our stay in the bi-national natural space posed no threat to anyone. Inside the canyon we could smell cattle on the Mexico side, but we never saw a soul on the rocks above. No one seemed to live anywhere near. At one point we did get out of the boats and climb into an enchanting spring-fed side canyon where the water ran light blue over white rocks. We guessed we could have followed the spring upstream and made it farther into Mexico at that point. No one would have cared.

Wayne took a matter-of-fact attitude about Mexicans coming into Texas, through the park and otherwise. He had interacted with Mexican immigrants his whole life. Nothing seemed wrong to him about people traveling back and forth as necessary. He had once taken a job working with Mexicans chopping out mesquite stumps and had seen how hard they worked in the hot sun. "They are good people and I think if they want to work and there's jobs for them, they ought to be able to come through." Then he shifted the discussion elsewhere: "I caught a lot of rattlesnakes back then, too." "Caught?" I asked. "Yeah, you catch them by the tail and hold it up high and they just try to crawl away from you. They don't think to turn back to bite you. They're just trying to get away." We had seen one small rattler near the boat launch, so we were glad Wayne was around. He wasn't a bad cook either. His filet mignon cooked on a mesquite fire was unforgettable.

|   |   |   |   |

Heading out of the park after two days of camping, I picked up a weekly newspaper at a café in Terlingua where we ate breakfast. A front-page article said that during the past week President Obama had taken a significant step toward establishing the Big Bend as a "peace park" between Mexico and the United States. He and Mexico's president, Felipe Calderón, who had just that week visited Washington for talks, had taken steps to protect important transboundary wild lands. They noted the long history of bi-national cooperation and specifically recognized the Big Bend National Park and the Rio Grande, including the Cañon de Santa Elena. They pledged to preserve this region of extraordinary biological diversity. It was a good step and a welcome article to read after scraping along on the bottom of the river while looking at Mexico beside us. The word "fragile" doesn't begin to capture the state of the river and the park. "Precarious" is more like it. At least the two presidents had given lip service to our mutual future and had signaled a hopeful note about international friendship.

| | | |

Leaving the national park and heading west on Route 170, we traveled through a landscape mountainous and parched, yet mesmerizingly colorful and diverse. Most of the land was uninhabited, with one exception: a gated golf community named Lajitas. Peeking through fences, we could see green lawns, and as we drove around a bend and craned our necks back toward the clubhouse, we saw golf greens. We couldn't understand how any humans could be so oblivious to their surroundings as to pump water to a golf course while living beside the barely running Rio Grande, the landscape around them dying of thirst.

A few bends farther we passed an old Hollywood movie set for a make-believe town named "Contrabando"—a name that captured perfectly America's fears of Mexico. We stopped and took a few photographs, realizing that what appeared to be solid old western buildings were nothing but façades. A few miles after that we stopped to say hello to five Latino *vaqueros* riding in an old gray pickup as they repaired livestock fence in the scorching heat just a few feet from the U.S. border. Their work was not at all a façade. Caught in the middle of their job stretching wire, they seemed happy to pose for a photograph and to mark a connection with someone who noticed. As we drove off, a simple joke about the border came to me: When they construct the border fence, who will do the work? I continued the thought: Who built the fence around the gated community of Lajitas? For that matter, who built Contrabando?

We turned northward and drove for half an hour before coming upon another Border Patrol stop. It was in the middle of nowhere and by then at least thirty miles from the borderline. The Border Patrol agent on duty looked into the driver's window where I sat and, after greeting us, began to ask questions. First, "Why do you have that map?" It seemed a ridiculous question for people driving along back roads near a tourist destination. Then, as we had grown accustomed to being asked, he wanted to know where we were headed. I lost my patience.

"Anywhere we please," I replied, giving him a sidelong glance. Hope took over. She answered, "We're leaving Big Bend and heading toward New Mexico." The officer nodded and after hesitating a bit to look into our car, said, "Thank you, have a nice trip," choosing to ignore my angry comment. He stepped back to let us pass, and we set off northward through a landscape strewn with boulders, scrub brush, and green and white vehicles. The Border Patrol trucks were everywhere: some parked, some off road, some driving by. Cooling down as we drove, I told Hope again how glad I was she had spoken up when she did. Some scenes at the border might be façades, I said, but border guards are all too real.

# TWENTY-FIVE

# Pancho Villa and the Pink Store

COLUMBUS, NEW MEXICO, AND PALOMAS,
CHIHUAHUA

HAVING DRIVEN THE LAST STRETCH OF THE TEXAS BORDER,
we followed back roads to I-10 and then drove a stretch of interstate as it curved around the westernmost corner of Texas along
the Rio Grande, heading back upstream toward El Paso for the
second time. For most of our trip through Texas, the borderline
we followed had meandered as the river meanders, but that pat-
tern was about to change. At El Paso we crossed the old passage
to the north again and continued without stopping this time,
leaving both Texas and the winding river behind. With the twin
cities of Juarez and El Paso disappearing into the wavy hot horizon behind us, we entered New Mexico at the midway point on
its southern boundary.

According to the Congressional Research Service, Texas's
border with Mexico measures 1,241 miles or about 63 percent
of the total U.S./Mexico border. Texas's border is much longer
than the other states' borders in part because rivers don't travel
in straight lines. New Mexico's border with Chihuahua, Mexico,
in contrast, measures only 179.5 miles—about 9 percent of the
U.S./Mexico border. That is because its line was shot by a transit
belonging to a team of surveyors headed by Major William H.

Emory of the U.S. Army's topo-
graphical engineers.

Major Emory, also the name-
sake of the tallest peak in Big
Bend National Park, mapped the
Republic of Texas in 1844 prior to
the United States' annexation of
the state. After the signing of the
Treaty of Guadalupe Hidalgo in
1848, Emory headed the commission that surveyed the area and
recorded the region's geography,
chronicling its flora, fauna, human populations, and more. The
three-volume work that resulted,
*Report on the United States and
Mexican Boundary Survey*, con-
tains hand-colored lithographs of
Native Americans. The set took
over seven years to complete.[1]
When the United States made
the Gadsden Purchase, Emory

The Pancho Villa statue just inside the
border wall at Palomas, Chihuahua.

was the go-to man that President Franklin Pierce's secretary of the interior, Robert McClelland, called on to mark the lines of the new thirty-
thousand-acre, $10 million acquisition.

Emory began the line at the Rio Grande near El Paso, heading due
west for one hundred miles. At the one hundredth mile, the line, as described by the Gadsden Purchase treaty signed December 30, 1853, jogs
"south to latitude 31°30' north thence due west to the one hundred and
eleven meridian; thence in a straight line to a point on the Colorado
twenty miles below its junction with the Gila; thence up the Colorado to

---

1. William H. Emory, *Report on the United States and Mexican Boundary Survey*

the former line." The Gila and the Colorado Rivers form natural divisions between the countries at those points and thus the border meanders a short distance. Other than that, there are just straight lines through the desert, telling not only of a surveyor's craft but also a tale of man-made divisions that only a combination of money and military power can buy. We have already learned about Gadsden's strong-armed diplomacy. Emory was the one who put his handiwork on the map.

| | | |

OUR PROBLEM WAS that the map in our car wouldn't lead us to the right roads. Our choice was Highway 9, but every road kept channeling us back toward I-10. It was as if the road designers had intentionally steered people away from the border. But with repeated stops to check and recheck, we finally found our way to the back road also known as County Road A003. We drove westward along the lonely and flat route, heading toward Columbus, New Mexico, which we hoped to reach before dark. We sped up and headed into the sun.

Columbus is where in 1916 Pancho Villa's army attacked the U.S. fort named Camp Furlong, causing an international scandal. In response, the U.S. military sent thousands of soldiers into Mexico to bring Villa and his hundreds of Villistas to justice. No other single site on the border had been more fraught with international controversy than that little town. Its population was only 350 in 1916, and though it had grown to 1,667 by 2010, the fort was still the main draw. Camp Furlong is mostly gone now, but Pancho Villa State Park, which boasts a few of the original buildings of the fort and a museum, has taken its place. It was a must-see point on our itinerary.

On the way, we drove through mile after mile of rolling landscape with white sands, tan and gray rock outcroppings, and dull green and brown mesquite and low-growing scrub brush along the arroyos. The land isn't much to look at for the uninitiated, and thus it was easy to imagine why some easterners ridiculed the Pierce administration in 1853 for buying what seemed a desolate place.

Fewer than ten inches of rain fall in the southern New Mexico desert annually, but to the trained eye, like those on Emory's botanical survey team, the plants and animals that live low to the ground and survive on minimal moisture are plentiful enough to fill volumes of writing. Even so, passersby like us don't really want to look down all that much in southern New Mexico. First, the mountains in the distance capture the attention. Then there is the sky, particularly as the sun sinks toward the horizon. Many have been enraptured by the view, including Willa Cather, who wrote in 1927 that there is more sky to look at in New Mexico than when one is at the ocean shore. She wrote in *Death Comes for the Archbishop,* "Elsewhere the sky is the roof of the world; but here the earth was the floor of the sky. The landscape one longed for when one was away, the thing all about one, the world one actually lived in, was the sky, the sky!"[2]

We pulled into Columbus late in the afternoon as the billowy clouds in the West were just starting to turn brilliant shades of pink and red, a scene we would come to realize is part of New Mexico's nightly show. We turned off Route 9 and down one of the few back streets of the town and easily found Martha's Place, a B&B recommended by our border angel, Sarah. It was only a block off the main route. We knocked, opened the unlocked door, and walked inside, calling out to Martha. Hearing our knock, Don Javier Lozano, Martha's husband, boomed his friendly greetings and met us in the kitchen. "Hello, come on in! Martha went to buy some groceries. She'll be right back." He told us to make ourselves at home in the living room and kitchen, the guests' and owners' mutual space. Martha was back almost before we took a seat, poured us glasses of water, and showed us to our clean and simple room she had decorated herself.

Martha, it turned out, was a relative newcomer to the community, but by marrying Javier, a Latino man whose roots run deep into the soil on

---

2. Willa Cather, *Death Comes for the Archbishop,* 232.

both sides of the border—in Columbus and Palomas—she was as close to local as any outsider can get. Her place was one of the few guesthouses anywhere near Columbus, and we were pleased Sarah had sent us her way. I was especially glad because of the man Martha married.

After carrying our things to our room, I returned alone to the kitchen to talk with Javier. Like Chad Foster, he said he was also in the last year of his term as the mayor of Columbus, but was not leaving behind his love for his town and its history. And he had the bloodlines and the experience to go with it. His great uncle rode with Villa when the soldiers attacked Columbus. A U.S. citizen with Mexican ancestry, the mustachioed and statuesque Lozano had also put on the costume of the man who would go on to become the archenemy of Villa—General John J. "Black Jack" Pershing—in annual dramatic reenactments performed in the town. Mayor Javier was a treasure trove of information about the area. While recommending that we visit the state park and museum the next day, he proceeded to whet my appetite for what I would see. He pulled out his stack of books and started telling what he knew.

He began with a date. On March 9, 1916, Villa's impoverished and hungry force of some 485 Villistas raided the Columbus Customs House, the arms depot, and the U.S. fort. Only 350 U.S. soldiers were present at Fort Furlong then. Most of the soldiers, along with the town's 350 inhabitants, were asleep when the Villistas attacked. Eight U.S. soldiers died, as did ten civilians, in the initial attack. But the counterattack was swift and effective.

Ninety Villistas died that night. Six more Mexican raiders were captured as they attempted to retreat and were later hanged. The surviving Villistas withdrew, mostly on horseback, into the state of Chihuahua. Meanwhile, the Thirteenth Cavalry stationed at Fort Furlong regrouped, joined with soldiers from other nearby forts, and awaited orders to give chase. General Pershing soon arrived with the plan for what became known as the "Punitive Expedition" and the columns of mounted soldiers gave chase. They would be gone for nearly a year in pursuit. They came back empty-handed.

Though tempers have cooled and people are ready to look more objectively at the battle, there are still no definitive answers regarding why Villa engaged in the suicidal attack. One opinion is simply that Villa was a madman and a terrorist bent on stealing guns from an innocent neighbor. But others say he was provoked and that the United States was no harmless bystander in the Mexican Revolution after all. We've already learned that early aviators at Fort Brown engaged in reconnaissance during the Mexican Revolution, drawing Mexican small-arms fire with the world's first aviation mission. It turns out that this was only one of many incidents.

In the early years of the revolution, the United States had been somewhat supportive of the opposition forces, Mayor Lopez explained. Two years before the attack, Black Jack Pershing had even invited Villa and other Mexican revolutionary generals to visit Fort Bliss where Pershing was commander. There are striking photographs of a smiling Pershing posed with Villa at the fort. In the photos, it appears Pershing is an ally, even as he and the U.S. military commanders continued their vigilance at the forts. Fort Bliss, where he was stationed, as well as Fort Brown had been reinforced because of the revolution and top commanders were there for strategic reasons. Yet the commanders remained at least outwardly neutral, particularly because they had no way of knowing exactly who was in charge at any given time or which Mexican leaders might prevail. Maybe they were simply playing all sides against the middle.

In the beginning of the revolution, the Mexican generals were all united in their common opposition to the thirty-year dictator, Porfirio Díaz. He was a man easy to hate, and because his dictatorial policies were so draconian, merely opposing him and advocating democracy and fair policies for the poor and landless majority was enough to rally the masses. It was an inspiring sight as the peasants rose to fight for freedom with no uniforms, guns, or even shoes, all believing that a revolutionary life was better than returning to what amounted to chattel slavery.

With Francisco Madero in leadership, along with Pancho Villa and Emiliano Zapata commanding their own forces in the north and south respectively, the alliance overthrew Díaz in 1910. As with many revolutions, however, ousting a dictator proved easier than inventing and leading an alternative government. Democracy was fleeting, and the vacuum that followed the victory gave Madero a chance to step up as president. Villa, Zapata, and Venustiano Huerta backed him initially.

Madero had seemed a logical successor to Porfirio Díaz, but soon after taking power he began to appoint his family members and other favored friends to cabinet positions and tried to rule unilaterally. Angered, the other revolutionary leaders pressured Madero to enact reforms, but he managed to put them off temporarily with empty promises. When no change came, the other revolutionaries prepared to fight again. The dissension between the leaders about how to begin gave General Victoriano Huerta, a holdover from the Díaz regime, just enough leeway to oust Madero and force his way into power. It was only 1913, three years after the revolution began, and already two different presidents had held office. After seizing power, Huerta arrested Madero on charges of corruption and forced him to step down from the presidency after having served only two years. Shortly afterward, Huerta had Madero shot.

When Huerta began to reinstate much of the Porfiriato era that Mexican people had so hated, Madero's backers and other revolutionaries, including Villa, rose up in opposition to the new dictator. A new round of fighting ensued, adding years to Mexico's revolutionary period. It was during those years that Villa, along with Venustiano Carranza, emerged as the famous leaders of the anti-Huerta forces in northern Mexico. Despite Villa's strong dislike for Carranza, they became allies of convenience in order to stand against Huerta's strong government-funded military. Álvaro Obregón, who would go on to become Mexico's president in 1920, also fought with Villa.

Villa's Division of the North consisted of several thousand cavalry and infantry. They fought mostly in the mountains of northern Mexico, using the familiar terrain to their advantage. Villa's forces were legendary for their guerrilla tactics and Villa himself garnered the affection of millions on both sides of the border, including Hollywood filmmakers and countless U.S. photographers who documented the Villistas' horseback exploits. To his credit, Villa insisted that half of any Hollywood film profits go to support his soldiers, many of whom were otherwise fighting without pay. Hundreds of photographs of this flamboyant general circulated, and they are still available as prints, T-shirts, and posters today. The famous writer of "An Occurrence at Owl Creek Bridge," Ambrose Bierce, among others, rode as a journalist with Villa and wrote about his exploits.

One of Villa's endearing qualities was that he had been born into a peasant family and continued to live as a sharecropper for much of his young life. He championed the poor, many believed, because he had been one of them. That he wore pith helmets and dashing cowboy hats, brandished bandoliers across his chest, and rode well at full speed while shooting his rifle with accuracy didn't hurt his image. His every move seemed to cultivate his mythological Robin Hood–like character.

It was during Villa's honeymoon period with the press in 1914 that he, along with Obregón and other Mexican officers, went to Fort Bliss to visit with General John J. Pershing. The photographs were so good because professional publicists made them. For a year or more afterward, Villa continued to receive U.S. government and popular American support, and this translated into financial gain for him. Some banks in El Paso accepted his pesos at face value. Others made him loans. For a fleeting time, Villa basked in the widespread support, surely thinking his reputation as a hero had been sealed.

But Villa's popularity soon began to wane, in part because of propaganda that his co-general in the north began to circulate. Villa had been right to distrust Carranza, who had begun casting rumors that Villa wasn't a man of the people after all, but a power-hungry celebrity. Villa, sensing Carranza's power grab, fought back by accusing his former ally of having dictatorial ambitions. Their split led to military skirmishes between the two generals, dragging out the period of the revolution even as Carranza upped his negative publicity campaign against Villa. Some of Carranza's words started filtering across the border into the United States, where they made an impact.

In the fall of 1915 Carranza dealt Villa a decisive blow by sending his ablest general, Álvaro Obregón, to attack Villa at Celaya. Villa suffered severe defeat and lost hundreds of his best riders that day. With a second and third assault, Carranza's armies nearly crushed Villa's forces, and then he hit Villa again at Sonora before his soldiers could regroup. Villa's men could do nothing but limp away to nurse their wounds. With few resources left and his support from banks and individuals in the United States dwindling, Villa turned to banditry as a means to keep his forces alive. It was during this lowest of times that a merchant from Columbus named Sam Ravel cheated Villa out of rifles and ammunition.

Meanwhile after the battles of Celaya and Sonora, Carranza persuaded the Mexican press to turn against Villa, and the U.S. press followed suit. The people's hero became an outlaw overnight. As Villa fell from grace, President Woodrow Wilson threw his support behind Carranza and even lent American trains for Carranza to use at Agua Prieta, where he outmaneuvered Villa.

This was a messy time for Mexico, and Villa was no saint, but the corrupt and power-hungry Carranza was far from deserving of U.S. tactical support. The Wilson administration needed to back the strongest man for strategic reasons, however, and as Carranza gained military advantage, the U.S. government recognized him as the legitimate president of the country before any election and even while Villa and other generals were still actively fighting against him. Whether Villa deserved anything more than what he got, as Mayor Lozano said, "The U.S. had gotten its nose in Mexican affairs." Uncle Sam was no innocent bystander when Villa attacked.

Villa went after Ravel's warehouse in order to procure the munitions he was owed and to exact his revenge. Ravel was out of town and avoided being killed, but he was not the only target, as one of Villa's officers reportedly yelled in Spanish, "We want revenge against the Americans!" Whether they were attacking the United States for backing Carranza or just were trying to get some desperately needed arms, they paid dearly in men, horses, and the loss of goodwill for what they got. After Columbus,

Villa's forces would never fight effectively again and the demoralized Villa would be on the run for the rest of his life.

| | | |

AS WE TOURED the fort and museum with Don Javier the following morning, the futility of the Villa attack was still palpable. Crossing the border in the night to capture promised arms could never have worked. With that move it was clear the revolution had faltered and the ideals that millions had died for had shriveled on the vine. In a tragic twist of roles, the great General of the North had been reduced to an outlaw on the run, while his antidemocratic and dictatorial rival gained power and the backing of the land of the free.

With Carranza in power, Mexico's revolutionary hopes gave way to cynicism, leading to PRI's (*Partido Revolucionario Instituto*) domination for the rest of the twentieth century. The word "Revolutionary" in their name came to mean anything but. Not even land reform would take hold until twenty years later when President Lázaro Cárdenas implemented the *ejido* system of common land ownership for the landless. Meanwhile, the United States had been stuck with a neighbor whose politics people have long fled rather than believe and engage in.

In 2005, while working on the documentary *The Guestworker*, two collaborators and I followed our film's main character, Don Candelario Gonzalez Moreno, to his home in rural Durango, Mexico. Don Cande grew up and lived on an *ejido* with his family during the winter. For more than half the year, however, he harvested tobacco and peppers in North Carolina, which is how we met him.

Candelario told us that his father and others had fought for the land where he lived, and, with the government's support, succeeded in establishing the common holding where his family and others raised corn, beans, and cattle. As the land yielded dwindling returns, Candelario began making annual trips to the United States while still holding on to his *ejido* claim.

Don Cande, sixty-six at the time of our filming, had traveled to North Carolina every year since 1966 with the goal of earning enough money to buy the family's necessities and pay his wife's medical bills. There was no retirement money for him, so he couldn't stop working. "A teacher can retire, and some people who work in factories can as well, but not the small farmer, not the worker in the U.S. fields," he said in the film.

When we met Don Cande in North Carolina and planned to travel with him to Durango, I had expected to find a difficult life there. I knew that he and others had to leave home to provide for their families, and to leave their land in order to keep it, and, sadly, neglect it in order to save it. When we arrived in his little community named Pánuco, I saw this in poignant and stark relief. The crops his ailing wife had tried to keep alive were shriveled, and their cattle were near starvation because of prolonged drought.

I knew before we arrived that something was broken on both sides of the border when a person of retirement age has to migrate every year to keep afloat financially. This was doubly true when, as with the Braceros, there was no retirement for a man participating in a U.S. government program. But unlike the Braceros fifty years ago, workers in today's H-2A program were not promised any benefits. All of this hit me hard when we arrived in Don Cande's home and met his family, but what I had no way to prepare for was the direct connection between Don Candelario and Pancho Villa.

The birthplace of Doroteo Arango, the poor *campesino's* son who would become Pancho Villa, was only thirty minutes from Candelario's *ejido*. Don Cande had to take us there and show us, so we borrowed a truck from the local labor recruiter and drove to the historic landmark one afternoon. Finding no one else there but the elderly caretaker, we walked into the adobe version of a sharecropper's shack and filmed under the towering statue of Villa erected beside it. Don Candelario, walking arm-in-arm with his wife, Doña Magdalena, began to shed tears and to speak about how important Villa had been to small farmers like him.

We rushed to put up the tripod as he began. "Tears of emotion, tears of respect and gratitude fall from my eyes when I think of the sacrifices this great man and the others made for the poor people of Mexico," he said. "It's only because of Villa that we have the liberty we have today." Luckily we captured the moment, and I am still struck when I watch the film and see how moved Don Candelario was by Villa. Don Cande went on to tell us on film how Doroteo Arango, like his father, had been born a sharecropper on a desert farm. I'll never forget the moment.

According to legend, Arango's fight against injustice began when the hacienda owner's son raped his sister. He first sought help from the local authorities, but when neither the *federales* nor the nearby Catholic father responded, Arango took matters into his own hands and stabbed the rapist. This began his years of flight from the law, during which he took the name Pancho Villa. From there, some say Villa pursued a life of self-promotion and crime. Others, including Don Candelario, believe he became a freedom fighter.

Inside the Villa museum at the site there were photos of his bullet-riddled car. Villa's bloodied corpse was photographed in 1923 lying across the hood of his killers' vehicle like a downed animal. A man many thought could never be brought down—one that even Pershing with six thousand cavalry had failed to catch—had been shot in an ambush staged by Villa's revolutionary rival Álvaro Obregón. The photographs now in the museum had been taken to prove and celebrate his demise.

Thus I learned from one of my heroes, a farmworker who spoke of his feelings at Pancho Villa's statue, that Mexico's revolution was no less important to Mexicans than the revolution led by George Washington is to us. The problem is what followed it. We know that France aided the United States as it built its democracy in the 1780s. What country aided Mexico as it tried to build a democracy after their revolution?

|    |    |    |    |

AFTER SAYING GOOD-BYE to Don Javier at his mayoral office, Hope and I went back once again to walk over the grounds of Fort Furlow, passing the old mess hall, then the old customs house and the railroad depot, the last vestiges of the buildings in Columbus at the time of Villa's attack. We walked up on the small hill above the museum, stood under an American flag, looked over the site, and talked about what might have been.

| | | |

BY 1914, GENERAL PERSHING had already distinguished himself as a commanding officer of the Tenth Cavalry during the Spanish-American War fought over the issue of Cuban independence. By riding with African American soldiers, Pershing earned the nickname "Black Jack." The moniker was not a tribute to his military prowess, but a kind of mockery: "black" was for the color of his soldiers' skin. But for Pershing, commanding black soldiers appears to have been more than mere duty, perhaps even a point of honor. His writings show that when he began commanding black soldiers, his respect for them deepened. Likely that respect began when Pershing taught black youths at the Prairie Mound School in Laclede, Missouri, near where he was born. Likely he learned from that teaching experience, along with his own escape from poverty through education, the value of building a society based on education and economic development for all. Maybe he distanced himself from racism through that.

After serving as one of Teddy Roosevelt's lieutenants at San Juan Hill, John "Jack" Pershing wrote that the African American Tenth Cavalry "fought their way into the hearts of the American people." Following Pershing's report, TR praised them as well, saying the African American soldiers fought on equal footing with his Rough Riders. It was impossible to tell whether it was the white Rough Riders or the African American soldiers of the Ninth who "came forward with the greater courage to offer their lives in the service of their country,"

Roosevelt wrote.[3] San Juan was a shining moment in African American history, as black historian Rayford Logan attested: "Negroes had little, at the turn of the century, to help sustain our faith in ourselves except the pride that we took in the 9th and 10th Cavalry, the 24th and 25th Infantry. Many Negro homes had prints of the famous charge of the colored troops up San Juan Hill. They were our Ralph Bunche, Marian Anderson, Joe Louis and Jackie Robinson."[4]

Unfortunately, Colonel Roosevelt later took an about-face, saying, "Negro troops were shirkers in their duties and would only go as far as they were led by white officers."[5] The motivation for his comments had to be a problem of stereotypes of the time, and was likely a political maneuver made in order to gain white votes as he ran for office, but it was not unrelated to his refusal to pardon the wrongly accused Fort Brown soldiers when he had a chance.

As the call to arms went out after Villa's attack on Columbus, soldiers gathered over a five-day period, as many companies were mustered under Pershing's command at the border. The Tenth Cavalry, all black soldiers, arrived from Fort Huachuca in Arizona to join Pershing's pursuit. Ultimately some six thousand or more troops would ride into Mexico. Their foray on horseback some five hundred miles into Mexico in 1916 with Pershing at the head of a long column of mounted soldiers—incidentally, during the middle of WWI—was what author Colonel Frank Tompkins calls the "last campaign of the U.S. Cavalry."

What remains less visible about the campaign is that the cavalrymen of color—men who grew up as sons of slaves and sharecroppers—served the U.S. Army having never held voting rights. They were soldiers who had never experienced democracy themselves and who remained

---

3. Frank N. Schubert, *On the Trail of the Buffalo Soldier: Biographies of African Americans in the U.S. Army, 1866–1917*, 6, 14, 331, 338, 404.

4. Rayford W. Logan, *The Betrayal of the Negro, from Rutherford B. Hayes to Woodrow Wilson*, 335; Frank N. Schubert, "The Buffalo Soldiers at San Juan Hill."

5. "Buffalo Soldiers and the Spanish-American War," last modified January 9, 2014, http://www.nps.gov/prsf/historyculture/buffalo-soldiers-and-the-spanish-american-war.htm.

in a segregated nation in the middle of the Jim Crow period. They were riding in pursuit of a son of a sharecropper from Mexico who had once led a column of bedraggled farmers in their own struggle for equality.

In chasing Villa over five hundred miles and engaging in many skirmishes, at least ten Buffalo Soldiers lost their lives in Mexico. They died in Parral, Chihuahua, killed not by Villistas, but by Carranza's forces. Some are still buried there. According to Mayor Lozano, one of their grave markers in Parral reads, "Praise the Lord, but keep your powder dry."

| | | |

LEAVING COLUMBUS, we drove a mile southward, parked in a lot made for tourists, and walked into the little town of Palomas, whose name means doves, a universal symbol of peace. Only the town had not been peaceful. In 2005, drug cartel members murdered Palomas's mayor because they believed he had been meddling in their affairs. The murder remains unsolved today. Yet Martha had told us to go anyway. "As long as you go in by day, there's no problem. And when you go, you have to visit the Pink Store."

We walked through the border entrance with only a wave to the guard. Just inside Palomas is an impressive bronze statue of Pancho Villa on his galloping horse, his hat blowing back off his head and caught by his chinstrap, his gun drawn. His eyes appeared fixed on the pink building across the street. We followed his gaze toward two indigenous women dressed in colorful traditional clothing who stood in front of the store greeting visitors. No other businesses around even approached the vibrancy of the Pink Store, and though the crowd was small, everyone we saw was headed there. Outside, greeters announced there were free margaritas and mariachi music within. "Please come in!" they said in accented but practiced English.

Dozens of customers were inside sipping their drinks. Some were in the restaurant. Others carried their drinks around as they shopped. Margaritas for brunch! Sizzling plates of fajitas went by as we looked at displays of glassware, pottery, and wall hangings from all over Mexico while we waited for our table. Glass pendants and other ornaments hung from every rafter. Every wall was filled with items for sale. Overwhelmed, I walked out to the store's courtyard to see their statue: Pershing shaking hands with Villa.

A broad smile was on Pershing's face, the same expression I'd seen in the photos. The handshake represented friendship and interchange between two countries; it also fostered good feelings about buying Mexican goods for American homes. I went back in to join Hope for a margarita and some enchiladas, and we listened to the band as its musicians meandered around the tables, leaning backward and belting out *ranchero* tunes and all the tourist favorites, including "La Bamba" and even "Feliz Navidad" six months early.

After we ate, we talked briefly with the Pink Store's owner, Ivonne Romero. Attractive, gracious, and eloquent in English, Ivonne surrounded us with her warmth as she does many other Americans every day of the year. She loved her job, she said, but her business had declined precipitously over the past few years. "No one wants to stay as long as they used to. They come here for lunch, but by four in the afternoon, they're all gone. We used to close at nine at night. Then it was eight. Now it's six!"

Ivonne then asked us why we had come, and we told her about our border sojourn. Though busy, she stopped and asked for more details, and seemed overjoyed. "Wait here a minute," she said as she went back into the store and returned with two handmade Christmas ornaments to give to us. "Thank you so much for coming, and please tell others about what you found here in Mexico."

On the way out I walked by the Pancho Villa statue again and noticed that pigeons had roosted momentarily on the horse's bridle. They should have been doves, but pigeons would have to do. We walked back across the border unimpeded—no passport required, just as the store had advertised. On the U.S. side of the line, an abandoned shopping cart sat empty beside the big wall on which we had spent billions. The scene said everything I could think to say about international trade and development in a single image.

# TWENTY-SIX

## Smoke on the Apachería

CHIRICAHUA NATIONAL MONUMENT, WILCOX, ARIZONA

WE SAW SMOKE ON THE HORIZON JUST OVER THE ARIZONA border when we were still some thirty miles or more from the Chiricahua range. Concerned about what was clearly a forest fire ahead, we stopped at the crossroads at Animas and asked two grizzled men in a pickup about a road heading south.

The lone grocery cart left in the United States alongside the border wall. Note also the new floodlights and road constructed by Homeland Security.

The map showed that a small road, Route 338, headed toward Mexico. "The fire's not close to the road," they said, "and since you don't have four-wheel drive there's no way you can go 338. There might be a road marked on your map, but nobody maintains it." We thought of the Minas Road and the flat tire. Thanking the gentlemen, we took Route 80 toward the Chiricahua. We had wanted to see mountains anyway. We just hadn't planned to see them in flames.

The Chiricahua Desert Museum parking lot on Route 80 was filled with firefighter vehicles when we pulled in—along with those of others assisting them, including the Border Patrol. We talked to a volunteer sitting at a food and water table. Already the fire on the mountain above had consumed fifteen hundred acres and the winds were up again, she said, with no rain in the forecast all week. As we talked, a plane spreading flame retardant flew over the peak nearby, the only visible sign of human activity. But she said there were hundreds of firefighters somewhere on the mountain digging trenches in the dry pine forests, trying desperately to keep the fire out of the park.

I asked the volunteer if it would be okay to talk with some of the Border Patrol officers I saw standing next to their vehicles in the second row. "You're welcome to walk in there," she said. I thanked her, put a donation in the box on the table, headed toward the green and white trucks, and approached two officers standing beside them.

"Hello, how is everything going?"

"Pretty well, considering."

"I'm surprised to see so many Border Patrol vehicles here. Are you helping with the firefighting?"

"No, we're here to catch the ones that run out from the smoke."

"Are there people hiding up in the Chiricahua wilderness?"

"They're everywhere!"

"Have you caught any people as a result of the fire here?"

"Not yet."

There were four other Border Patrol trucks in the parking lot besides theirs, all of them new, large, and equipped with the most powerful Cummings Diesel engines—the top of the line.

Hope and I had driven and walked through much of the Chiricahua National Monument the previous year and I remembered the remote and difficult terrain well. In the heart of the park, hundreds, maybe thousands, of tall, chimney-like rock formations stand like columns of some massive ancient cathedral long decimated by time. We walked a trail to see the columns up close, and the heat there was so dry and intense that we had to ration our two quarts of water. We wanted to drink it all in the first mile. At the higher elevations tall ponderosa pines and Douglas firs tower above the rocks, so large that little vegetation grows beneath them. They were the ones I feared could burn.

As with all the other deserts we had passed through on foot, I couldn't imagine someone lasting for more than a day or so on these peaks without bringing massive amounts of water and other provisions—particularly someone who is not indigenous to the place, as once were Cochise and his people.

Cochise and his kin were the Chiricahua, a subgroup of the Apaches who survived in these rocks for years while on the run from the cavalry. From certain vantage points in the park, one can see the upturned profile of Cochise's face in a mountain range; his curved nose is one peak, his brow ridge another, his chin a third. He is resting, not dead, the legend goes; he was so tough that his spirit still remains alive in these hills.

Cochise and his people knew their territory well, and they used the borderlands of Mexico and the United States, particularly the labyrinth of rock formations that would become the real draw of the park, as hideouts. The U.S. Cavalry, who often had to dismount to navigate this place, never found the Chiricahua, and Cochise and his beleaguered family survived long enough to go down in history as victors of sorts, though they had to live on the run to do so.

As Hope and I hiked through the tall and thin spires of rock with their many overhangs and nooks, arches, and caves, we talked about the countless hiding places in this maze of rock. There were boulders on top of others providing natural shelters. The place was perfect for concealing oneself, but it was clear to us that without the water we carried with us for a morning jaunt, we could not have survived more than a day. To imagine dozens of people traveling with their children and hiding there for weeks was nearly impossible for me. Yet somehow the Chiricahua people possessed the needed hunting and scavenging skills and knew how to find water, and so they lived.

Could an uninitiated person who had inadvertently dropped into this landscape make it? No way in hell, I thought. But clearly the Border Patrol disagreed. I had to assume they knew what they were talking about. After all, there were Cochise's people who had survived a previous government search, and not even Black Seminole scouts could find them. Starting back then, how many U.S. dollars had been spent on border hunts like that? The donation box for the firefighters couldn't possibly compare.

| | | |

AS WE DROVE southward paralleling the Chiricahua range, the smoke suddenly billowed higher and then flames leapt up over the closest ridge, and trees at its top burst into flames like torches. I knew many more resources and person hours were going to be required before that wildfire was out. Back in the parking lot, part of me had wanted to say something about the priorities in our national budget, but I knew the officers had nothing to do with making those choices. They were like the cavalry riding after Cochise: they had a job to do and they remained faithful to it.

We drove south on 80 with the Chiricahua range a safe distance off to our west, though we could still see smoke for many more miles. The fire continued to dominate our conversation until a state sign riveted my attention: marker for the site of Geronimo's capture ahead, it announced. I stopped at the marker, got out on the hot roadside, and read the plaque on the tall stone obelisk. The graffiti-marred text said that in nearby Skeleton Canyon just off to the east of where I stood, Geronimo and his thirty-five bedraggled men and teenaged boys—along with 101 women and children—had surrendered to the cavalry. The year was 1886.

Several years before that, Geronimo and his people had agreed to live in the San Carlos reservation in the southeast Arizona Territory, but in 1885, hungry and suffering the indignities of captivity, they broke out, deciding to live the nomadic life again, which included raiding to survive. They headed toward the open mountain ranges some called the Apachería and made raids into both Mexico and the United States. For over a year, they lived as fugitives along the border near the Chiricahua as over five thousand troops and their auxiliaries pursued them. Then, after their discovery, they could run no more and they surrendered.

While on the run they had killed over seventy-five settlers and nine soldiers. They had lived in a desert where in May the sun can beat down at a hundred degrees during the day and get to near freezing at night. The cavalry and their scouts under the command of General Nelson Miles had finally tracked them into a dead-end canyon with high walls. There was no escape route. According to the plaque, this surrender "forever ended Indian warfare in the United States." The famed Buffalo Soldiers had completed their mission.

Geronimo said in his autobiography that he had been tricked, and he had never agreed to go to a reservation to begin with. Following their capture, what was left of his tribe was taken to Fort Sam Houston in San Antonio and then later the families were split up and sent as far away as Florida and Alabama, and never allowed to return to their homeland again. Geronimo himself would experience something else.

Though his actual name was Goyaaté, this shaman-warrior later became a performer in public events and parades known as Geronimo. We still shout his name when jumping from high places. He has never left our language, or our imaginations. After their capture, he and his warriors were taken by boxcar toward captivity. On the way to Fort Sam Houston in September 1886, Geronimo and fifteen of his men were taken out of the boxcar on a hillside and photographed. Somehow even held at gunpoint and defenseless they still managed to look proud.

There is another well-known photograph of Geronimo with three warriors, all armed with rifles and wearing headbands, long sleeves, pants with loincloths, and high moccasins. They stand together in the desert looking straight into the camera. Taken year of the Skeleton Canyon capture, the photograph has remained iconic, even a symbol of American freedom. Today it appears on T-shirts sold in stores all over the Southwest. The four Apache men stare at the camera, seemingly daring anyone to pass. A common caption under the photo reads: "Homeland Security: Fighting Terrorism since 1492"—an ironic response to 9/11. Geronimo's face is recognizable today in part because he appeared with Teddy Roosevelt and Buffalo Bill Cody's Wild West Show before thousands of spectators. He is remembered today in part because he played himself in the shoot-'em-up shows.

The Geronimo's Capture monument, erected in 1934 by the city of Douglas, Arizona, tells of the end of one people's freedom and the taming of this once feared place. The capture would also help usher in the state named Arizona in 1912, a state that would by 2010 become synonymous with the enforcement of borderlines and catching trespassers with sophisticated technologies. The place would never be home to people who live outside of boundaries again, and the life Geronimo had surrendered would never return. Now Homeland Security had come to mean something quite different from the scene on the T-shirts we still love to buy.

# TWENTY-SEVEN

# A Grandmother Mourns at the Wall

DOUGLAS, ARIZONA, AND AGUA PRIETA,
SONORA

THE NEXT DAY WAS HOPE'S AND MY ANNIVERSARY, SO WE
decided to head directly to the mining town turned tourist destination named Bisbee, Arizona, to celebrate. That meant bypassing the Douglas/Agua Prieta border crossing and leaving
it for the following year. Knowing I would likely be back in Arizona with students the very next year, I said, "I'll just go to Agua
Prieta and Douglas out of sequence." The story that unfolded
proved that sometimes things work out best when we forget
about being linear.

When I flew to Tucson in 2011, the students I helped re-
cruit—eight of them in all—had just completed their two-week
orientation at BorderLinks, during which they had learned firsthand about the border and immigration challenges. I had said
to them before they left that Arizona is ground zero of the U.S./
Mexico border and immigration debate as well as the best place
to study and work on border and immigration challenges. BorderLinks and other nonprofit organizations in town had been
excellent partners for our DukeEngage on the Border program
since its inception in 2007. This was our fifth group of students,
and they had just completed their homestays with immigrant

families and started their work assignments—some of them working directly with migrants, others on policy and education.

As part of their orientation, the students had traveled to visit the border wall at Douglas, Arizona. They were still talking about their experience when I walked into the BorderLinks office. Before they saw me, one of them said, "The Border Patrol is tearing it down . . ." I greeted everyone and then asked what they had been talking about. They explained that they had just visited a makeshift border shrine dedicated to Carlos La Madrid, a nineteen-year-old U.S. citizen who had been killed by a Border Patrol officer. Being nineteen- and twenty-year-olds themselves, the story of the young man's death hit them hard, especially when they learned he was an American. "Why do they have to tear down the shrine?" one of them asked, stricken with grief. I didn't know the answer, but I started reading more about the case that afternoon.

According to media reports, La Madrid was a soccer player,

The grandmother of Carlos La Madrid mourning at the shrine erected at the site of his shooting near Douglas, Arizona.

guitarist, and solar technology buff. The night he died, Carlos was driving a vehicle that the Border Patrol considered "suspicious." He and a friend had parked the vehicle and then ran for the fence—from the Douglas side toward Mexico, heading toward Agua Prieta. Family members reported he was on his way to visit his father, who lived there.

There are conflicting reports about what happened after the Border Patrol officer arrived in his truck and tried to stop the young man as he scrambled up a ladder heading south. The other youth with him was already on the wall when the officer approached. According to the officer, one of them threw rocks. Carlos refused to come down and kept climbing.

As the officer moved closer in his truck, a rock, perhaps two, hit his windshield, he said. He demanded the young men turn around. Allegedly more rocks pelted the truck. Then the officer shot. Carlos was hit four times, three times in the back, once in the shoulder. He died at the scene. At this writing, the case is still open. No weapons were ever found at the site. Even the rocks are in dispute.

I asked the students if anyone would like to go back to visit the shrine with me. Michelle Lozano, a child of immigrants from Mexico and a junior majoring in public policy, volunteered to go with me. She wanted to take more pictures of the shrine, she said, and had some free time after work the following afternoon. She said she remembered how to get back to the site and would guide me.

Michelle was finishing up her work at the Southside Presbyterian Church's day-labor center when I arrived. She completed her record-keeping, writing down which workers got jobs that day, where they went, and how much they were paid. We helped some of the workers still there pack away the chairs and the snacks the church provided, and then we left. We drove east on I-10, exited at Route 80, Jefferson Davis Highway, and headed south for Tombstone, Arizona, where we had decided to have a late lunch.

We got out of the car just in time to see actors wearing western clothing fight it out with six-guns in the middle of the street in front of us. Several shots rang out and then an announcer on the street corner shouted to the gathering crowd that we could see more down inside the OK Corral, where actors would replay the Doc Holliday and Earp Brothers' 1881 shootout with the Clantons and McLaurys.

Before that visit, I'd only seen the town in a film—the documentary *Crossing Arizona*. I learned from the film that Tombstone was home to the Minutemen founder, Chris Simcox. A local newspaper owner and reporter who had grown frustrated with the influx of immigrants, Simcox started the organization in 2002, operating it out of his small press office. To draw media attention to their cause, Simcox and the Minuteman Civil Defense Corps began organizing patrols along the border of Arizona and Sonora, Mexico, in 2006. Their stated goal was to apprehend and turn over undocumented people to the Border Patrol. They were well armed and patrolled in groups. They used walkie-talkies to communicate with one another while hiding in the desert waiting on the unsuspecting migrants.

Their ultimate goal was to embarrass the government into sending additional National Guard troops to the border and to strengthen the wall. The national media gave the group lots of attention. A gathering of hundreds of civilians with guns, ammunition, and lots of American flags who said they were there to capture Mexicans was certainly newsworthy. Shortly afterward, the Bush administration saw that the Secure Fence Act of 2007 passed. Many credited the legislation to the publicity the Minutemen garnered. The day we arrived, it didn't seem out of place that the Minuteman movement had been born where men shoot it out in the streets every day, though I'm sure the Minutemen didn't load blanks.

|    |    |    |    |

WE CONTINUED SOUTH to Douglas. Our first stop there was the Mexican Consulate, where we picked up literature intended for Mexican families about the dangers of crossing the border—well-designed posters and small pocket-sized booklets about why people should avoid the desert. "*No vale la pena*" (It's not worth it), one poster said. Michelle asked, "If someone makes it to Douglas, how could those materials help them?" Excellent point. At least the materials showed the Mexican government had tried to educate its citizens. The free resources also showed that they considered migration a humanitarian issue rather than a crime. Though we had just walked in without an appointment, the consulate employees gave us their time and copies of everything they had about immigration, and even removed one of the posters from the wall and handed it to Michelle.

We then drove south to the gravel road the Border Patrol had made and headed eastward toward Calvary Cemetery. I stopped to ask an officer parked on a knoll overlooking the fence if there was any problem with our driving there. The officer looked stern, trying to figure out a middle-aged white guy and a young Latina student traveling together. Without exactly giving us permission, he said simply, "You must avoid all restricted areas." I thanked him and we drove away slowly, though still stirring up clouds of dust behind us.

Michelle knew she would recognize Carlos's shrine if she saw it again. But as we drove several miles, we began to worry we were too late, that maybe the shrine had already been removed. I even asked Michelle if we had gone the wrong direction. Then suddenly she saw it ahead. "It's even bigger than last week!" she said. The family had been busy.

Encircling an area some thirty feet across were white rocks arranged in the shape of a heart. At the top of the heart near the wall was a large cross, imprinted with a permanent color photograph of Carlos. Placed around the perimeter were colorful artificial flowers. Hanging on the border wall itself were handwritten posters and papers with messages; some of them venting anger, some poetic laments, all emotions of love and grief. On one large poster, Carlos's sister had printed in large letters a message that began with the scathing salutation, "To the Border Patrol Who Killed My Brother." No one was anywhere around when we stopped, so I got out of the car and took pictures of everything, and we stood staring at the place, letting the deep emotion of the scene sink in. Then we drove on to see more of the wall ahead. I wanted to see the Chiricahua Mountains from the west to link the places that Hope and I had skipped the year before.

We stopped where the road crossed the last of the Chiricahua foothills. There was only a small rise there, but I could see it connected to the range as it lifted higher and extended north toward the horizon. We got out of the car, and I was looking toward the mountains when, without saying a word, Michelle began shimmying up one of the border wall posts. In less than a minute she was sitting on top of the fifteen-foot fence. I scanned the horizon for any sign of any vehicle stirring up dust. Nothing came. Then Michelle slid down having conquered one section and tried it again in another spot, scaling the wall several more times as I looked on in amazement. When she was satisfied that she had climbed enough, we got back in the car and doubled back toward Douglas. She didn't say why she had done it.

As we neared the shrine on the return trip we could see a maroon Ford pickup was parked beside it. On the back window facing us, there was a full-color sunshade photograph. We realized quickly that it was the image of Carlos La Madrid—the same one as on the cross—a full-body portrait of him standing beneath white clouds. At the wall, a young woman we would soon learn was Carlos's sister stood with her young son in diapers and watched her grandmother make her rounds ensuring that all of the adornments she had left earlier were in place. We got out of the car as reverently as we could.

I asked Michelle if she would approach the family to find out if we might talk a little with them and maybe take pictures. I waited beside the car, but decided not to bring out the camera unless Michelle gave me a signal. Michelle approached the sister and told her our purpose for being there, about our DukeEngage delegation and the students' work. Our hope, she explained, would be to share photographs and help bring attention to the grandson's death. Carlos's sister talked quietly with the grandmother, who nodded, and Michelle waved me in.

Then the grandmother—clearly bereft with grief and saying nothing—walked toward the cross. She draped her arms around it as if embracing Carlos's body. With tears running down her cheeks, she looked up and explained that she had not visited the site since his death. The day we were there had been exactly four months since he died and it was a tradition for her to return. She leaned over and embraced the cross again. My photographs began to feel like offerings.

Then Michelle noticed the posters on the border wall were gone and asked what had happened to them. The sister said the Border Patrol had removed them, saying they were inappropriate for the wall, but mercifully they had left the shrine in front of it untouched. I couldn't believe that I had just documented the site a half hour earlier and already it had changed dramatically. Then Michelle took her own pictures, and later wrote further about the ensuing exchange on her DukeEngage blog. The excerpt that follows tells what happened next:

> The grandmother moved back to the memorial and inspected all the candles and other items to check they were unharmed. From time to time she would remember something else and the tears would start again. Charlie turned to me, can you ask her if I can give her a donation? *Dice el senor que quiere darle una donación, para que pueda seguir luchando para que dejen en paz esto. . . .* She nodded "yes" slightly and I turned to Charlie and said yes. He took out a $20 bill and handed it to the lady. So you can buy more candles, he told her in Spanish. *Mira, me lo dio para que le pongamos velas de su parte* [Look, he gave me this so we can put out some candles for them], said the grandmother to the younger woman. Carlos, *mira te van a poner mas velas* [Carlos, look, they are going to put out more candles for you], the younger girl said to the picture on the cross.

After saying thanks and good-bye to Carlos's family, we drove along the wall through Douglas and on to the western side of town where the wall skirted the edge of a sewage treatment plant. Realizing the road stopped there, we turned around to leave. At the exit to the plant we met up with a Border Patrol officer named Garcia. He waved us down and asked what we were doing there. "I'm a university professor and this is my student. We're studying the border and immigration," is how I started, and then explained we didn't know the road along the wall ended there.

He seemed eager to talk with us. He said he felt sympathetic with the migrants, but was quick to add that if we were studying the border we should learn all sides of the issues. "We're trying," Michelle said, explaining they had been to the Border Patrol regional office the week before. Officer Garcia said he would be glad to have us ride with him; all we would need to do is to go to the national office and get permission. I'd love to do just that, I told him. Having just left Carlos's shrine, part of me wanted to bring up the rocks and windshields and ladders, but I knew no officer would be able to discuss a pending case. So I swallowed it all and just said thanks for the help and the offer.

As we started to leave, Agent Garcia offered something totally unexpected: "If you're going along the border you should follow the new road. You'll need to take the first left just outside of Douglas near an abandoned ranch and that will take you right there. You can follow the road all the way to Bisbee." We thanked him and followed his directions, turning south onto the newly graded North Cattleman Road, which soon intersected with W. International Avenue, a gravel road paralleling the wall just as it had done east of Douglas. Not a soul was there.

We stopped at a spot on a hill where we could see in all directions, and as soon as her car door shut Michelle headed for the wall again and was up on top in no time. Then she tried it again in another spot. No problem. Then I got into the spirit, though I knew I'd better not try to go vertical. I found an open floodgate at an arroyo covered with a few strands of barbed wire and simply ducked under the wires and walked into Mexico.

I gazed southward at the colorful dry hills of Sonora and mourned a family's loss. I thought of Carlos's grandmother and the candles. At least because of the shrine a few small fragile flames might shine their light onto the huge metal wall behind it. I gazed at the hills, took a few minutes of silence, and summoned my best sense of hope for change. I sensed that Michelle, who was sitting silently on top of the wall staring into the distance, was doing the same. Then I turned and crawled back through the barbed wire and stepped into the United States, Michelle clambered down, and we drove back toward Tucson.

# TWENTY-EIGHT

# Fences and Neighbors

NACO, ARIZONA, AND NACO, SONORA

HOPE AND I CELEBRATED OUR ANNIVERSARY IN BISBEE WITH several great meals and a walking tour of the town. On the way into town, we passed the old copper processing facilities and the copper mines gouged into the earth like massive rock stair steps, marveling at the environmental and economic impact the industry had made on the region. Without the mines, the town of Bisbee would never have been on the map. Today tourists go for the food and art, but a few signs of mining have been preserved for artistic and educational purposes. An exhibit at the museum explains the mining process, but I noticed little was said about the miners themselves. Later I started hunting.

Searching the Internet using the terms "Bisbee and miners," I quickly came upon an infamous event I'd never heard of called the "Bisbee Deportations" and started reading. We had seen no historical markers, no exhibit references, no educational aids about the incident, so I called the tourist bureau in town to make sure I hadn't missed something. An elderly woman named Martha answered and confirmed there was nothing official in the town to commemorate the event, but she had heard some of the stories and started telling them.

In 1917, the last year of World War I, demand for copper to make bullets was high. At the same time Michelle climbing the border wall near Douglas, Arizona.

over twelve hundred miners had struck against the major mining company, Phelps Dodge. Though wages had increased some, the company had started paying immigrant and minority laborers less than the whites. No worker was happy with the inequality, even as those making the highest wages were scared that their jobs were in jeopardy. Yet instead of fighting each other, the workers organized and went after the company. The union called International Workers of the World, known alternately as the IWW or the "Wobblies," backed them.

The company cracked down in retaliation. Over two thousand armed men, one with a mounted machine gun, moved in to round up the striking workers and their supporters at the mining headquarters in Bisbee, marched them at gunpoint to the railroad station two miles away, and loaded them onto twenty cattle cars. Martha said people still talk about the event. "There were mothers snatching their children out of the lines," she said. "They were just kids." Many arrested alongside the miners had never worked for the company.

The vigilantes loaded the miners and others onto cattle cars inches deep in manure, all ethnicities together, and sent them eastward into the desert of the New Mexico Territory, putting them out in Columbus of all places. Finding no place to keep them, the company men backed the train to Hermanas, New Mexico and left the men there for over two weeks without shelter. Guards kept them there until federal troops arrived. They had water and a little food, but that was it.

"They just left them there," Martha said, "in the middle of the desert!" No one was ever prosecuted for the incident. The federal government could find no statute the company violated, so they sent it to the Arizona courts. Nothing happened there either. Following that, the federal government became proactive in its own official deportations, including the deportations of supposed anarchists in 1919, two million Mexicans in the 1930s because of the job shortage during the Depression, and the Operation Wetback deportation initiative in 1954. The Japanese internment during World War II involving the involuntary relocation of 120,000 should also be added to the list.

I tried to end the phone conversation with Martha on an upbeat note, not singling out Bisbee: "Well, it's good to know we've made some progress in labor laws since then." Martha snapped right back, "I think sometimes things are getting worse." I knew she was right. I should have gone further, as she may have talked about how we are deporting more people now than ever before. We could have talked about the overloaded detention centers. I just didn't have the emotional strength to go there that day. I didn't want to be on the phone either. After all, this was a tourist office I had called, and the romantic place where we celebrated our anniversary.

| | | |

BEFORE HEADING TOWARD Tucson to meet the DukeEngage students, Hope and I decided to drive down to the nearby border crossing at Naco in the early morning. We wound down the mountain and drove easily through the Naco crossing, around the labyrinth of barricades, and into Mexico almost without thinking. As we passed the gate, to our left were a series of children's paintings on rusted sections of the border wall. Those sections were secondhand sand-colored military aircraft landing platforms from the first Gulf War, now prettied up with multicolored children's paintings of families holding hands among flowers. "Art without Borders" was painted on the end panel, and that was the only interpretation offered. The juxtaposition was haunting for me. I couldn't decide whether local elementary school students had humanized an inhumane scene, or if the paintings of innocents had been used to normalize the violence of the wall. Either way, there was dissonance.

Naco, Sonora, a border town with a combined population of only five thousand inhabitants, is full of not-so-obvious history. A miners' strike there had been a precursor to the Mexican Revolution. Later the siege of Naco became that conflict's longest battle, when Villistas and Carranza's forces fought in 1914–15 for nearly four months. A century later the crossing became a popular drug and human trafficking route. It had also been host to a humanitarian outpost: the Migrant Resource Center staffed mostly by retirees and church volunteers. The organization provided rooms and food for migrants traveling north, as well as help for those deported back into Mexico, an essential service in such a small and lonely place.

We could have stayed to visit the center, but since we were scheduled to be in Tucson in the afternoon, we decided we would only cruise through, turn around at the end of the main street, and be on our way. The visit inside Mexico took all of five minutes.

As we approached the Immigration Control and Enforcement station from the south, officials came out to meet our car, asked for our passports, and checked the trunk. No other cars were anywhere near. From our observations, we were likely the only ones to approach the crossing that morning. We explained we had just driven through town for a few minutes and were now heading back. I asked naively, "Didn't you see us as we went through?" But the official was in no mood for talking. He took our documents and disappeared into his office, staying inside for at least ten minutes. Then he returned for what we thought would be a typical "thank you and have a nice day." But instead he told us to pull under the shelter next to the headquarters. We complied without complaint.

When we had parked, his voice got harsher. "Step out of the car and stand over to the side." I reached for my camera before doing so, and he barked, "No picture taking. Leave the camera!" A second official came out of the building, and now both began going through our trunk and our back seat, and then they gathered the documents we had in the front seat, including maps and Hope's small trip diary. They took the documents and walked back into the office.

A Latino man heading into Mexico in the pedestrian lane said to no one in particular, "I've seen this on television, but I've never seen it in person." I felt I was part of some reality crime show. A few minutes later the ICE official returned with a different officer who asked Hope why her passport had been stamped in El Salvador. "I went there for my work," she answered, bewildered. The document and car searches continued as we stood under the shelter and watched, complaining a little under our breath.

We waited for nearly an hour until finally something must have checked out on their computer and a clearance came. Without apology or excuses, they told us we could reload our things and that we were now free to go. "So much for our quick morning jaunt to the border before heading to Tucson," Hope said as we drove off. Now she was mad at the border guards.

We drove Route 80 to Route 90, also known as the Buffalo Soldier Trail. The names of many of the roads now had resonance with the stories I was starting to uncover. A few hours south of Tucson, we stopped at a roadside restaurant in the hamlet called Sierra Vista. While we waited for a table, we struck up a conversation with a woman about seventy years old who was working the cash register. I asked her if she had lived in the area long. She said she and her husband had retired to Sierra Vista and now lived in a travel trailer in a nearby campground. The climate was much better than the cold one they had left in Michigan, she said. She had applied to work lunches at the café to earn a few extra dollars.

I asked her what she thought about living near the border wall. Her tone took me by surprise. "I think we ought to put armed soldiers along the entire thing!" she replied. I probed for more information. She said she had not experienced any violence or danger herself, or even seen or heard of any problems nearby, but since she had moved to a rural area in Arizona she wanted to feel safe. I didn't know what else to say but, "It already seems pretty safe here to me." She replied, "You can never be too sure." Then our table was ready and we turned to thank the cashier.

It wasn't until after lunch as we were driving off that Hope reached into her bag for her little book, intending to jot down some notes about the restaurant, and realized she didn't have it. We had taken a business card from the restaurant, so we immediately called back to ask if we had left it there. "No, we haven't seen it," replied the same cashier, asking the others to be sure.

Then it dawned on Hope: "The ICE guy took it into his office!" In her little book she had written down every crossing we'd made, every place we'd stayed the night, and many of the names of people we'd met and their contact information. She even had notes from other trips she had taken. We'll never know for sure if they kept it, but we never saw the notebook again. Maybe we have an ICE file and it is in there, along with their notes about Hope going to El Salvador.

# TWENTY-NINE

# Ground Zero of the Border Crisis

TUCSON, ARIZONA, AND NOGALES, SONORA

AFTER SPENDING YEARS ORGANIZING DukeEngage SUMMERS of service in and around Tucson, I'd grown to love its mountains, the desert with its unmistakable saguaro cactus, and its university town funkiness. But no matter how picturesque the place, I'll always associate the town with the migrant deaths in the Sonora Desert. And the people and organizations that have long worked on border justice issues will forever be in my heart.

Pulling into the parking lot at BorderLinks felt simultaneously like a homecoming and redeployment to a war zone. I had been away for a year. Meanwhile dozens of

These crosses bear names of the migrants who have died near the border. The wall they are mounted on was constructed from landing strips used during the first Gulf War. Nogales, Sonora.

volunteers and staff people of numerous nonprofit groups had been fighting to keep migrant deaths a humanitarian cause rather than fodder for some politician's idea of the need for a secure America.

We parked among BorderLinks' fifteen-passenger vans. Since the nineties, BorderLinks had used their big vehicles to take their delegations to the border, particularly Nogales, Agua Prieta, and other nearby border towns. I'd helped pack and unpack every one of their rooftop luggage racks for trips southward. I knew already that most of the students would be inside that afternoon in the air-conditioning waiting for their debriefing session with the staff. Arriving just in time for the meeting, I was eager to attend. I couldn't wait to hear their stories.

Hope would head back to North Carolina the next morning, but we would have at least a few hours together with the students that evening. Then I would complete the rest of the trip alone. I consoled myself with the fact that I would be with the students a few days before setting out again, and I would be among people who would understand my trip.

The work of BorderLinks and other humanitarian groups in Tucson, including No More Deaths/*No Mas Muertes*, Coalition for Human Rights, Border Action Network, The Samaritans, and Humane Borders, to name some of the most prominent, are worth a book of their own. Indeed, there are several volumes and films already in circulation. Collectively the groups comprise a hodgepodge of students and recent grads, retired people, longtime Tucson residents and newcomers, people who speak Spanish as a first language and those just learning Spanish, Mexican Americans, American Mexicans, Tohono O'odham people, indigenous Latinos, Guatemalan Americans, Asian Americans, African Americans, and whites giving their time and energy to this present-day Civil Rights movement.

Why Tucson? The main reason is the Sonora Desert and the "funnel effect" created by the militarization of the United States–Mexico border. With some 645 miles of physical barriers erected by 2010, much of it reinforced with high-tech detection devices and Border Patrol checkpoints at the major crossings, migrants have been routed into dangerous desert routes. Those who intend to head to Tucson must first pass through a parched landscape where the only water for dozens of miles is the little amount that migrants might carry or find in putrid livestock tanks.

The Sonora Desert just south of Tucson has become a killing zone. According to the Tucson Human Rights Coalition, over two hundred people had already died in the Sonora in the six-month period between January and the time we arrived in June. July would be worse. More than five thousand had died there since Operation Gatekeeper and Operation Hold the Line brought border walls to San Diego and El Paso. The deaths had reached crisis proportions.

If the government believed sending people toward the desert would be an effective deterrent and that the stories of hardship and failure would filter back to the migrants' villages and stop the hemorrhaging, they were dead wrong. Even after the thousands of deaths accounted for and publicized, the migrants have continued to cross the desert. Although slowed by fences, sensors, guards, and then the economic downturn, they keep risking their lives in hopes of earning enough money to support their families. Their money might save a child or parent, pay for an education, or build a house. The pull is so strong that they have kept coming, and dying, even as immigration has slowed.

In addition to serving as police, Border Patrol officers often act as first responders, rushing dehydrated, injured, and hyper- or hypothermia victims to hospitals. Humanitarian groups have also arisen and now stand in the gap between our government's policies and the reality of the border deaths. Volunteers provide water and information and advocacy. Many say we are criminalizing the poor and catching them in nets we have set for the bad guys. No one I know is against law enforcement, but the call to help people in trouble simply outweighs the need to support the government's apprehension of the undocumented.

| | | |

ARIZONA IS ALSO the place to learn about anti-immigrant forces at work in the United States. In addition to the Minutemen, Sheriff Joe

Arpaio of Maricopa County is one of Arizona's best-known personalities, and he has many followers. Even as Arpaio made Phoenix the stronghold of the anti-immigrant forces, Tucson, with its university population and a strong history of activism and asylum for refugees, emerged as the locus of border humanitarianism, creating two competing ideological fortresses just hours apart in the same state. With the two factions in close proximity, southern Arizona became the immigration epicenter, with leaders on opposite sides becoming national spokespersons for their competing causes. Tucson has been the perfect place to send our DukeEngage delegations each year to learn about immigration. The students have volunteered to go, I believe, not because they are leftists, but because they are humanitarians.

The old building that houses BorderLinks once served as the head-quarters of the local musicians union. It is now crowded with desks and meeting rooms in the front end while the back is sectioned off into cubicles with bunk beds for housing delegations of up to forty people. The organization has a large kitchen and even features a small garden out back. It is the epitome of a low-budget operation, boasting plenty of heart and hard work along with low salaries, secondhand furniture, and hope for the next grant. Our students join with BorderLinks and other groups for eight weeks, learning from the inside about the stresses, rewards, and sometimes the conflicts of working in nonprofits.

When we first proposed the project at DukeEngage, the program's executive director, Eric Mlyn, asked me point-blank what we would say to the press if he got a call asking if we were aiding "illegal immigrants." I answered that we should say that our students are probing the root causes behind the polarizing debate and trying to understand how immigration affects those suffering most from our policies, particularly the families of those dying to get into the United States. "Our project is about the students meeting real people and understanding the issues from a personal perspective," I said. That includes talking personally with Border Patrol officers, judges, doctors, and many others. Michelle, the student who traveled with me to Douglas, was right about our hearing all sides, although when people are dying from the collision between their

economic needs and our wall, immigration and the border become more than a partisan debate—it's an emergency.

Migrant Walk between Sasabe and Tucson, Arizona. The peak in the background is the Tohono O'odham sacred mountain named Baboquivari.

Students almost always rank their homestays with new immigrant families at the top of their lists of favorite activities. The relationships they build are life-changing. I always tell the students that before they make up their minds about immigration and the border, they should listen to an immigrant's story and hear what it is like to leave home and walk across the desert. I encourage them to learn about new immigrants' dreams for their children and to compare what they learn to their own family's story of immigration. Before you make up your minds about immigration and border policies, I tell them, get to know an immigrant.

Putting people in touch with each other is BorderLinks' central mission, turning statistics into stories that delegation participants can carry with them back to their schools, churches, and homes. There is no indoctrination, but guided experiences through which members of delegations touch, see, and hear about immigration directly. So far no one in our group has left disappointed, though a few have gone home exhausted. Many stay involved once the summer is over and they return to North Carolina. The first year's DukeEngage students returned to campus to start a Humane Borders chapter that has continued since.

| | | |

TWO DAYS AFTER I arrived in Tucson, the annual Migrant Walk organized by the Human Rights Coalition's Kat Rodriguez was just setting out. Several hundred people had signed up to walk between the border at Sasabe, Sonora, and Tucson—a sojourn that lasts a week during the hottest part of the summer. Before leaving North Carolina, the students and I signed up to join them for the first and last days of the journey.

We arrived by van on the first day at Sasabe, a small border town mostly on the Mexican side. We parked among dozens of cars and vans alongside the road and crossed into Mexico on foot. Just south of the border wall, we stood in a large circle and joined hands. Some who did not want to cross reached through the posts of the border wall from the U.S. side and we formed a bi-national circle. Before walking, we participated in a blessing ceremony led by a Native American healer. Then Kat Rodriguez distributed white wooden crosses bearing the names of those who had died in the desert, and each bearer read the name and date on the crosses aloud. Mine represented, as did many others, someone who had died unknown, someone likely still in the Tucson morgue. When my turn in the circle came and I read what the cross said—"¡*Desconocido!*" (Unknown!)—the word caught in my throat. By the end of the ceremony, there were no dry eyes.

We formed a line and walked back through the border checkpoint, each of us showing documentation to the ICE officers, who allowed us through quickly. We walked single file on back roads and headed through the Buenos Aires National Wildlife Refuge. Each person in the long line carried one or more crosses. I carried the "*desconocido*" cross I was given fastened to my backpack.

That year the Pima County Morgue already had 150 unidentified bodies in white bags in their cool storage—from 2010 alone. Hundreds more from previous years remained in the cooler, necessitating refrigerated trucks for the overflow. Sometimes tattoos, phone numbers, photographs carried by the victim, or dental records help with identification. There is also a dedicated group of forensics experts—medical examiners, pathologists, and anthropologists—who do their best to identify the bodies. But too many remain unclaimed.

Some human rights advocates believe that given the harshness of the desert and the prevalence of coyotes, vultures, and other wildlife, for every body found, there are perhaps as many as five others unaccounted for. In the most desolate areas the injured and weak often have to be left behind. No one, especially those being led by a guide traveling at a fast pace, could bear another person's weight for long. In part because of increasing Border Patrol numbers, migrants must go into ever more remote places. This helps the traffickers in the same way Prohibition helped bootleggers—scarcity sends prices skyrocketing. More policing equals more profits. As the risk increases, the need for a guide increases, giving those at the top of the immigration pyramid reason to charge more money.

Border Patrol officers are often as concerned about the deaths in the desert as anyone, but put them alone in the desert and sometimes their choices go awry. I experienced this one morning when I joined the Tucson Samaritans on a water and food run. Two retired women volunteers, one of them a doctor, and I drove into a remote area an hour south of Tucson to a well-known migrant path and got out to look for anyone in distress, bearing jugs of water and plastic bags of food to leave along the trail. About two miles in we met a Border Patrol officer walking toward us on the same path. He was alone. We greeted him and offered him water and food, which he declined, and then we continued walking in opposite directions. After placing our last jug under a tree, we doubled back not a half hour later along the same path. As we approached our first water drop we realized that someone had slit with a knife the two plastic jugs we had left beside a tree. All the water had run out onto the bone-dry sand. There were no other people anywhere near.

| | | |

THE EIGHT DUKEENGAGE students and I walked single file among the Migrant Walk participants stretching out over several hundred yards. All held up fairly well by wearing hats, sunscreen, and long loose clothing, and drinking the copious amounts of water one must consume to stay hydrated. We felt boosted when a few supporters, including a Buddhist monk and several other onlookers unable to make the walk themselves, stood and waved in encouragement as we passed by them in the 110-degree heat. I walked behind a Catholic Franciscan brother who wore a long brown frock. The cross on his backpack also read "unknown." After the first day, we left the walkers as they set up camp in an open field.

A week later, we met the group again, this time on their way into a Tucson park south of town for their final day of walking. For the entire week, dozens had slept in tents and relied on water provided by the Humane Borders trucks—the same ones that refill water stations scattered throughout the most traveled migrant paths. Arriving at the city park, participants laid the crosses they had carried for the week (including those we had carried for a day) one by one at the base of a large mesquite tree, a plant whose roots can reach more than a hundred feet into the ground. Then the pilgrims read statements before the media. Representatives of many faiths, from Catholic to Presbyterian to Muslim to Tohono O'odham, united at the ceremony. There were prayers, singing, and testimonials. There was also a foot-washing ceremony. Several ministers made their way around the large circle and trickled water over tired and hot feet and then washed and dried each one.

Later, I visited the room at the Human Rights Coalition where Kat stores the crosses year-round. "We'll keep them forever," she said, reverently handling the crosses in their storage boxes. "They can never be discarded." Their storage room had become a sacred space.

| | | |

THAT SAME WEEK of our walk our delegation attended an Operation Streamline federal court session. In brief, this federal court facilitates migrant deportations in groups of seventy-five nearly every weekday of the year in order to speed up the process and save the U.S. government money and time. With the droves of poor people still attempting to cross, there seems to be no problem catching seventy-five. But the rest of the story is there are many more than seventy-five, in Tucson alone, to process every day. For that reason, some advocates believe this is merely about sending a message to angry citizens who live far away, not speeding up the court system in the end.

After passing through a metal detector and leaving our cameras and phones behind, we filed into the courtroom and sat together toward the back. We were the only spectators. Attorney and Human Rights Coalition Board Chairwoman Isabel Garcia met us inside the courtroom before the proceedings began. She gave us a quick briefing, bracing us for what we were about to see, and told us she would return to talk after she had represented a few of the clients in the court session. A Latina, longtime legal advocate, and national spokeswoman for human rights and immigration reform in Arizona, Isabel gave us a brief but strong personal introduction and her take on the system. Several students had seen her on TV already, particularly following the passage of Arizona Senate Bill 1070. She had become a regular interviewee on CNN and other national networks. Still she was able to take time for us.

Magistrate Judge Thomas Ferraro entered and we all stood. The court-appointed attorneys were at the front. We sat down again and waited for the defendants to enter. We began hearing the jangling of the leg chains before the door opened. Then the incarcerated migrants began to file in and to sit where they were told. The seventy-five nearly filled the remaining courtroom seats, perhaps explaining the otherwise arbitrary number. All of them were Latinos. There were a few women, but the vast majority were young men, most with the dark skin of the indigenous. They were exactly the profile of farmworkers today: 85 percent are young men between ages sixteen and forty and from rural parts of Mexico.

They were dressed in the clothing in which they had been caught, some of them having been jailed weeks prior. Presumably they had been wearing jumpsuits in the meantime. Some still bore the marks of the desert on their skin and clothing: scratches from cacti, stains on jeans, though some had already spent a month or more in private centers run by corporations like Kellogg, Brown, and Root, Halliburton, and Corrections Corporation of America among others. They sat on the judge's right, to our left and all the way to the back row, some of them in the back, just across the aisle from us. Some glanced over at our group when they sat down. I tried not to stare.

The hardest part was deciding whether to look at all, and if so, how. Some of the men were the students' age or younger. Should we look toward the front or meet their eyes? Should we send them a supportive smile? Should we shake our heads at our disgust with the charade of justice? Would that be the right emotion? Not a word could pass between us, and we would likely never see each other again. At least we were there, I thought for a second, but then I remembered that this happened daily, and we were there for one day of a long year of deportations.

Each prisoner received a set of headphones and instructions on how to put them on, but their handcuffs gave them some difficulty. Judge Ferraro, a white man, perhaps Italian American, looked about sixty-five years old. He seemed compassionate, but also serious in carrying out his duty to uphold the law as it is written. He spoke in English and a nearby translator spoke into a microphone transmitting a Spanish translation through the seventy-five sets of headphones simultaneously.

"I want to be sure each of you can understand this process and that you can hear me. Please answer 'yes' if you can hear me and understand." There were a few seconds of hesitation as the translation went through the headphones, which we couldn't hear. Then a loud and nearly simultaneous "Si!" arose from the seventy-five.

Those not processed this way are taken to detention to await trial, or perhaps back directly in buses to the borderline and deported in groups. A very small fraction of those caught are detained with charges like drug possession or robbery. The overwhelming majority of them are charged with illegal immigration and nothing more. They had done nothing but cross over to work.

No official in the courtroom that day seemed to feel good about being there, including a court representative who talked with us afterward. From the beginning, everyone knew that all the people going into court would be "streamlined." All of them were led through the litany of guilt together. All of them would be driven back to the border and let out, most likely to walk into Mexico on their own under the watchful eye of the Border Patrol. From Tucson they would ride a bus to Nogales or Naco, places they may have never seen, and fend for themselves. Of course none of them had money to spend when they got to the other side.

Those in the courtroom were called by name to stand and then led in groups of seven or eight before the bench. An appointed lawyer stood behind each one. Most attorneys had multiple clients. They may have met their clients for a half hour beforehand, attorney Garcia explained. The judge asked if each defendant understood they had entered into the United States illegally. "Si!" they answered in unison.

"Do each of you understand that if you were to enter this country again without proper documentation that you would be charged with a felony and serve a much longer sentence, perhaps five years?"

"Si!"

"Do each of you promise never to return to this country illegally again?"

"Si!"

Then each was given a chance to respond individually or to ask clarifying questions. A few were brave enough and had the presence of mind to say something—and they made statements in Spanish that were translated to the judge, who in turn responded as the law required. One man who looked about forty-five said between sobs that he had not wanted to break the law, but that he had come into this country because of a sick daughter. He asked the judge to forgive him and again he promised not to try to come back again. Other stories voiced were equally heartbreaking. One man apologized profusely and then asked for special help.

"I'd like to say I'm sorry for entering your country without permission and I won't do it again," went the translation. "I crossed with my son and he was separated from me. I would like to ask for help to find him."

Judge Ferraro answered, "I have no power to do that. Your lawyer says she'll try to find him in the system—if he's been caught."

Then to the whole group still standing before him in their cuffs and shackles, he gave this lecture: "I'm not an immigration lawyer. But I urge you to go back to Mexico and seek a way to come back legally. We're a nation of immigrants. We want you here legally."

In another group of seven a woman spoke up: "I have three children to support. Their father died a month ago."

Ferraro replied, "It's not going to do those children any good for you to be in jail. You can have good reasons to come to the U.S. Try to enter legally. Even if you get in illegally, you're still going to have to live in fear."

None of the migrants' words mattered in the end, of course. This was no place for sentimentality—though they had a right to speak. Any tip of the judge's hand toward leniency would have sent every one of the migrants to their knees in front of the bench with similar stories. So all were treated the same: politely, firmly, and efficiently. No words of apology or tragedy helped any cause. And then they were led out, still in chains, and deported.

A few things were obvious about the defendants in the windowless courtroom in Tucson. Every one of those people was dirt poor. Most had had little chance of education. Some spoke indigenous languages and knew little Spanish. Ms. Garcia told us they must receive a special translation in their own tongue. Anyone could tell most of the prisoners were afraid. Most seemed defeated by their jail time and sentencing. And none left the courtroom with any solutions to the problems that sent them north to begin with.

Would they try again? I had to guess they would, even those who spoke tearfully and promised not to. They were, by and large, not people who migrated by choice. And by the time they reached this point most had borrowed, or had been extorted for, huge sums of money, some for twenty thousand dollars or more. There is no way to return home with that kind of debt. If a violent or vindictive *coyote* is in the picture, then it is worse. And what of those going back broke to face a sick daughter who needs treatment or to tell children left fatherless there is nothing more a mother can do?

As one man filing out in leg irons and handcuffs met my eyes, I thought about what I would do if I were in his place. I nodded to him, forced a slight smile, and tried to show as much empathy as possible with my one-second gaze. Then a large uniformed deputy with a shaved head reached for his arm and ushered him gently through the open metal door, and he was gone, his chains clinking to the rhythm of his walk.

Attorney Garcia asked us after the session ended, "How many terrorists did you see deported today?" The answer was obviously none. She continued, "The anti-terrorist groups sold this to Congress. They said down at Del Rio the border is wide open and there's uranium there. They passed this zero-tolerance policy we see in action today." The students were incensed that the prisoners' only experience of our American justice system had been this display.

There was a strange disconnect in the numbers, attorney Garcia reported. The Border Patrol officers in the Tucson sector say they apprehend nine hundred people every day. Seventy-five were paraded before the bench in the Streamline court. "How are they chosen?" she asked and then answered, "It appears to be up to the discretion of the Border Patrol." The rest are "voluntarily returned."

"In January 2010," she continued, "the Warren Institute in Berkeley showed that of the $10 billion allocated to border security, some $3.5 billion was going to transport, incarcerate, and deport migrants, along with the court processing costs. We're paying $13 million a month just to the Corrections Corporation of America for incarceration. Their stock was plummeting prior to 9/11. Now, of course, it's back.

"If you prosecute all these people for illegal entry, there's not enough money left for arms, narcotics, and violent and organized crime!" She asked rhetorical questions of the students: "Is it constitutional? Are clients without any experience of our justice system competent to waive their rights?

"I'm ashamed about Operation Streamline," she concluded. Then she spoke of the drug cartels. "We love to hate them. We're spending millions, maybe trillions, to fight the smugglers. But it's our own creation, our own drug consumption. Our own militarization creates political refugees. We're trying to squelch part of the world spirit. Humans migrate. You can't stop that."

|   |   |   |   |

A WEEK LATER, I went alone to see the detention centers in Florence, Arizona, the little town that holds thousands of immigrant detainees. The town has built its entire economy around the industry of incarceration, with both private and public facilities nearly adjacent to one another and together covering hundreds of acres—nine different facilities in all. Though the population is only twenty-five thousand, thousands more are employed there.

Prisons are one solid growth industry that Arizona can boast of. We have already seen the Border Patrol's numbers—they are another. According to the American Civil Liberties Union, in the year 2011 there were 429,000 people held in 250 facilities across the country, with a daily capacity of 33,400. During that time, over two thousand of them had been held daily just in the Corrections Corporation of America's center in Florence alone. That didn't include the county, state, and federal facilities all within the same mile.

I know the distance well because I walked along the road between the facilities, the sun baking down on me, drinking water constantly and snapping photographs late in the afternoon. There seemed to be no division between the private and public facilities—the courthouse sat adjacent to the private detention facility, which was just up the road from the federal one. Drab warehouse-like buildings spread toward the others, creating so little to catch the eye that I waited fifteen minutes for one grackle to land on a wire to add a point of interest in one shot. With thousands of people inside and between $122 and $164 spent per detainee each day—amounting to $2 billion a year, according to the ACLU—how could an exterior photograph possibly show that?

I had ridden from Tucson that morning with Cindy Schlosser and several other staff people who commuted every day to Florence. After going with them, I didn't have to ask why they didn't just move up there to live near their offices. I knew from just one day that the setting would destroy one's optimism. Yet on the day I rode up with them, four dedicated people, none of them much over thirty years old, were carpooling together into the detention world, telling stories and jokes, and laughing their way into hell.

Their organization is called the Florence Immigrant and Refugee Rights Project. The mission statement says it "provides and coordinates free legal services and related social services to indigent men, women, and unaccompanied children detained in Arizona for immigration removal proceedings." Their main work was to help the unaccompanied children traveling into the United States looking for work and/or their parents who may not know their whereabouts. Their statement of purpose continues: "The FIRR Project strives to ensure that detained individuals have access to counsel, understand their rights under immigration law, and are treated fairly and humanely by our judicial system." Having just seen Operation Streamline at work, I knew what they were up against.

I spent half a day helping them research why Guatemalans were ending up in such large numbers in Arizona prisons. Using the organization's computer, I wrote out some facts about Guatemala's genocide in the 1980s and about the economic turmoil in the country since. It was enough work to at least pretend for a day that I was part of the project, and sufficient to show me how small this organization seemed when compared to the Goliath complex one can see up and down the road from their parking lot. Yet, after that single day, especially after I went with Cindy through security at the federal facility to witness a court hearing for a migrant, I knew their work as witnesses and advocates is what America stands for. These talented people could be making good money working in some beautiful place with a view, but they cared enough to spend their days working for the huddled masses here. As far as I was concerned, they were the torchbearers of all we say we believe when we pledge allegiance to the flag.

During their week of orientation, the students and I went with a BorderLinks leader to visit the regional office of the Border Patrol. We met with Commanding Officer Jim Stout for an hour.

Pablo Peregrina, a volunteer for Humane Borders, replaces a vandalized flagpole marking a water drop for migrants.

He began his presentation in a windowless classroom by saying his organization is the "tip of the spear" regarding immigration. It's a term used by the military to signify the part of an organization (or a weapon) that is the first to go in. But he was quick to stress that their mission is "to help people. Our humanitarian efforts are the largest anywhere. We have our own version of humanitarianism, which includes an EMS service, BORSTAR search and rescue, paramedics, and even cadaver dogs."

"But," he continued, "we look like a SWAT team because that is what we are." He showed a PowerPoint presentation of Homeland Security's numbers for detentions and deaths: in FY09, 165,934 detained, 94 deaths.

In FY10 thus far, he said, there had been 171,246 detained, 114 deaths. That was fewer than Humane Borders had counted. I never learned the reasons for the discrepancy. Along the entire border, he added, "We have been arresting over a million a year; 1.5 million in 2009. We've never taken that many prisoners of war ever! We're moving, housing, feeding a million people. That's got a price tag this nation's never seen." He compared the border to the thirty-eighth parallel in Korea. And then he said, "We've also got the OTM's—Other than Mexicans." They would catch 9,873 in 2010, most of them Central Americans. "Ninety percent of them are human trafficked!"

The students asked some hard questions. What about the controversies over whether border technology works? Mr. Stout answered straight, "They [meaning Boeing and other companies contracting with the government] make a bazillion out of this! But having a fence has made a difference. So has our ability to be armed. We've gone crazy trying to get the stuff to do our job!" Gas and ammunition were in short supply at times, he said, even in Arizona, which he called "the state of Wyatt Earp," where presumably ammo should be no problem.

He didn't tout the electronic sensors much, or the drones either, but spent most of his lecture time on the job of the individual officers. "We carry a pistol, baton, pepper spray, and Taser," Officer Stout said. "And you have to be tased to carry it." We couldn't believe our eyes when he passed around a standard-issue M4 carbine and let us hold it and even cock it. He guaranteed it was not loaded, but told us not to point it at anyone just the same.

"It's good pay," he said about working for the Border Patrol. He seemed to want to entice some of college students to join. He bragged, "The Border Patrol is like a paramilitary organization. We're at war against the cartels."

But there were some ambiguities. In response to a student's question, he said that on one side of the border equation there are cartels, but the other side reveals an entirely different story. He asked incredulously, "Deporting people just trying to do his job as a gardener?" His answers came at times as if he were two different people, or maybe he was speaking from both heart and head. I wrote the following quotes down as he spoke: "Kicking the poor out of the best country in the world?" Followed by, "People have become contraband!" Then, "We're here to get the bad guys!" Then sensing his logic was hard to follow, he left us with this clincher: "Are there officers who quit because of this? Yes!" We had to appreciate his frankness.

After the lecture he led us to the parking lot where he showed us the inside of a Border Patrol vehicle. He opened the door and let the students climb up and sit on a bench made for detainees. He wouldn't let them take pictures of the scene, but sitting inside a metal container for humans that felt like a dogcatcher's vehicle was unforgettable for the students, and that was with the door open.

|  |  |  |  |

I'D TRAVELED WITH BorderLinks to Nogales, Sonora, to see the border wall from the other side on several occasions. Once DukeEngage students and I happened to be walking alongside the wall looking at the innumerable crosses someone had placed there to memorialize the dead—eerily similar to the ones we had held on the migrant walk—when we saw a Wackenhut bus stop a hundred yards or so from the wall on the U.S. side. The bus door opened and deportees began to file out and walk toward the border.

There was a corridor of fences through which the deportees walked. They moved slowly southward en masse. Some talked among themselves, but most walked silently alone. They carried small plastic bags. We saw some of them later outside the office of Grupo Beta, the humanitarian agency run by the Mexican government, and realized the bags were imprinted with the Homeland Security insignia. Inside were the few belongings they possessed when they were arrested. Having been processed in the courtroom, they now walked toward the fence knowing there would be no family members to greet them. Their slumping bodies said they were the tired, the poor, those yearning to breathe free, but nothing about the scene made Emma Lazarus's poem ring true. They had gone to America to work and had been sent home empty-handed.

Other organizations, mostly staffed by Americans on the U.S. side near the border entrance, served coffee and food. Some provided free phone calls. Grupo Beta also had phones and showers. Together the organizations offered something of a welcome in Mexico, but I had not realized how little we in the United States gave the captured migrants until I saw them on the other side. Some had gotten nothing more than water and peanut butter crackers for several days while inside U.S. detention centers. Some never had an opportunity to shower, they told us. One deportee named David Lucas Alonzo laughed as he showed us his U.S. detention "meal." He had somehow resisted the temptation to eat his crackers, and he reached into his Homeland Security bag and pulled them out to show us. I took a picture. To be locked away in the jails of the richest nation on earth in a prison system, funded to the tune of billions—over a hundred dollars per night per detainee—and to receive peanut butter crackers to survive on for twenty-four hours? One of the students said we treat our stray animals better.

After leaving the Grupo Beta office, we walked along an incredible gallery of border art wrought by the late Alfred J. Quiroz and other Mexican artists. These original works on the south side had been placed there for free. The artist, whom I had met on an earlier trip, told me he survived on donations alone. He had crafted some of his images from stainless steel; others were metal painted in full color. Every one of them was worth a photograph: skulls inside trucks, images of water jugs in deserts, migrants entrapped in dollar signs, and symbols representing the powerful forces of government and corporate interchange. Somehow in the face of militarization, closed borders, and deportation, art emerged. On the U.S. side, no one can attach or paint anything. The south side had been made into a canvas for just about anyone who wanted to leave a statement. Graffiti was everywhere. In the face of the massive border wall, the art made our spirits feel strangely uplifted in the face of shame. We were all circulating with our cameras snapping away.

| | | |

THEN PEDRO CAME. He had been among the deported on the Wackenhut bus, had already gone to Grupo Beta to make his phone call, take a shower, and get a few bites of food. He must have had a few dollars on him, because he had also somehow found a place to have several drinks before he met us. He first approached the students while I was in the middle of taking photos of the border art. I turned and noticed everyone gathered around him and went to see what the commotion was about.

His English was nearly perfect, if slurred. He was emotional from the start, tears just beneath the surface. He began to tell his story to our group. Pedro said he had been picked up after working and living in Phoenix for fifteen years. He no longer had close family in Mexico. His wife and children were in the United States. By the time he was into the middle of story, he had raised his voice a few decibels and the tears had started to flow. He turned his frustrations with the U.S. immigration system on the students, some of them children of immigrants themselves, some of them Latina.

"You think you're going to come here and change things! You come here to see, but there's nothing you can do," he said. "You should go back to where you came from, to your college or wherever, and go on with your lives, because you can't change anything!" They tried to answer him, but he couldn't be consoled.

Ceci, our BorderLinks leader who had grown up in Nogales, stepped between Pedro and the students and quieted him with her eyes. She calmed him as a mother would, hugging him as the rest of us walked slowly away, leaving her to say something to him in a whisper, her arm now around his shoulder.

Several of the students were crying when they got to the van. They replayed the story several times as Ceci got back and let us all in and started the engine and the AC. She put the van in park and turned from the driver's seat to talk with everyone. She had lost loved ones in the border crisis, she said. She had others who now lived on both sides, some of them living in the shadows unable to obtain documentation. She still believed in change, she said, and that acting on one's beliefs was better than doing nothing. She said that Pedro didn't mean what he said, but was just lashing out because of his own pain, all fueled by alcohol. She also hugged several of the students at our next stop as we all descended from the van to see more of her life story.

Down the hill from where we stood, huge new factories had mushroomed, taking up hundreds of hectares of the best flat land. High fences topped with razor wire surrounded them, and there were tractor-trailers pulling in and out, hauling goods to the United States. Once I'd gone inside one of the factories and talked with some of the young women, some of them sixteen, none older than twenty-five. They assembled small electronic parts with their nimble fingers, bending over a table doing piecework.

To our left and down the steep hillside lay a squatter's village put up by workers who had recently arrived to take jobs in those plants. Whole cities of non-landowners had tried their best to put down roots.

We gathered around Ceci in a semicircle as she told us how she had witnessed her small village change to this, of how in a decade she had seen Nogales go from a peaceful agricultural town to a major industrial center where tens of thousands, then hundreds of thousands, of people had migrated and set up neighborhoods in makeshift fashion, without government infrastructure to support them. Almost none of the newcomers had potable water and sewage systems. They had packed themselves into the maquila barrios and made do even as they worked ten or more hours in the plants. Their average wage was no more than ten or twelve dollars a day—nowhere near enough to live any other way. It was easy to see why so many had fled that part of Nogales for the United States only a mile away. No one would want to live there in a squatter's hut if he or she could get out.

After experiencing losses perhaps of greater magnitude than Pedro had ever known, this grandmother in her sixties had gone to work for BorderLinks, an organization committed to hiring Mexican staff people to balance its U.S. team. It was a philosophical commitment of the group to have equal numbers of people on both sides and to pay everyone a living wage.

It was easy to see why they had hired Ceci. She exuded a powerful personal strength only a hard life could create—one that would either kill you or make you strong. She still had a small-town resident's love for neighbors even as she watched her hometown be overtaken by polluting factories whose owners take from, but make no return commitment to, the communities around them. Her husband had been disabled and she was the only breadwinner. One daughter and her family had left to start farm work in North Carolina. Still, somehow she found the energy to educate U.S. youth about the realities of border life and the effects of policies on people she knows.

She had seen other Pedros before. But she chose to work to promote the positive and not to listen to the naysayers. Rising from a well of inner faith she held deep inside, she had found a way to live and work against despair. One could point out that she needed the modest salary Border-Links paid her and that it was reason enough to work with these students and drive them around as a guide. That is true, but no one had paid her to hug an angry deportee.

# THIRTY

# Altar and Sacrifice

NOGALES AND ALTAR, SONORA

IT TOOK SPECIAL DISPENSATION FROM RISK MANAGEMENT AT Duke to get us there, but the students had argued successfully that their experience wouldn't be complete without witnessing the staging ground for immigrants readying to cross the desert into the United States. We were on our way with Ceci at the wheel. We drove southward from Nogales toward Altar on SON 43, where our learning experience continued en route.

Just south of the city of Nogales, we came upon a row of a dozen shrines to *Santísima Muerte* (Most Holy Death) erected alongside the road. I asked Ceci if we could stop. She said she thought we would be safe enough, but she didn't want to get out because she had no use for the "saint of darkness." She pulled over and I clambered out to get some quick photographs, feeling some trepidation mixed with a healthy dose of curiosity. Seven of the students followed, all with their cameras drawn.

No two shrines were anything alike. I started at the top of the rise and began working my way downhill, looking into each and photographing its contents. Each had some form of a human skeleton inside representing the saint. Some held three-dimensional skeletal icons dressed in queenly finery and seated

in ornate chairs. Others had only a painting of her surrounded by a variety of candles, artificial flowers, and other decorations. I'd visited many sepulchers in Latin America, including many examples of the bloody figures of Jesus, Stephen, and other martyred saints, but they had not prepared me for the ominous feel of the shrines to death herself. Something seemed unsettled, and I felt the need to look around to see who was watching and felt especially protective of the students.

One of many shrines to Santa Muerte built south of Nogales, Sonora, on the road to Altar.

According to some, La Muerte is the Virgin Mary's skeleton. Others say she is the Aztec goddess of the underworld syncretized into a Catholic saint. But what really made me uneasy was the description Ceci gave just as I had jumped out of the van: "The *narcotraficantes* put those up to ask La Muerte to help them in their drug trade." The last thing I wanted to do was to have to explain to one of the shrines' owners why we were out there taking pictures. We passed along the whole line of shrines quickly, and then I hustled everyone back into the van and we were on our way again. "It's good to know about such things. It's part of our education," I said to the students, trying to shake off my uneasiness.

But it was the town of Altar that had scared me most—especially in its heyday, when thousands of migrants passed through the town every day on their way to the Sasabe desert crossing sixty miles to the north. Altar is the staging ground. From there, vans take the migrants to the beginning point from the Mexico part of their trek on foot to El Norte, some five miles from Altar. If they survive the trip, they end up near Sasabe, the same border crossing where the *Derechos Humanos* Migrant Walk began.

With temperatures sometimes exceeding 130 degrees Fahrenheit in June, this was no easy terrain to walk even for a day, but I'd witnessed the town center filled in summer with men and women readying themselves for the journey north. In the winter months it was even more packed. Now the numbers had started dwindling, but the infrastructure I'd seen on previous visits was still in place.

We saw *coyote* vans parked alongside the church square waiting to take migrants through a restricted *finca* (plantation) entrance on the Sasabe road. The Migrant Prayer for those heading north through the desert was still hanging at the church altar. There were flophouses where dozens of migrants waited as they searched for the right *coyote* to guide them. And there were stores like Super Plaza that specialized in black clothing for hiding from helicopters. There were black backpacks, shoes and socks, lightweight foods, and water jugs for sale. The whole town had organized itself around the business of receiving and sending migrants from all over Mexico and Central America. Even the local baseball team was named the Coyotes. The church had started up a ministry just for the migrants.

But by 2010 the massive river of migrants had dwindled to a trickle. Part of the reason was the slowdown in the U.S. economy. Militarization of the border also contributed. But the most ominous part of this operation was that our border crackdown had led to increasingly sophisticated means of crossing, which then gave rise to a mafia-like infrastructure for human trafficking. The worst of the *coyotes* had ramped up their trade in people. A process that had at one time been individualized had now become more controlled, and criminals had gotten hold of the means to get people across the line. The prohibition of migration had led to more profitable trafficking and the drug cartels had entered the business. Now it was more dangerous than ever to be a migrant in public. Kidnapping and rape had become more prevalent.

Many migrants are no longer able to choose Altar as an option and must sell themselves into the world of the traffickers, often as drug mules. Payments of human flesh might mean safe arrival. Passing through Altar had been the old way by which migrants made their way to the church square. Their prayer to the Virgin came first. Afterward they would find a guide who would take the money for the van. Though it was dangerous as hell, the individual migrant still retained a small amount of agency.

But now those who had erected the shrines to *Santisima Muerte* were in charge. They don't stop at a church before setting out. Their routes are secret, their destinations less certain and controlled by hidden forces. Delegations like ours would never see them.

But even with the drastic reduction in numbers, the students and I were able to meet and speak with a few migrants. We had been asked by church members to pass out flyers about the migrant hospitality house called CCAMYN (*Centro Comunitario de Atención al Migrante y Necesitado*). I walked up and introduced myself to two young men named Efrain and Lorenzo and told them there was free food and housing a few blocks away. They thanked me, but said they were waiting on a *coyote* to line them up with a van so that they could leave that morning. They already had their backpacks full of food and water, their cheap flat-bottomed tennis shoes were in fairly good shape, and they had on hats, loose shirts, and long pants. They had been through the desert before and felt fairly comfortable with the trip, they said. Still, I could see fear in their eyes.

I couldn't imagine situations in which human beings would be more vulnerable than these two were at that point. The traffickers, the sun, bandits, double-crossers, poisonous snakes, bad water, and La Migra—the

U.S. authorities—all awaited them. Of course they really couldn't trust me either, but I posed no real threat standing there in front of the church. When asked about jobs, some migrants answer, "Whatever I can get." But when I asked these two, they knew their destination exactly. They were heading back to the northern California strawberry fields where they had worked before. They knew they would have to travel at least a thousand more miles from Altar, going through Sonoran desert on both sides of the border and nearly the entire length of California, to end up on a farm they already had worked on.

I asked Efrain and Lorenzo if I might take their photograph, and they nodded and looked directly into the camera. Their resolve said they were going no matter what, but I thought I could see in their eyes that they didn't want to do this. I knew this wasn't a choice; it was a sacrifice. I gave them the common blessing said to travelers in Spanish, "*Vayan con Dios.*" They looked down at the ground and said *gracias*.

Every year of the Altar migration phenomenon, the congregation of Nuestra Señora de Guadalupe del Altar, the church in the center of town and the sponsor of CCAMYN, makes a pilgrimage from their sanctuary to the beginning of the migrant trail where the vans pay their entry fee to the landowner. The pilgrims pray together inside the church, read aloud the Migrant Prayer posted on the wall, and then walk toward the entrance

The words "La Familia" and "Mujeres Migrantes" are inscribed on two crosses erected by the Catholic church in Altar at the beginning of the often-used migrant route through the desert.

to the Sasabe road, some five miles away. At their destination they had planted three twenty-foot-high white crosses with black lettering. One cross read "*Familias Migrantes*," another said "*Mujeres*," and the third, "*Niños*." When the walkers arrive at the crosses, they light candles and pray for all migrants who pass there.

I made that pilgrimage along with seven students on our first delegation of the DukeEngage program. We walked with the Mexican townspeople following behind Padre Prisciliano Peraza, a stocky man dressed in a white robe, a wide-brimmed cowboy hat, and boots. We arrived at the tall white crosses and began to encircle the father. He had already started praying when several vans pulled up at the guardhouse not more than a hundred feet away from our group.

With my head bowed, I looked out of the corner of my eye at the attendants emerging from the little wooden house as they approached the vehicles. I saw them ask each migrant to pay a fee of fifty dollars U.S. per person just to pass through. The migrants were essentially paying an entrance fee into the most dangerous corridor on the border, the corridor that had taken the lives of many people like them. Then, with cash exchanged, the attendant opened the gate and the vans sped northward, leaving a cloud of dust wafting toward us.

In silence, one by one, each of us lit our votive candles and stood them upright in the sand under the crosses. They burned next to spent ones that had fallen over. At the end of our service, people gathered the used glass canisters from previous pilgrimages. The red wax had melted and spilled from each of the old glasses and hardened in the sand beneath. It looked like blood.

# THIRTY-ONE

# Phoenix Rising

PHOENIX, ARIZONA

ON THE WAY INTO TUCSON TO SEE THE STUDENTS I HAD PICKED up a flyer at a gas station about a pro-SB 1070 rally called Phoenix Rising. I noted the June 5 date would be on the Saturday during my stay in Tucson. I knew I had to go, and I invited the students to go with me. There were three students who had not been able to go to Nogales and Altar because of complications with

their visas or because of lack of parental approval and had stayed behind disappointed. The group voted that they would be the best candidates to accompany me. They eagerly

Sheriff Joe Arpaio makes a point to an admiring audience at the Phoenix Rising rally in support of Arizona's SB 1070.

agreed. They were a diverse team, all of them female: one whose parents were from India, one Latina—the descendant of Cuban immigrants with very light skin—and one Korean American. I told them the night before that we would go to observe and document, not to take sides or confront. I had no idea what we might witness, I said, but I knew we would see different people from those they had been working with in Tucson.

We left the next morning, heading northwest from Tucson on Interstate 10, which took us near the center of Phoenix. We parked two blocks from Bolin Memorial Park several minutes after the rally began and were surprised we could get so close. We thought at first we had the wrong location or, worse, the wrong day. But we continued walking, and as we rounded the block at the capitol we saw the flags and banners, more of those than people it seemed, for as we soon discovered some had left their banners and moved to the shade. With the concrete and pavement of downtown, the heat was especially intense that day. The thermometer in the car read 107 degrees. We had put on hats and packed lots of water, but we still felt dehydrated after walking only two blocks. We knew those cheering up ahead, particularly the elderly or out-of-shape people, had to be dedicated to their cause to stand out there at all.

The controversial bill had already passed both state houses by the time of the demonstration. So the point of the demonstration was to rally the troops behind SB 1070's author, Russell Pearce, and push back against the criticisms the state had gotten for passing it. Right after the bill passed, thousands had begun boycotting the state in protest. The Arizona Tea company had to send out a disclaimer explaining that their drinks weren't really made in the state after all. Even the Phoenix Suns professional basketball team had started identifying themselves defiantly as Los Suns. National pro-immigrant groups said Arizona was racist and xenophobic. Those rallying on this broiling day were angry and fighting back.

Putting those emotions together with intense heat in an open-carry state made me worried, so I pulled the students into a huddle and told them that no matter what people said, we would need to be very polite in return. "Do not argue with anyone. Don't talk back if anyone speaks to you disrespectfully. It's fine to ask questions, but don't challenge," I said.

The lineup of speakers read like the who's who list for the national anti-immigrant movement. Russell Pearce, the man who introduced the bill, spoke right after we arrived. Then the former congressman from Colorado, Tom Tancredo, also a lightning rod on the immigration issue, followed him. Tancredo had become famous for shouting in one political debate, "Don't give us your tired, your poor, your huddled masses!" He was explosive that day as he led the crowd in several chants, including, "Americans first! Close the Border!" The signs and banners held by the protesters surrounding him were even more direct: "*Mi Casa No Es Su Casa!*"; "You report 'em, We deport 'em!" And so on. Some flags for sale depicted President Obama in a variety of mocking images. One poster showed the president in Sheriff Joe Arpaio's prison stripes. One depicted Obama's face superimposed over crossbones and filled with faux bullet holes. Those particular flags sold for five dollars. I noted that some of the people selling the posters and flags with make-believe bullet holes were packing real guns at their sides. Chris Broughton, the guy who took a loaded assault rifle to an Obama campaign event in Phoenix, was reportedly in the crowd as well. Since Arizona is an open-carry state, these folks were just practicing their rights, as they reminded everyone. But the students witnessing the vitriol amidst the open display of guns for the first time were visibly shaken.

One man who dressed as a cowboy and identified himself as Bud Hart rode his horse "Biggun" through the crowd and surprised us all. He held a sign that read, "SB 1070 Will Cause More Harm Than Good!" The *Phoenix New Times* quoted him in their article on the rally: "These laws are already on the books," he said. "They can arrest these Mexicans if they want to, but I contend that if they're going to arrest Mexicans, go after the big wheels. The Mexican Mafia, the Sinaloa cowboys, get after those dogs. They're the ones that control the drugs and all the god dang crime. It's not the dishwashers and the landscapers."[1]

---

1. Stephen Lemons, "Pro-SB 1070 Phoenix Rising Rally: Neo-Nazis, Nativists, Crackpots, and More," *Phoenix New Times*, June 7, 2010.

Kevin DeAnna, representing Students for Western Civilization, took the stage early on. He spoke as a beleaguered patriot fighting the university systems, college administrators, and multiculturalism. He talked of enemies threatening him with death, but he countered, "We have fifteen chapters around the country!" He had attended William and Mary College several years earlier. Maybe he talked the crowd into believing he spoke for masses of students, but those I was with thought he seemed a little too old and angry to be college material. He also had a page on the Southern Poverty Law Center's website that documented some troubling connections he had with neo-Nazis both in college and since graduation.

DeAnna and others talked of our civilization losing its focus on morality and of how new immigrants are diluting the country's traditional values. I had to believe those sentiments were one reason Senator John McCain, an immigration reformer only three years earlier and a cosponsor of the McCain-Kennedy immigration reform bill, ran his campaign in 2010 using the slogan, "Secure Our Border." It seemed that fear had won that day, which usually means that hate isn't far off. We ran into one Latina organizer from North Carolina at the rally and she said, "I feel such hate here." I was pretty sure she wasn't just imagining things: as I photographed Tancredo, I stood behind a motorcycle gang member wearing a menacing vest with the slogan "White Boy Society" surrounded by some Nazi imagery.

Some people didn't just disagree politically with Obama and other opponents—they seemed to want to shoot them. At least their flags, T-shirts, and posters gave that impression. A gang calling themselves "Bikers Against Illegals" roared on their Harleys around the capitol building throughout the rally with American flags waving behind them. It gave the event extra noise as the small and relatively older crowd stayed in the shade.

The keynote speaker was Maricopa County's own sheriff, Joe Arpaio. Because I had a nice camera, people thought I was a member of the press and gave me leeway. I got very close to him and was a foot behind the sheriff when he argued with a Latino counter-protester. I followed him up the stairs as he took the stage as well. Suddenly people were coming out from under trees to see him. He didn't disappoint. He was not backing down to all the national pressure, he yelled. Neither Washington, attempting his public embarrassment, nor anyone else would tell him what to do! "As long as I'm elected I'm going to uphold the law!" Though no law explicitly said that he could set up traffic checks exclusively in Latino communities or parade prisoners in pink underwear or black and white stripes down a public street, he would do it anyway. These were his means to intimidate people into obeying the law. He said he was not ashamed that he had used those kinds of tactics, even if he was already under investigation by the U.S. Department of Justice for human rights abuses.

Regardless of the criticism he had experienced, Sheriff Joe said he would keep doing his job of catching illegals and building detention facilities to hold them. "I'll keep building detention centers all the way from here to the border if I have to!" Then, realizing that Tucson would be in the middle of that corridor he had just described, he added that he would put all the liberals in Tucson in the same jails. The crowd roared with approval. The students looked at one another and then back at me as if asking if we could beat it, but I smiled reassuringly, and they collected themselves and went to interview some bikers standing under some shade trees.

With the loudspeakers blaring and motorcycles roaring, it was hard to realize there had been another group in the shadows of the legislative building

George Clifton, identifying himself as both a Marine veteran and ex-CIA, holds a sign in support of immigrants during the anti-immigrant Phoenix Rising rally at the Arizona State Capitol.

across the street all along. We found them singing church hymns softly in Spanish and standing in a circle in front of a simple altar to the Virgin. We met Pati Madrigal out front. She had been returning to the site every day to sit under a small umbrella near the shrine, she told us. Contemplating an all-out hunger strike, Pati had been eating only minimal food and surviving mostly on water in prayerful meditation. She was praying for a peaceful and humanitarian solution to immigration reform, she told the students. She was wearing a black cap saying that her brother had served in the military in Iraq. She was there, she said, because of the discrimination against Latinos. Seventy-five feet away, local United Farmworkers members held aloft a huge black and red flag bearing the eagle logo. The eight men grouped under it all looked younger than thirty.

By then the students were exhausted emotionally and physically, but I bargained with them to talk with just one more person before we headed back to the car. We chose a man standing on the street corner who was holding a sign and facing away from us. He was a white man in his sixties who wore a suit and kept his gray hair neatly trimmed. He could have been a street preacher, I thought. From behind it was impossible to tell which side of the issue was he on. As he turned to talk with us, we saw that his sign said, "Ex-Marine and CIA." He could have been an Arpaio supporter or perhaps someone standing up for veterans unrelated to the protest. But the rest of the sign read, "I stand for all immigrants."

"George Clifton," he said, shaking our hands. He had served his country officially because he believed in freedom, he told us. But he had gone to the Arizona capitol square that day because he thought the country was heading in the wrong direction regarding immigration. "All of us are immigrants or we're descended from immigrants," he said. "I feel cowardly if I don't do anything. After all, I lucked out, my mom had me here." He turned and held his sign aloft toward the oncoming motorcycle gang.

Not wanting to keep the students in the heat any longer, we thanked Mr. Clifton and left him standing on his corner alone. As we crossed the street heading back to the car, the Harley riders in black leather with their American flags flying behind them roared around the block again.

Mr. Clifton looked small and unthreatening in that scene, but I couldn't help but think of him as the boldest man out there.

| | | |

DRIVING BACK DOWN the interstate toward Tucson after dark, I told the three students about the Japanese internment camp I had visited with the previous year's delegation. After doing some research, we had stopped some forty miles south of Phoenix at a small settlement just off the highway and found the nearly hidden public monument put up by the families of those imprisoned in the Gila River Internment Center. Plaques at the monument said the detention centers like the one at Gila had been built in response to President Franklin Roosevelt's Executive Order 9066, a decree that had forced 110,000 people of Japanese descent already living in America, mostly on the West Coast, into camps in inland deserted places far from cities.

The U.S. government wanted Japanese Americans out of circulation, where they couldn't aid the enemy, though we now know they were as loyal to the United States as anyone. It was 1942, the same year the Braceros came for the first time. Some of the imprisoned had never seen Japan. Many were native to the United States. The internment was based on race and lineage alone, not on personal connections.

Against the wishes of the Akimel O'odham native people already living on their land, the U.S. government had designated part of their tribal territory near Rivers, Arizona, as the Gila River Internment. The Akimel lands only belonged to the Native American tribe because of their own relocation and government treaty years earlier, and that fact, along with the Akimels' sovereignty over the land, gave them strong reasons to oppose the use of their land for incarceration. But the government forced them to accept the plan anyway. The people placed on the reservation through no choice of their own had to live with an internment camp in their midst. Opened on July 20, 1942, the Gila River Camp housed people of Japanese descent in barracks. Almost all of the imprisoned were from California, mostly the Sacramento, Fresno County, and Los Angeles areas. The peak population numbered 13,348 people.

In 1995, with "grateful acknowledgement to the Gila River peoples," descendants of the Japanese prisoners erected a monument alongside the road near the turn to the ruins of the center. The Akimel people we talked with at a local store were welcoming, but they asked that we not enter the lands without someone from the tribe to guide us. No one was available to take us to the site on the day we stopped, so we decided to make do by standing at the roadside monument, which included some photographs of the internment site, and have a discussion there. The monument said that over 1,100 citizens from the nearby camp had served in the U.S. Armed Services. The names of twenty-three Japanese American war dead were listed on the sign. Ninety-seven students graduated from high school in the internment camp, it added.

Standing in the scant shade of trees beside the plaques in the late, and cooler, afternoon, we couldn't fathom how hard it might have been to maintain one's dignity while living in groups in unair-conditioned barracks for three years, keeping some semblance of a family and community together despite the harsh conditions. We read the plaques aloud and then stood in silence.

What got to me most was learning that nearly one thousand of the Japanese American prisoners worked as farm laborers on the eight thousand acres of farmland around the Gila River Camp, planting and harvesting vegetables and raising livestock. I assumed part of what they raised was used for feeding the prisoners. The plaque makes it sound dignified, and I'm sure those who were interned maintained self-respect as they performed the grunt work put before them. But, particularly with all the layers of labor and loss I'd been uncovering on the border, I couldn't help but connect that suffering to the long history of mistreatment of those who have fed our citizens from the time of slavery to the present, with the factor of race present at every turn. The Gila location off I-10 is but one of many such places where pain is written into the story of American agriculture.

| | | |

"DOWN THERE TO our right is the Japanese Internment monument," I said to the sleepy students returning with me from Phoenix. The camps had such an eerie resonance with everything we had just heard in Phoenix that I decided to stop even if I woke them. I pulled off at the ramp and pointed southward. "We're only about fifty miles from the border here. And just down the road a mile or two was an internment camp, and along the road is a monument we went to visit last year. You're too tired and it's too dark to stop, but you can read about it all online."

We sat on the ramp for a moment, and then I asked: "How might you relate what you just heard at the rally, especially the part from the sheriff of Maricopa County about detaining Mexican immigrants, to the history of the Japanese internment camp on Gila land?" The car remained quiet for several minutes as we drove toward Tucson, that bastion of liberalism where, as Sheriff Arpaio joked, everyone should be locked up in the huge immigrant detention centers he would build—the advocates alongside the "illegals." Then the talk began.

# THIRTY-TWO

# Tohono Sacred Peak and Desert Deaths

SELLS, ARIZONA

ONE OF THE MOST TOUCHING SCENES IN THE DOCUMENTARY film *Crossing Arizona* is the moment when Tohono O'odham tribal member Mike Wilson finds dozens of water jugs—plastic gallons he has put out for thirsty migrants crossing through his reservation's desert land—slashed and the water spilled into the sand. He shows no visible anger, but instead exhales with a sense of heartbeat for those—he is fairly certain it had to be a member of the tribe—who would do such a thing. "A sacrilege" is what he calls it. When he realizes

Mike Wilson, a Tohono O'odham leader in the humanitarian response to migrant deaths on his reservation, shows his tribal membership card to DukeEngage on the Border students.

he has lost the containers, he returns to his truck, fills his wheelbarrow with new jugs, and replaces the old ones. "Must continue to put out water," he says under his breath as he pushes.

The story intensifies as Mike is unloading replacement jugs from his truck and a lost and dehydrated immigrant walks up to him on the deserted dirt road. Seemingly unconcerned that he is being filmed, he tells Mike that he has gotten separated from his *coyote* and the group of friends and relatives with whom he traveled into Arizona. It's obvious that the man is exhausted and disoriented, and as he tells his story, he begins to cry. He believes he has failed his family, particularly his wife, who is sick and without means to get help. Calling the stranger *"Hermano"* (Brother), Mike gives him food and a gallon of water, but then tells him he should turn himself in. He shows him how to walk down the road to find a Border Patrol truck. Mike explains that he couldn't transport an undocumented migrant in his truck, even in an emergency, without risking arrest and prosecution.

Mike was living on the edge of the law in several respects. He could put out water on tribal land without fear of arrest, but one young volunteer named Walt Staton was fined and threatened with jail time in 2009 for placing plastic water jugs on trails inside the boundaries of the Buenos Aires Wildlife Refuge just a few miles away. The federal authorities convicted Staton for littering, even though his organization, No More Deaths, always managed their water drops and cleaned up any emptied or damaged jugs. As he reported, Mike could leave jugs on Tohono O'odham land, but he couldn't transport anyone, even to a hospital, without risking government intervention. He had to send the migrant away. The moment the broken man turns to walk away is as poignant as any I've seen on film.

Mike Wilson came to meet with our delegation at BorderLinks a few days after the students had watched the film for the first time. His ponytail, his floppy hat he wore to protect his face from the intense sun, and his military boots made him easy to identify, particularly because an hour before he had been in the desert carrying water. As he walked into the room, he seemed larger than life.

Mike told the students about his volunteer work with Humane Borders and about how it feels to join the effort as a Tohono O'odham member. He said he was the only tribal member participating in the water program on their reservation. He had received open criticism from tribal leaders for doing so, he said, but instead of cowering, he dished out his criticism of the tribe in return, for their turning a blind eye to those in need. He referred to the migrants as brothers and sisters who happen to be crossing the reservation in search of work in the north. Many get to the reservation knowing nothing about the terrain. Many lose their way and die. The Humane Borders death map shows that more bodies have been recovered on Tohono land than in any other border sector.

As with all the borderlands, Tohono reservation land ownership and use is politically complicated. Though long considered Tohono O'odham sacred space, the land itself belongs to the federal government, and therefore the Border Patrol enjoys free access to most of the territory. The Bureau of Indian Affairs works with tribal leaders to set policies and functions as the local government for the land where Mike had created drops, but government agents have free access to it as well. Mike could put out jugs without being accused of littering there, but the Border Patrol officers could drive anywhere they pleased as well, though some of the land is too steep for any vehicle.

| | | |

VISIBLE FROM ALMOST anywhere on the reservation is the mountain named Baboquivari, the Tohono O'odham's most sacred place. High on the mountain, the first Tohono ancestor named I'itoi emerged from a cave the tribe considers the navel of the world, which is represented as a labyrinth in Tohono art. Legend says that early Spanish conquistadors tried to dig their way into the cave in search of gold, but the ground under them opened and swallowed them. They were never seen again. Since time immemorial, Baboquivari has been the central locus of the Tohono people and land, and from that peak, I'itoi continues to watch over them today. The peak itself, however, is actually inside the wilderness area adjacent to the Tohono O'odham reservation, not inside it. The federal government protects it, not the tribe. And since the place is so remote, it has become a route for the migrants.

Equally complicated is the fact that traditional Tohono O'odham land is on both sides of the border. After the U.S. government surveyed the line, tribal members who were once united on the same land ended up in two countries with two different national languages. In America they were required to speak English in schools despite having their own mother tongue. Official membership in the tribe is still not contingent upon national origin. Despite pressures to acculturate, Mexican and American tribal members, particularly the old ones, still share their indigenous language. Many tribal members in the United States, including Mike, know some Spanish as well. Ceremonial gatherings in the U.S. often have family members from Mexico in attendance.

Mike's difficulties with his own people are a microcosm of the national debate about immigration. For the Tohono O'odham, though, the debate isn't abstract, but about whether to help those walking across their backyards. Some believe giving water to the dying migrants encourages, even abets, the drug smuggling and human trafficking. Should they just stay out of the fray and let the Border Patrol handle it? It seems that is the tribe's de facto position. Mike begs to differ based on his belief in showing basic human kindness toward others.

Yet another complication for the Tohono O'odham tribe is that many are poor themselves, with few more opportunities than some of the migrants. The 2010 census showed that a majority of Tohono people lived below the poverty line, and community agencies reported that they subsisted on diets that cause and exacerbate health problems. Type-2 diabetes is rampant. Many tribal members know that without some help from the Bureau of Indian Affairs, they would be homeless. Should they aid strangers crossing Tohono land? Should they turn them in? Many simply would rather not be involved.

Mike Wilson, a seminary-trained Presbyterian lay leader, knows exactly where he stands on these questions. He cites biblical verses when asked if one should give water to people breaking immigration law and entering the United States by crossing Tohono land. "Jesus said, 'Giving to the least of these is giving to me,'" he quotes. For him the parable of the Good Samaritan illustrates that the Bible leaves no ambivalence about what is the right thing to do when someone is in danger. The interesting twist on this well-known parable is that the protagonist, the Samaritan who helps a fallen traveler, is the immigrant who helps a citizen. The foreigner without rights of citizenship, in other words, is the one who comes to the aid of the local guy who has been beaten and robbed. Mike's belief in giving water to migrants also derives from Native American history. Growing up on the margins of America and enduring racism as a member of an indigenous nation has given him connections to others who are downtrodden.

But his membership in the Tohono O'odham tribe and his adherence to the Christian faith still do not explain his crusade entirely. Many members of his tribe are also Christians and live just as close to the border. But tribal Christianity is where Mike is most critical of his people. He says the tribe used to have a tradition of hospitality, of offering food, water, and shelter to strangers, but they have shied away from it. "We used to be just like the ancient Israelites, and all the desert people on the planet. But now they're worried about how much putting out water will cost. I fill up my water barrels with my garden hose while the water tankers for our nation drive by. They care more about their cows and horses than they care about human beings."

He left his position in the Presbyterian church in Sells, Arizona, for just that reason. Before doing so, he had pleaded before the session, "Your brothers and sisters are dying in the desert." He had urged them to adhere to "higher universal law" and forget about man's law. Otherwise, they have "no moral authority" to argue their own case as native people before the government. He said, "We have the blood of migrants on our hands!" But the church and the tribe had refused to act. "We were the oppressed," he said. "Now we've learned from the oppressor and we'd rather let other brown-skinned people die in the desert. That's why I left that church."

That still didn't explain how Mike had found his calling. So in the Q and A period following his talk, I asked him point-blank about what happened in his life that gave him this kind of compassion. Surprising all of us, he said his change began with his tour of duty in the U.S. Army Special Forces in El Salvador.

I had guessed he might say the early sanctuary movement in Tucson, particularly because members at the Southside Presbyterian Church had given shelter to refugees of the same war in the 1980s. But back then Mike had been an adviser to the right-wing Salvadoran government forces, about as far from being a peace activist as one can get. A popular uprising had taken the country by storm and was supported by many Latin American religious leaders, including, most famously, Archbishop Oscar Romero. The U.S. government, meanwhile, took the side of the military junta and sent advisers to help them, while also training many who would go on to become death-squad leaders at Fort Benning, Georgia's "School of the Americas." As the documentary *School of Assassins* reveals, thousands had died at the hands of the squads led by officers trained there, including four U.S. nuns who worked with the poor in a small village. Archbishop Romero was also one of their victims.

But Mike's conversion didn't come after learning of those assassinations or by realizing that he was a representative of a government's campaign against the poor. No major battle or death of comrades had changed him either. Rather, his reversal began quietly at a dinner table over a meal he shared with a poor family of *campesinos*.

No one who has spent time in Latin America would be surprised that a visitor, even an American in uniform, would find himself sitting at a table being fed by people who have nothing themselves. A poor farm family would kill its plumpest chicken for a guest and sit smiling with only tortillas and salt while the guest ate. Mike had just shared such a meal with the family when the father began counting out his week's wages on the table in front of him. The father had left home to work on a larger farm to earn extra cash to cover their expenses.

As the man placed the few crumpled bills and coins on the table, Mike saw firsthand how little his work had yielded. He witnessed the expressions on the faces of the man's wife and children as they watched. That, he said in answer to my question, was the moment he began to change. Upon his return to the United States, Mike pursued a seminary education, a lay ministry position, and then eventually began his voluntary ministry of giving water to the thirsty, food to the hungry, and advocating for the migrants.

Every day that he makes his rounds, he knows many in his tribe will criticize him. He knows some of them will slash the plastic jugs. Yet he continues his campaign to convince them he is right. This isn't just a white man's problem, he says. "But why is no one holding our nation accountable?" He answered his own question, "Because white America would rather not raise this because of their historical persecution of people of color. They don't want to be reminded of ethnic cleansing, Manifest Destiny, of the dominant culture from sea to shining sea!"

Though angry about the Tohono nation's stance, along with the billions the U.S. government has spent on border technology and militarization even as it neglects its native peoples, he continues his methodical daily work of putting out water—alone. He returns prayerfully to his rounds day after day and carries water with the discipline and strength of a Special Forces member and the heart of one who has seen the other side of immigration. Maybe he thinks of the family in El Salvador sitting at the table together as he pushes his wheelbarrow filled with water jugs toward the drops he manages. Perhaps he imagines his own ancestors parched from desert travel receiving a gourd full of water given by a stranger. "Must keep putting out water," he says, knowing he is the only one.

# THIRTY-THREE

# Campesinos Sin Fronteras

## SELLS, ARIZONA, AND SONOYTA, SONORA

I COULD SEE THE UNMISTAKABLE BABOQUIVARI OFF TO MY left as I drove alone from Tucson on Highway 86 toward Sells, the largest town in the Tohono O'odham Nation, in the early morning on the final leg of my journey westward. I passed the turn to the Sells Hospital where I had learned with the previous year's student delegation about its work with injured migrants. According to Dr. Karen Moriah, with whom we spoke inside the hospital, some migrants had found their way there on their own. But most of those treated in the Sells Hospital go there because Border Patrol officers escort those too injured to go directly to detention.

As we were touring the hospital, we passed an officer stationed in the hallway outside a room with a partially closed door. He nodded to us as Dr. Moriah whispered he was there to guard the migrant under arrest—the one in the hospital bed being treated for severe dehydration and horrible blisters on his feet. Later in her office she began to cry when she spoke of migrants she had personally attended to, a touching moment for all of us, particularly the students who thought they might become physicians.

From Sells I headed due south through the Organ Pipe Cactus National Monument and then toward the Sonoyta border crossing. Thinking of what had happened to us at Naco and elsewhere, I got out of the car to check with the ICE officers stationed at Sonoyta before driving out of the country. I wanted to know if I could legally drive along Mexico's Calletera Federal 2, a highway within sight of the border fence. Both officers standing there just nodded impatiently without saying a word. I returned to the car and drove into Mexico.

The "Hassle Free Vehicle Zone" sign south of Rio Colorado, Mexico, indicates that U.S. vehicles, including produce-hauling semis from Imperial Valley, can travel on this road without extra immigration documents.

Out on the highway, heading west, I passed a large road sign that said "hassle free zone," which I learned meant the area is a trade corridor so

close to the line that extra documentation and lengthy checks aren't required—at least for transport trucks. The road was built in order to miss
the U.S. mountains just north of the line, and it made sense as the least
costly route. The road led me through some of the harshest and most uninhabited desert landscape of my trip. At times I could look for miles in
every direction and see no sign of any significant vegetation or anything
man-made at all, except of course the road and the border wall, now so
stark and jarring that at times it offended the eye. Picture a photograph
of a sand-colored landscape and rocky hills that someone has taken a
ruler and felt-tip pen and drawn a perfectly straight black line across. But
aesthetics, of course, are just one of the problems with our borderline.

The Sierra Club and other environmental organizations have documented others, such as stresses the wall has caused on wildlife populations, where everything from snakes to deer and wildcats are prevented
from migrating. Animals have been photographed standing in front of
the wall looking lost. The worst are the animals found dead next to the
fence or with their heads or antlers caught in its mesh. Of course, cam-
paigns to save wildlife always raise questions regarding whether supporters care more about wildlife than they do people.

Then there are those who care about both. One year one of our delegations heard from Sierra Club organizer Dan Millis. He deftly interconnected the environmental concerns with his advocacy of human
rights. We had learned before we met that Dan was one of fourteen per-
sons, along with Walt Staton, who had been ticketed in the Buenos Aires
Wildlife Refuge for littering by putting out plastic gallon water jugs for
migrants. Convicted by a lower court, Dan's case was later overturned by
the Ninth Circuit Court of Appeals. According to the *Los Angeles Times*,
the court ruled simply that "Water didn't meet the definition of waste."

Dan told the *Times* that the victory made him feel more sadness than
triumph, and added, "The day we change our border policies to show
more respect for human life is the day I'll feel vindicated." This was the
same man who advocated for the environment, for snakes and deer. For
him, there is no division. Of course he would never throw out litter in a

natural area, but he had found a fourteen-year-old Salvadoran girl's body. She had died alone—of thirst. He was quoted afterward by the *New York Times* as saying, "People are part of the environment." The students sat glued to his every word.

When I got out of the car to take pictures of the desert landscape, my body heated up immediately and sweat was gone as soon as it formed. As I ventured into the desert hills, clamoring over rocks to get a sense of the lay of the land, I was careful where I put my feet. I knew so few people were around that if I stumbled in that heat, now reaching 115 degrees, or happened to step on a snake, slip, and hit my head or break a leg, I could die in an hour. There were signs every mile or two picturing Gila monsters, scorpions, and rattlers with warnings in Spanish of the dangers of heat, poisonous animals, and paths that lead to dead ends. "No vale la pena!" some said, using the same words I'd seen at the Mexican Consulate. "Family members are waiting," said others. At one point when I had been driving I saw two men disappearing over a hill. I had no way of knowing where they were headed, whether there was a ranch or settlement just over the rise where they lived, or whether they were two migrants on their way to the United States, but I wondered how they could survive out there at all.

| | | |

THE IMMENSE DESERT that I was driving through made it almost unfathomable that, according to the map, I would soon be heading into one of our nation's most prolific agricultural areas. But the map showed brown changing to green with a straight line dividing them. I had read earlier that nearly all of the winter vegetables consumed in the United States are grown in the area near where southwest Arizona meets California. And the melon crops produced there in summer were some of our most important. Yuma is the largest of the towns in the corridor. Not by coincidence, the Mexican Federal Highway 2 leads right to it, passing through San Luis Rio Colorado and its U.S. twin called simply San Luis.

When I got there I realized I had been traveling on a produce road and many of the big reefer trucks I had been seeing were carrying food.

Ironically, Rio Colorado, the Mexican town named for the Colorado River, no longer has water flowing through it. As soon as I crossed the border into Arizona again I saw why: San Luis soaks up nearly all of the Colorado River water before the river reaches the border. In the United States, I was soon driving through flat, huge expanses of irrigated fields that lay in every direction. Lettuces, spinach, and other greens are the main winter crops grown there. Melons follow those in succession, with harvests that beat the Florida crops. Cantaloupe harvest was under way when I arrived. Plumes of black smoke rose from wheat fields being burned after grain harvest.

Passing dozens of farm trucks filled to overflowing with melons, I knew I was in the center of farmworker country. I had no appointments, no one to visit, and little information about what to look for when I got there. I was simply heading to the agricultural place I knew as Yuma, driving and hoping something might materialize.

Immediately beyond San Luis, I entered Somerton, Arizona, and passed a sign at a small strip mall that read, "*Campesinos Sin Fronteras.*" I braked hard, whipped the car into the next shopping center, and did a U-turn. I drove back to the front of the office and saw it was open. I entered a small waiting area where there were posters and handouts in Spanish about farmworker health and workers' rights. One young family with two small children sat quietly in chairs waiting. Then a woman came out to talk with them, and they followed her through a door. I waited, not knowing quite what I would say when she came back. A different receptionist returned to her desk, saw that I was reading the brochures, and asked if she could help me. I explained my trip in brief and asked if it might be possible to talk with someone about the organization's work. Ten minutes later I was speaking with the director, Emma Torres, and telling her about my trek. She treated me like a trusted friend.

Emma had been a veteran of farmworker struggles and had once worked closely with the United Farm Workers (UFW). Though she was a fighter, I could tell she felt beaten down that day. When I asked how things were going, she said she was tired from all the anti-immigrant sentiment surrounding SB 1070 and was worried for the workers she served. "They're afraid to leave their houses," she said. "They're unable to participate in community activities. They can't even go to their children's schools. They used to be able to cross the border to visit relatives in Mexico, but no more."

"I was part of the César Chávez movement," she said. "I never felt hopelessness then, but now I'm seeing despair and oppression engraved on the hearts of the young. This despair is, of course, what they want."

But Emma wasn't quitting. She told me that in a few hours, she and other community leaders would gather to tell the public about SB 1070 and answer their questions at a hearing in the town hall. "Would you like to go?" she asked. "Of course!" I replied.

Before going to prepare for the meeting, she introduced me to Chayito Sanchez, one of the organization's outreach workers. Chayito spent a majority of her time in the fields doing health-related outreach, but she happened to be in the office that afternoon. Chayito and I spent a half hour talking in her small office, and she asked me then if I would like to accompany her on her rounds the next day. Since Emma was speaking that night, Chayito offered to accompany me that afternoon to the SB 1070 meeting. Afterward, we could go to the United Farmworkers Union headquarters and to César Chávez's office and the house where he died. "I'd like you to meet my husband, too. He works as a mechanic on a farm."

On the way to the meeting, Chayito confided, "People just don't have the spirit to talk right now. Some are driving home after dark to avoid any trouble. They're driving three hours, all the way from Mexicali to the fields in the morning, every day. We're all damaged, injured, just because they want to work. I know of pregnant women who are working in the fields just because they're afraid to stop."

She had been a farmworker herself. She knew the feel of melons in her hands and what they did to her arms and back after lifting them for days.

She knew the ways that farmworkers suffer mentally as well, as when people seemed to consider them outlaws. She had dedicated her life to helping change their lives, a task both insurmountable and essential at the same time.

Some two hundred people representing numerous ethnicities and backgrounds attended the hearing in a carpeted room with fluorescent lights. A majority of the audience was white; some of them looked like they might be transplants from other states. I realized that farmworkers most affected by the new state law were not in the room. They were either in the fields . . . or the shadows.

Emma and the other officials sat at a table in the front and shared a few microphones, first giving short presentations, and then answering specific questions about the new bill and its effects. They asked for comments afterward. No one seemed openly pro-1070, and the discussion remained civil.

One speaker at the front table, a man with brown skin and jet-black hair pulled back into a ponytail, was the first to speak. He openly criticized the bill. His name was Chris Deschene, the first Navajo tribal member to run for secretary of state—Arizona's second-highest office. Both a veteran of the U.S. Navy and a lawyer, he told the audience he was worried that the new law could mean he and other Native Americans could be stopped and questioned based on their skin color, along with the Latinos. Deschene's critique enlivened others. One Latino man in nice clothes stood in the back and said, "Here in Somerton, 98 percent of us are Latinos. They're after our kids and they're not going to stop! The hatred shows!"

Chayito and I went from there to César Chávez's UFW office in San Luis, near the border. The child of an American Chicano small farmer in Yuma who later lost his land to foreclosure and was forced to turn to migrant work, César rose to fame when he helped organize, alongside Dolores Huerta, the United Farm Workers in the 1960s. The organization successfully led national lettuce and grape boycotts that brought workers safer conditions and more wages per pound harvested. He and other UFW leaders became major civil rights figures and he befriended

Attorney General Bobby Kennedy. But he never forgot where he came from and died working in his office near the Arizona fields.

Chayito and I walked along the street to where the office and UFW headquarters were still located. The small one-story building was newly painted red and emblazoned with a large black eagle UFW insignia. Afterward we walked down the street and stood staring at the simple rental apartment where Chávez died. There were no historical markers or other signs besides the green street sign named for him. A mile or so away, Chayito took me to a community center gym to see a mural dedicated to the man whom Cardinal Roger Mahoney called a "special prophet to the world's farm workers." Outside the center was a small statue of Chávez with a short-handled hoe at his feet, but nothing more in town said a man who had changed the world had lived and died there.

| | | |

I SPENT THE NIGHT in Yuma and met Chayito back at her office the next morning at six. We got into her Tahoe and drove toward the fields. She had health-related flyers to hand out—with information about AIDS and other sexually transmitted diseases, pesticides, and more. I had no agenda other than to accompany her and to meet workers in the fields. It didn't take Chayito long to find people already working in the early morning sun.

She drove up beside a field where a large conveyor pulled by a massive John Deere tractor was crawling across a cantaloupe field, its wheels straddling the rows. Behind and on both sides of the harvester, dozens of workers were picking melons in both hands and hoisting them up to the moving machine where women and older men stood packing the melons into brown waxed boxes that said "Arizona Cantaloupes." Young men, one of them wearing a bandana that looked like it was made of twenty-dollar bills, stacked the full boxes on a trailer pulled directly behind the tractor.

They were halfway across the field when Chayito got out of her car, walked across a board over the irrigation ditch, went down a row, and approached the foreman. A seasoned and sympathetic-looking Latino man who probably had worked his way up from the harvesting jobs, he greeted her warmly. Chayito told him who we were and asked him if we could talk with the workers. She turned and motioned for me to come in. "He says it's fine, and you can get up and ride up on the machine if you want." I climbed carrying my camera up on the slow-moving machine and rode with the crew as the machine made its way across the ten-acre section. The work continued apace as we talked.

The women, who worked on the boxing part of the machine, had covered their faces almost entirely with scarves, which served as sunblock and protection from dust from the field, they said. I began photographing them at work, trying to capture the scenes of sun on irrigated green, the crawling machines, and the fluid human handwork.

One of the men shouted from the field as a he placed two cantaloupes on the conveyor, "Get a picture of Rosa's eyes." Another woman nearby pointed toward Rosa. Rosa paused for a few seconds in her work and allowed me to approach with the camera. Her aquamarine eyes were all I could see of her face, but in moving closer, as cameras allow us to do, I realized she was no older than sixteen, a girl who might still be in school but instead was out picking melons before sunrise and on through the day.

Chayito waited in the shade on the side of the field while I rode with the crew until they finished the field and took a break underneath the harvester. Then she approached the group with her materials and gave a short tutorial about pesticide exposure, heat stroke, and other dangers of working in the field. The workers seemed eager to take the free pamphlets and pens she was handing out. She asked me to take photographs for her to use in her work.

The conversation turned to SB 1070 soon after. One of the women asked Chayito a question about how to get more information on the new law, and Chayito gave her spiel on workers' rights. But there are few protections to offer, she said, visibly frustrated by the bill. Chayito later said to me in the car, "We come as workers and we're treated as criminals." And decades after César Chávez's death in 1993, a new Arizona law passed that had vilified farmworkers—again. The fields where people work hardest for the lowest wages to feed us are also where people are most afraid of arrest, separation from families, detention, and criminalization.

I rode with Chayito back to her office and got my car. The Cruze's thermometer was already climbing near 100 degrees and it was only 10:30. I flipped on the air-conditioning and drove past other fields of other workers, but now I had at least a few names and faces I remembered. Rosa and the others would have to stand for some forty-five thousand farmworkers who work in the Yuma/Somerton area, all of them woven, often invisibly, into the fabric of the American food system.

|  |  |  |  |

THANKS TO A PHONE call from Emma Torres, on the way out of town I was able to stop by the Mexican Consulate's office in Yuma. Señor Miguel Escobar Valdez, the consul himself, seemed happy to see me, even on short notice. He had an extra half hour before his lunch meeting. He was quite eloquent in both English and Spanish and spoke in both, and I was surprised by how open he was with his views on immigration and the border wall—which turned quickly to critique. In the middle of the conversation, he pulled out a copy of his book, *El Muro de la Vergüenza* (*The Wall of Shame*), inscribed it, and handed it to me. The following quote is a good sample of what is inside:

It is lamentable that the theme of migration has been subordinated under other agendas such as the fight against terrorism and the war on drug trafficking. . . . It is deplorable that we end up confusing migrants with terrorists. . . . What has resulted from this unilateral perception is that migrants are almost "criminals."

We have to realize together that these migrants, both men and women, are the most dynamic and imaginative, and possess the best work ethic. They are the bridges between the global marketplace and rural places. They are the bravest and most ambitious people we have. They're workers, not criminals.[1]

I left his office thinking this: if all the American politicians who have voted in favor of bills such as SB 1070 could spend just one day toiling in the Arizona sun and harvesting cantaloupes alongside people like Rosa, the mutual realization and appreciation that Señor Escobar Valdez writes about in his book would likely come faster than we think.

---

# THIRTY-FOUR

# The Wall of Shame and Entrepreneurship

CALEXICO, MEXICALI, AND IMPERIAL VALLEY,
CALIFORNIA

THE ALL-AMERICAN CANAL CHANNELING THE COLORADO RIVER
was to my right as I drove Interstate 8 from Yuma's green fields
toward California. Leaving air filled with the smoke of burning
wheat stubble, I had reentered the dry heat of the desert where
nothing grows, and the air seemed clean again. Then, there it
was in the middle of the desert: 26,000 cubic feet of water per
second was heading toward another agricultural oasis of 630,000
acres, one that was formerly one of the driest places in America,
the Imperial Valley. That's where I was headed as well.

Many migrants know when they leave Mexico to work in the
fields of Imperial Valley they are taking a great risk. But most
first-timers have never experienced a desert like this one I was
in. Just walking through, their shoes and clothing begin to deteriorate. Their backpacks are cheap and their water containers
are just the store-bought gallons, sometimes only liters. Water
runs out fast.

Those who place water in the desert for the migrants know
that human bodies require more water over a twenty-four-hour
period in that environment than a person can carry. A gallon
weighs eight pounds. Four gallons, weighing thirty-two pounds,

is about all anyone could imagine carrying while walking for any long distance, and most people can't possibly take that much. I have seen migrants traveling on foot wearing a backpack and holding their water jugs in their hands—eight pounds in each and more in the flimsy backpacks they wear. That is still not enough.

Water drops along pathways are essential for migrant survival. Groups like the Border Angels in California and Humane Borders in Arizona have been leaving water at regular outposts for years. They have saved lives, but they know the chance of having the water in the right places at the right time is always slim. Even so, they believe they must try. To do nothing is to condemn people to death. That lesson was never more obvious to me than in the heat of the Imperial Valley, particularly in the Algodones Dunes where everything in sight is bleached white—which is not the reason for the name, but "cotton" fits nonetheless. There was not even a dead cactus to provide shade.

The Sonora Desert south of Tucson, in contrast, is greenish brown and filled with plants that survive on a few inches of rain.

Rosa and her coworkers harvesting and boxing cantaloupes in a field near Somerton, Arizona.

Plants nurtured by the scant rain in turn support animal life. The saguaro cactus, for example, provides a home for the elf owl. One Tucson resident once told me a visitor from Saudi Arabia went to the Sonora and said, "That's not a desert, that's a forest." In the Imperial Desert, without the canal that is, any Saharan probably would feel at home. The desert outside the agricultural area made it obvious that the half-million acres of green vegetables in the Imperial Valley could only exist by damming the Colorado River. But having seen San Luis and its border sister town only the day before witnessing this, it seemed like the United States was kicking sand in the face of our neighbors to the south by using all the water. When I delved deeper into its history, I realized that I was pretty close to the truth.

The idea for the canal came about because American leaders once thought the snow-fed Colorado was limitless and unstoppable. There was so much water in the river that it sometimes flooded naturally into the Alamo River, which then channeled the Colorado's water northward into the giant dry Salton Sink, a basin where the river deposited layers of rich silt as the water evaporated. The deep alluvial soil of the area gave early settlers an idea: if they could get water to the Salton Sink consistently, the deep soil there would jump in production, providing food for export back east and limitless profits for the farmers.

Most notorious of the early Imperial developers was a transplanted Ohioan named O. M. Wozencraft, a doctor who had left his family behind in Louisiana when they contracted cholera. He rose to leadership in California, though he went down in history for having proposed that African Americans be excluded from the new territory—"prohibiting the negro race from coming amongst us," as he put it. He later landed an appointment from President Millard Fillmore as Indian agent for the state of California. In that post he traveled around the state, writing bogus treaties, eighteen in all, with various tribal groups. When the treaties made it to the U.S. Senate, not one was ratified. All were so inflammatory that they were sealed from the public record for fifty years. Shortly after that debacle, Fillmore removed Wozencraft from office. Robert Heizer wrote in 1972 in his book *The Eighteen Unratified Treaties of 1851–1852 between the California Indians and the United States Government* that "one cannot imagine a more poorly conceived, more inaccurate, less informed, and less democratic process" than the one Wozencraft championed.[1]

Despite this, Wozencraft still became known as the "Father of the Imperial Valley." He had recognized the valley's potential early and hired a California acquaintance named Ebenezer Hadley, county surveyor of Los Angeles, to route a channel for the entire Colorado by way of the Alamo River in Mexico to the Salton Sink. With Hadley's surveyor's report in hand, Wozencraft traveled to Washington to present his proposal that he called the Colorado Desert Irrigation Plan.

He received a cold reception. One member of the committee he spoke to described his proposal as a "fantastic folly of an old man."[2] Wozencraft died in Washington having garnered no funding for his proposal. Thirteen years later, however, the canal first known as the Alamo would begin anyway. Apparently our folly can continue to live on beyond us.

Following several floods in the 1880s and 1890s, when the Colorado River overflowed into the Alamo and filled the sink with water, a Canadian engineer named George Chaffey formed the California Development Company and began making plans to divert the Colorado into the Alamo on a permanent basis. After he began his work, he and his colleagues changed the name from Salton to Imperial, with the express hope of luring people to this land below sea level, where—and this would not be in the promotional literature—the annual rainfall is less than three inches and high temperatures can exceed 120 degrees Fahrenheit. Chaffey and his company began construction on the canal in 1900 without permission from the Mexican government.

By 1901, the Alamo Canal was complete and the Colorado River was diverted and controlled by the Chaffey Gate at Pilot Knob. A great quantity of the river could now be channeled to the Imperial farmland with the opening of one lock. But the agricultural developers of the valley

---

1. Heizer, *The Eighteen Unratified Treaties of 1851–1852 between the California Indians and the United States Government,* 5.

2. Thomas E. Sheridan, *Arizona: A History,* 226.

wanted even more water than that. A year later they increased the flow, and they increased it again in 1903. But by 1904 the silt, a known byproduct of the Salton flooding from the beginning, began building up in the Alamo Canal and stifling the flow of water. Farmers dependent on the waters from the canal pressured the California Development Company to do something to get around the blockage.

An engineer named Charles Rockwood devised a plan to dig a breach directly into the banks of the Colorado, an opening that would not require a gate and therefore wouldn't silt as much. He went four miles south of the Chaffey Gate and broke through the Colorado's banks, flooding the water into the Alamo River without devising any controls. The Colorado started heading into the below-sea-level Salton at a tremendous rate; at times the entire river flowed northward into the Imperial Valley. At the breach itself, a waterfall crashed downward over eighty feet at times. For a while, every farmer in the valley was elated at the abundance of water in the desert. Then the floods of 1904 through 1906 came.

The Salton Sink had developed over millennia as a means to evaporate the excess floodwaters of the Colorado. When silt settled out during a flood, the mud would eventually dry out in the intense heat. With the new channel sending most of the river into California, however, the water overwhelmed the ecosystem and formed what is affectionately known today as the Salton Sea, one of the saltiest bodies of water on the planet. Increasing in salinity by 1 percent per year, it never evaporates entirely. During its formation, the Salton Sea also flooded out the Torres-Martinez, an indigenous group that had long survived there. Salt processing companies that had occupied the basin since the arrival of settlers were submerged.

A lawsuit brought by the salt processors bankrupted the California Development Company and its assets passed to the Southern Pacific Railroad. But the farmers refused to give up. In 1911 they formed the Imperial Valley Irrigation District with the express purpose of guaranteeing dependable means to get water to their fields. But by 1915, H. T. Cory, an author writing in a journal for the American Society of Engineers, was calling Charles Rockwood's maneuver a "blunder so serious as to be practically criminal."[3] Regardless, the sea remained, while thousands of nearby acres continued to be irrigated by the Colorado River, though without the guaranteed flow the growers wanted.

In the late 1930s, New Deal legislation provided funding to begin building the Boulder/Imperial Dam north of Yuma and to construct a new channel known as the "All-American Canal," which would run entirely north of the border, bypassing the Alamo River altogether. The new canal would start at the Imperial Dam and direct the Colorado water first toward the fields of Arizona and then to California's Imperial Valley by way of a concrete canal some eighty-two miles long. When the project was finally completed in 1941 as part of Franklin Roosevelt's WPA efforts, it was considered one of the great engineering feats of the world. In a government-sponsored newsreel, the narrator says, "The Imperial Valley, once dry and barren, with the help of water from the Colorado, yields rich crops when irrigated." "Help" was an understatement. Without the Colorado, not one carrot would sprout and grow in that heat.

Today most of America's winter carrots, lettuce, broccoli, and cauliflower, along with spring melons, come from the valley. Yet no one is sanguine about the river's sustainability or the canal's miraculous qualities anymore. With wheat fields belching their columns of smoke into the sky and the temperature on the car thermometer rising to 115 degrees, I felt I was witnessing Armageddon.

Somehow no one seemed to foresee in 1941 that water shortages would be a problem in the future. Seventy-five years ago, the area was going through one of the wettest periods on record. Since then, starting in the 1930s, millions of people have moved to the region. Now global climate change is taking hold and rainfall patterns have worsened, even as the population of the valley has boomed and the towns have sprawled all over the deserts. Los Angeles is the scariest example of what the artificial transport of water can create—and it is obvious to many that large populations in a desert can't be sustainable. Eight additional U.S. municipalities also depend on the same canal for their sustenance. Wells are depleted and the area has been in severe drought since 2000.

---

3. Harry Thomas Cory and William Phipps Blake, *The Imperial Valley and the Salton Sink*, 1290.

The once mighty Colorado that flowed through Mexico and on to the Pacific Ocean at the Gulf in Baja has at times been reduced to a dribble in Mexico. Marc Reisner wrote in his 1986 book, *Cadillac Desert*, that the United States built the dam "on the pretension that natural obstacles do not exist."[4] This of course makes Mexico's water usage from the Colorado, including in its agricultural fields and for cities, even more precarious than ever. The *Los Angeles Times* reported on November 20, 2012, "To the dismay of Mexican fishermen and of environmentalists on both sides of the border, the river often is barely a trickle when it finishes its 1,400-mile journey to the delta and the Gulf of California."

Ken Salazar, secretary of the interior for the Obama administration, brokered a deal in 2012 with Mexico as I was writing this book, offering them more security in some dry periods in exchange for more regulated usage on both sides during normal periods. He proclaimed the Colorado a symbol that more than any other makes us one people with Mexico. He didn't mention our history of hogging the water. He also didn't mention the huge number of workers from Mexico who labor in the fields of the Imperial Valley because of the water. Despite the huge amounts of water being siphoned away by the Imperial Water District, and vegetables and fruits leaving the Imperial Valley by the truckload, the long-term prognosis for water on either side of the border remains bleak. And we have to remember that as fields once watered by the Colorado dry up, those who work in the fields south of the line must go somewhere.

The canal passed under an Interstate 8 bridge and was now on my left. The Colorado's water was entirely contained in concrete, a measure to save water from the seepage that used to occur when water seemed limitless. Its blue color reflected a cloudless sky seemingly defying an intense June sun and the immense Sahara-like desert that stretched out in all directions. I thought of the myth of Icarus.

| | | |

---

4. Reisner, *Cadillac Desert*, 1.

I HEADED TO THE border crossing at the twin cities of Calexico, California, and Mexicali, Baja California. Mexicali is a sending town for many migrants who work in the Imperial Valley. At one time many authorities looked the other way when the workers crossed, knowing of the mutual dependence. Now the new wall has channeled people elsewhere—away from the official border crossings. But finding desperate people willing to try is still essential for growers.

From the Mexicali border crossing I walked south in the shadows of the wall, shielding myself from the sun as I passed a few struggling stores and mostly empty buildings. At midafternoon I was the lone pedestrian walking southward against the flow of Mexican people headed north toward the United States in their cars. Seeing little to pique my interest, I decided I would head back through the gate to El Centro, California, where I planned to stay for the night.

On my way back, however, the red vests two young men wore as they dodged and danced through the slow-moving traffic caught my attention. They were leaving slips of paper under the wipers on car windows as they waited to enter the United States. Running back and forth, they shouted to one another and tried to capture the attention of the drivers. I thought they might be selling lottery tickets. Then I realized when I saw one guy run inside a building and return with a tray that they were selling drinks made to order. One of them called out to me in English, "Hey man, come and try us out!" They were selling coffee drinks and smoothies, he said. Intrigued, as well as hot and thirsty, I headed toward the shop, ordered a mango smoothie, and sat down to talk with the waiters while I sipped.

The sole reason for their business's existence was the long lines where every day thousands trying to leave Mexicali to head northward into Calexico must sit and wait. Every car takes minutes, maybe an hour, to search. Some are asked to pull over to the side. Some may never make it. Lists of terrorist suspects must be checked. Sometimes there is real evidence of wrongdoing, but the vast majority gets through—eventually. Since you can't be in a hurry, you might as well have a cool smoothie, or a caffé Americano to stay awake. The red-vested young men were not the only food and drink vendors, but they hustled the most.

Hector was the one who called out to me in English. He introduced me to Rebecca, the barista who made the drinks, and Gerardo, his co-seller. Gerardo was originally from Guatemala, he said, but he had been a migrant to the United States and now after being deported just across the border he was stuck in Mexico. Hector had also been deported, but he assured me he was culturally American and could feel comfortable nowhere else. He resisted speaking with me in Spanish.

He became intrigued with the idea of my writing about the border and asked several questions. "How do you get books published like that?" I knew he probably had a better story to write than I did, though we didn't have much time to talk about his situation between his constant jaunts to and from cars. I did learn he was put out at the border in Mexicali. Now he was running drinks there—not drugs—and living as a single man, sharing an apartment with other friends who were working within feet of the U.S. border wall. His goal, he told me, was to stay in Mexico just long enough to make money to return to the United States. "I have to get back to see my wife and children in California," he added. "If I can work here and make money, I'll have enough to go back." Then he dashed out again to take a frozen drink to a customer holding pesos out his window. How many more smoothies and coffees would it take before Hector might head to the desert to try his luck crossing in the night?

I finished my smoothie, said good-bye, and headed back on foot toward the United States in a short pedestrian line where my passport felt like gold. As I walked toward the immigration line, I pushed my hand into my front pocket of my pants and gripped tight the blue-covered booklet with the U.S. seal that bore my likeness and proof of my citizenship inside. It felt like having a first-class pass to a lifeboat on the Titanic. When I got to the other side and walked toward the place where I'd parked, I looked back at the fence and saw through holes into Mexico where the hundreds of cars were still stranded. I could also see the occasional flashes of red moving among them as the two young men from different countries worked like crazy, making a peso tip at a time, trying to do with hard work what I had received by birth and through no effort at all.

# THIRTY-FIVE

# Graves of Unknown Farmworkers

HOLTVILLE, CALIFORNIA

I FIRST LEARNED ABOUT THE GRAVESITES FROM THE BOOK *Working in the Shadows* by Gabriel Thompson. Before that, I'd planned to see the valley's fields that produce the incredible tonnage of food I had heard so much about and had hoped to meet some of the people living and working there. But after reading what Thompson said about the Holtville cemetery, I knew I had to visit the farmworkers who had died in the valley as well.

I had no idea in the beginning how hard it would be to find the graves themselves; that yet again I would have to search without a map for lives forgotten. But

"No mas" reads the cross in the migrant cemetery in Holtville, California. Unlike most, the person buried in this grave was remembered by name: Raymond Muzzy.

I had become an archaeologist of the invisible, digging through rumors and myths in an effort to find the truth beyond the map, sometimes stumbling into amazing discoveries, but just as often becoming lost and unable to find my way. This time I wasn't even sure I had the right name, but I had to assume there would be people in the town to help me.

I drove into Holtville in midafternoon and found a small *tienda*, walked in and bought a Gatorade, and then asked the young woman working behind the counter, "Have you ever heard of a cemetery nearby where they bury people from Mexico?" I knew I was being blunt. She answered that she had heard of it, but had never been there, and then she added specific directions that made no sense to me even when I repeated them back to her. I'm sure all of the turns and landmarks would be perfectly understandable to someone who lived there, but the way I took led me on an hour-long search up and down streets and through a series of farm roads and additional stops to ask for more directions, and still I was lost. I started to wonder if I even had the right town. I drove down every street in Holtville, then headed out to the agricultural fields surrounding the town and got lost on a sandy one-lane farm road. With the car tires kicking up dust, I pulled alongside a group of cantaloupe harvesters just finishing their day in the fields.

They had picked every melon in sight and filled the last tractor-trailer parked alongside the road. I slowed and rolled down the window, apologizing for detaining them another minute in the heat, but they seemed to want to help and walked toward the car. I asked, "Do you know of a cemetery near Holtville where they bury migrants from Mexico?" A group of five men crowded up to my window and answered as a team, "Yes, it's close by, go right up this farm road, take a left, and when you get to pavement you go to the left again. You'll see the sign that says Holtville Cemetery on the left." I thanked them and drove on, winding through the melon fields and believing against all evidence to the contrary that the farm road would eventually lead to hardtop.

Not surprisingly, the graveyard was just down the road from the agricultural fields. I turned into the cemetery entrance, but first impressions said the place seemed too tranquil, too well kept, and too green to be the place I'd read about. There were granite markers, artificial flowers, some benches to sit on, and even a nice row of shrubbery lining the back of the plot. An elderly white man who had driven up in an old Buick sat on one of the benches near the graves. This couldn't be the forsaken place I'd read about, I thought; this graveyard was for longtime residents, people with a little money to bury their family members in caskets and have preachers for funerals under green funeral home awnings. I decided I'd made a mistake. I would give up and leave because I was just too worn out to try again. Then I noticed a gap in the back hedge.

I walked toward the opening and up to the chain across the driveway. There was a "no trespassing" sign on the other side of the shrubbery, placed just out of sight of the public front. I could now see a couple of acres of disturbed ground. I glanced around to make sure no caretaker was nearby. By then the old man was pulling onto the highway in his car and driving away. I was alone, so I stepped over the chain and walked around the hedge. I realized the field was full of graves, just unkempt ones.

There was a pile of dirt from the front graves and last year's plastic flowers and broken wreaths—refuse that cemeteries keep out of sight of bereaved families. Beyond that lay an open field of uneven dull red dirt lined with red painted brick-sized concrete markers three feet or so apart. There was not a green sprig in sight, not even an upright plastic flower. Many of the bricks had white wooden crosses in front of them, some leaning, some prostrate on the ground. It was clear someone had been there to visit the graves, but not recently.

Driven into the ground among the graves were several tall official metal signposts that warned people to stay out because the ground could cave in. I could see it had already given way in several places, and there had been recent bulldozing, probably to smooth over some sinkholes from earlier collapses. I shuddered to think of falling through the thin layer of clay and landing in a wooden box next to a body. Then I realized I didn't know if they had boxes. Maybe there would be body bags?

I set out walking among the graves anyway, stepping cautiously and stooping to read the crosses and markers. Then I realized they continued into the distance—eight hundred or more in all. Some of the little crosses read only "*No mas*" or "*No olvidamos*" (we won't forget). Many of the red concrete rectangles serving as gravestones showed only the date of burial. Some said merely John Doe. A few had names and the dates, but the majority of them were unidentified.

For years I had known about the thousands of bodies found in the Sonora Desert south of Tucson. I had heard from No More Deaths volunteers who had found them, from Humane Borders people, from the Border Patrol. I had seen bodies in photographs and film footage. I had heard forensics experts speak in Tucson. All of them told of desiccated bodies found with a few personal effects, maybe a backpack, maybe a letter, or even just a few scraps of clothing strewn around by animals. The mental picture I carried was of victims of dehydration, hyperthermia, and even hypothermia during the extremely cold nights, but mostly it was thirst for water that killed them, I thought.

Part of me wanted to get the hell out of the place, but I forced myself to walk among the unclaimed and to bend over and read the scant records written. I made myself listen for their unspoken stories.

I read later that a San Diego–based organization called Border Angels/Los Angeles de la Frontera, a humanitarian group started by Enrique Morones in 1986, had put up the white crosses. Morones, the director of Border Angels, paraphrased a familiar scripture from the book of Matthew on his website: "When I was thirsty, who gave me to drink?" But dying of thirst, it turns out, wasn't exactly the whole story of that eerie place.

It wasn't until later that I learned, partly from a *Sixty Minutes* segment I saw online, the bizarre fact that a majority of the people buried there had died from drowning. The CBS piece was entitled "The All-American Canal." I learned later that the canal's water travels eight feet per second in a concrete trough 225 feet wide and 20 feet deep and that the concreted, sloped canal was built with sides at an angle approaching 45 degrees, nearly impossible to scale, and with no lines or buoys for self-rescue. Even after crossing an intensely hot desert, the first thing those who try to swim the canal experience is the chill of hypothermia. The water coming from beneath the impoundment above the Imperial Dam is only 55 degrees

Fahrenheit, and sometimes it is even colder at night when migrants usually think it is best to cross. Experts told the *Sixty Minutes* reporters that not even Olympic swimmers could swim straight across water traveling at thirty miles per hour, and even they would have to wear wetsuits to ward off the shock of the water temperature. The steep, smooth sides make it impossible to gain a handhold even if one reaches the other side. The drowning ones keep washing further downstream.

When human rights activists first attempted to convince the water authority to erect emergency lines, they got nowhere. Some resorted to installing them illegally on their own, only to have them immediately torn down. So drowning in the desert continued, and the All-American Canal became a killing tool. Now hundreds of drowning victims lie beneath the hard, dry ground of Holtville.

Over the years of learning about too many migrant deaths, I've heard of the touching sacrifices that other workers, brothers, cousins, and friends of the victims make to send the bodies of the deceased back home. Farmworker crews donate hundreds of dollars from their meager wages to buy caskets and pay bus fares or even to rush the bodies back home in a casket in the back of someone's pickup—all so the dead can be buried in their hometowns. No one should be alone in death, they believe. Catholics are especially sensitive to this, and often memorialize both the burial sites and the places of death. That fact makes it especially painful to visit Holtville. No Day of the Dead observances are held there. No wreaths. No flowers. No candles. Not even identification of the bodies in many cases. Only small wooden crosses.

| | | |

OVER A YEAR AFTER my return to North Carolina, representatives from a coalition of farmworker and immigrant groups in Florida stopped by the Durham office of Student Action with Farmworkers on their way to Washington, DC, to lobby for immigration reform. A group of us provided a potluck meal for them. I also decided to buy a votive candle adorned with the image the Virgin of Guadalupe for each of the approximately twenty-five people.

Most of the travelers were seasoned workers and intrepid organizers who had fought the long fight in the fields. They had done this trip before. They knew Washington. Some had even met César Chávez personally. But one member of the group was different. She was seventeen years old—by far the youngest in the delegation. Her name was Embrilly, and she was traveling without family or close friends. She had been born in Mexico, but had come to the United States as a baby carried by her parents. She was a "dreamer," she said, meaning she was among the number of undocumented youths dreaming of pursuing an American education. She was participating in the trip in part to help fight for a way to go to school.

She mentioned in her testimony before our group that she also had been part of the organization called Los Angeles de la Frontera in California and had helped place crosses on graves in Holtville in the Imperial Valley. Visiting the graves had inspired her to work more on immigration issues, she said, and then to join the delegation going from Florida to Washington. I doubted if many others of the easterners in the room knew what she was talking about. But I couldn't think of anything else.

After the closing ceremony in which we all sang a song together, I gave each of the participants a candle for the journey, and told the group they were a symbol to take to Washington on behalf of the rest of us. After I'd passed them around to everyone, I still had one candle left over.

I approached Embrilly, holding the extra candle out in front of me. I thanked her for her story and asked her if she would like to take the candle. "I've also been to Holtville," I told her, "and it's very special to meet someone who's put up the crosses I saw there." She thanked me and said unexpectedly, "I'll definitely be going back to California when I get back from Washington . . . and I'll be sure to take this other candle to the cemetery with me."

# THIRTY-SIX

# Desert View Tower and the X-Men

## IN-KO-PAH MOUNTAINS, CALIFORNIA

DRIVING CALIFORNIA'S 140-MILE BORDER WITH MEXICO FROM the Arizona state line near Yuma to the Pacific Ocean is possible in a few hours—if you stay on the interstate. But after leaving Holtville late, I decided to stay in El Centro, California, for the night and finish the final leg the following day by taking the back roads. I headed west along Route 98 at seven the following morning.

Many workers were in the Imperial Valley fields by then—men and women moving with machines as one across the fields, the boxes and melons piled high around them. They wore broad hats, bandanas, and long sleeves. Their gloved hands worked quickly moving through green vines. Only their eyes were uncovered. I had eaten a fruit salad that morning in the small restaurant at the motel. The salad had contained cantaloupe. As I drove by them, seated, well nourished, and cool, I held my hand up toward the crouched workers as if in benediction, hoping that could mean something even if they didn't see.

Soon the road channeled me back to Interstate 8, the Kumeyaay Highway, the only road that crossed the In-Ko-Pah Mountains up ahead. Leaving the last of the irrigated fields of

the Imperial Valley, I glided up smooth roads through the high desert just as the eastern red sky began to turn golden and heat up fast. I reached the higher altitudes X-men, wearing the discarded clothing of migrants who pass through this way, guard the Interstate 8 underpass near the Desert View Tower.

by the time the sun was baking the sand again. Halfway up I realized the air was cool enough to roll down my windows and let it blow over me.

Near the top of the mountain, I spotted signs for the Desert Tower Museum. I took the next exit and was the first visitor of the day. I got out of the car in the chilly air, put on a jacket, and met the proprietor emerging from his house. He waved to me as he headed to unlock the door to the museum and tower. "Hello, I'm Ben Schultz," he said.

Ben told me he had owned the museum only a few years, and seemed happy to invite me inside. I could tell from the age of the dusty collection that included Native American lore, mounted animal heads, and an assortment of photographs and memorabilia ranging from desert history to the American Revolutionary War alongside desert books, plant life, and more, that he had changed little about the inventory he purchased with the place. He loved describing the place and continued talking as I scurried up the spiral stairs and out onto the lookout platform to capture the soft morning light with my camera.

After I headed back down, Ben asked about my travels. He was intrigued and said that as a Quaker he was a contributor to the San Diego American Friends Service Committee office that worked with migrants and immigration reform policy. He had plenty of personal stories to tell as well.

Since arriving at the tower, Ben had seen hundreds of migrants traveling over the mountain pass along the interstate near his place. He had seen countless footprints and had found water bottles and clothing left by migrants. "They always come right through the canyon below here; the paths funnel them toward a gulley over on the other side of the interstate. Often at night a Border Patrol agent parks his truck at the bottom of the hill and the landscape funnels the migrants toward him. They just walk right up to his vehicle and he loads them in. It's sad. You can walk there from here—you just go under the bridge and then follow the path up the hill. You'll see their clothing and all the footprints in the sand."

I asked him what he thought about all the agents parked nearby. "The way I see it, the Border Patrol is just one big federal jobs program," he told me.

A "Roadside America" entry I had seen online about Desert Tower characterized the migrants as a tourist attraction, quite different from Ben's take: "Tourists who carry their own binoculars might spot the U.S. Border Patrol apprehending illegal immigrants streaming across a nearby crossing in the mountains. Prime your camcorders if you leave via East I-8—you might witness parades of the recently arrived escorted along the shoulder. No stopping allowed!"

Ben added before I left, "You have to see W. T. Radcliffe's sculptures before you go to the other side." I went to the sculpture garden entrance. The introductory plaque explained that the rocks were natural quartz and granite outcroppings that an out-of-work engineer in the 1940s had carved into a variety of shapes, including birds, mammals, reptiles, and monsters. Radcliffe used red, black, and white paint for accents on the gray rock. All seemed whimsical at first, but over a rise was a profile of a skull with a painted eye staring back that stopped me in my tracks. Behind that sculpture, on the other side of the interstate, I could see the path where the migrants traveled, likely some of them just a few hours before. Juxtaposed, the skull rock and its background told a story Radcliffe couldn't have been privy to then, but that captured today's border story perfectly.

The last thing Ben asked me before I left the parking lot to head toward the migrant trail was, "Did you see the X-men on the way in?" I had no idea what he meant. He explained: "I have a crazy neighbor who finds discarded clothing left by the migrants and uses yucca stalks and makes scarecrow-like creations." He assured me I would see them if I walked down the hill toward the interstate bridge.

A platoon of X-men awaited me at the bottom of a steep sandy incline. They stood close to human height, though some seemed bent in various stages of agony. One knelt as if falling on his face dying, or perhaps in prayer, or both. An "X" of yucca stalks made their arms and legs. The articles of clothing are left by migrants who drop them as they head under the bridge, perhaps running or suffering from the heat, or maybe just tired of the extra weight. Though the figures are headless, the dried flowers of the yucca protrude through the clothing and give the impression of fingers or hair. There are migrant footprints everywhere around the X-men, as signs of real migrants merge with their unnerving representations.

From what I learned from Ben, this was not necessarily sympathetic art. The figures started to become ghosts, border scarecrows, death angels all led by the head Grim Reaper waiting to harvest new victims. I took pictures as I slipped past them, being careful not to touch as if on a sacred burial ground, and also trying not to run. I knew they were just man-made creations, but they had started to come alive, and I couldn't make myself stay any longer. Migrant footprints were all over the pathway leading from there to the Border Patrol parking area just as Ben had said. One blue off-brand athletic shoe lay on the path leading over the ridge. Had the wearer lost it fleeing? Had he gone on with just one? Every piece of clothing, water bottle, and food wrapper strewn over the ground evoked other stories.

Just down the hill a mile or so was a blue flag flapping hard in the morning wind. It marked a water drop maintained by the Humane Borders group. I wondered how many migrants had stopped there. Inside the plastic bin at the base of the thirty-foot flagpole were packets of food, Band-Aids, and almost always water. But many, of course, never made it that far.

| | | |

I DROVE THROUGH Jacumba on Route 94 and stopped for lunch at Barrett's Junction Café and Mercantile: a bar, dance hall, souvenir shop, and grill rolled into one. Mexico was playing France in the Copa Mundial on TV as I sat and ate a sandwich and fries. Several local men were watching along with the proprietor and I joined them. Elsa, a Latina woman who spoke little English, took the orders, cooked the meals, and served them. She glanced up at the TV occasionally as she worked, but showed no emotion about the game.

While I was eating, a Border Patrol agent walked into the restaurant. His head was shaved and he wore high black boots. He was one of the more intimidating officers I'd seen. His pistol, handcuffs, and other equipment on his belt passed close to my shoulder as he walked by. I leaned back a little, and we nodded and said "hello" as he brushed past. He ordered at the cash register and then stood at the counter while Elsa prepared the eleven burgers he ordered for himself and his crew.

Elsa worked fast and then nervously handed the bag to the owner, who in turn walked over to offer it to the officer. The officer looked in the bag and realized he had gotten the wrong number of hamburgers— he was one short. He told the owner, who shouted back to Elsa, "Uno mas!" and Elsa scrambled to fix the missing burger. The agent waited patiently, looking over at the soccer game and chatting with the other men watching. He seemed not to notice Elsa at all. Elsa got the other burger ready and handed it to the owner, who passed it to the officer. The officer thanked the owner and walked out in a hurry.

A few minutes later, I stood up to leave. Mexico was leading France, and things were looking good for the underdog. Leaving a bigger tip than usual, I got up from the table, walked over to thank Elsa, waved to the proprietor and nodded to the patrons, walked out into the California sun, and drove toward Imperial Beach.

# THIRTY-SEVEN

# Walking Alone through Friendship Park

IMPERIAL BEACH, CALIFORNIA

I CHECKED INTO THE SAND CASTLE INN IN SAN DIEGO COUNTY. It was the cheapest place I could find, and I liked the name. The owners were a family of immigrants from Thailand who made me feel as if I were a visitor in their home. Their motel was spotless and I could see the Pacific from my door! And I had gotten there by three—perfect.

I unloaded my bag, rested a few minutes, and then returned to the office to ask about Border Field State Park. I had a map that could get me close and I could see it on Google Maps, but I had seen no road signs that mentioned it. I needed some

After receiving a warning on their radios, Border Patrol officers prepare to race away on their ATVs near the border wall's end in Friendship Park, California.

local knowledge. Luckily the owners did know something about the park once called "Friendship" and said I would need to get on the interstate to find it. The son drew a map for me showing me roughly where I had to turn, and I set out for the border again, driving south this time along the strand in the mild California afternoon sun. I wished for a convertible and a good stereo pumping music as I drove through the Imperial Beach strip, but the Chevy sedan and its radio had to suffice. The station I played as I cruised with my windows rolled down was *ranchero*.

There were no exits off the interstate for the park, and no signs indicated its whereabouts. It was now obvious that few people go there, and it seemed that the government wanted those who don't know about it to pass by without noticing. But I had to find it—it was the final destination of my quest. After several wrong turns and doubling back, I finally drove through a small ranch into what seemed a dead end and arrived at an abandoned entrance. I parked my car where a chain stretched across the road prohibiting anyone from driving farther. Luckily there were no "do not enter" signs, so I started out on the long sandy road heading toward the beach. Halfway there, as I walked by deserted overgrown fields and mudflats, a Border Patrol truck zoomed up to me and the officer asked me what I was up to. I replied that I was just walking and wanted to see the beach. I didn't go into the full explanation. I braced for a reprimand or worse, thinking maybe the place was off limits after all, but he zoomed away just as fast as he had arrived.

I walked a mile farther, reached the beach, and put my hand into the chilly Pacific. Throughout my walk there had been Navy helicopters flying test runs, their blades whopping as they took off and landed at the naval air station or outlying field just north of the border. There are tens of thousands of test flights from the base every month. Even at the water, they continued to be louder than the ocean waves. I can't say they seemed out of place as I neared the wall, as militarized as it was.

I walked southward on the sand, where I started seeing innumerable tracks of what had to be Border Patrol ATVs. They had covered every inch of the beach. Strangely the park signs still said it served as a bird sanctuary, even in the midst of all that driving and helicoptering. But somehow a few birds still remained. Some gulls and a flock of pelicans flew by, though not one beachcomber or bird-watcher was there to witness. Not one wader or swimmer was anywhere near either.

It was strange to be alone on a beach on a sunny afternoon just south of where millions of people live. It didn't seem natural for the place to be so desolate, particularly because I could see people on the Mexico side having fun. As I walked I realized my whole trip had been a journey into solitude and many of the places I'd gone had seemed strangely lonely and sad, not at all what Mexico seemed to be experiencing at the moment.

I had seen the fence from a distance as I walked toward it, and all of it had seemed foreboding. Yet as I got closer, the chinks in the border armor became more obvious. The metal wall, with its numbered military surplus sections, had looked impenetrable, but up close the posts driven into sand on the beach and into the surf had begun to deteriorate, with some leaning and literally dissolving into the Pacific. The rusted and broken posts looked more like pilings from an old pier that had been taken out by a storm. Swimmers of moderate ability could easily make it around them, particularly at low tide. Close to the wall there was a lighthouse on the Mexican side not very different from the lighthouse at Boca Chica, though this one was maybe a little better kept. Both white towers had been built as markers of safe harbor, signals of hope for those lost at sea. But a lighthouse next to a border wall was at best a mixed message.

There are old photographs of the fence that once stood at this place back when it had been called "Friendship Park." First Lady Pat Nixon had gone there in 1971 to dedicate the 370-acre park made from land taken from the naval base. At that time there was only a five-strand barbed wire fence between the two countries, basically a livestock fence that people could crawl through if they wanted. The United States had constructed a park for visitors there, complete with an attractive entrance, picnic tables, and, most importantly, an area where families divided by immigration policy could visit with one another and even embrace across the low fence.

The *Los Angeles Times* reported then that during Pat Nixon's visit to the park, a member of her Secret Service detail cut the topmost strand of barbed wire as the First Lady prepared to walk up to it. Though we know now that her husband's policies were at the forefront of some of the United States' first efforts to further strengthen the border fence, at least at that moment in August, she approached the fence with one strand intentionally removed and said, "I hate to see a fence anywhere."

Then she shook hands with a father holding a child on the Mexican side. She hugged the little boy wearing shorts and tennis shoes. "I hope there won't be a fence here too long," she said, looking at the child. I have no idea who the child might have been, but he would be near fifty years old by now, if he's alive.

In 1994, two decades after her visit, the border fence began going up there first, and the other major urban border cities were not far behind. Fifteen years later, in 2009, with three parallel walls now complete, people couldn't touch through the fence at all and the park was all but abandoned. The picnic tables left on site looked unkempt and sad.

I walked in the ATV tracks toward the wall and came upon four Border Patrol agents sitting on their ATVs up on a sand dune overlooking the wall's western end. I decided to approach them first before walking closer to the fence, partly as a precaution and partly just to have some human contact. I clambered slowly up the dune to greet them. They weren't exactly welcoming, but they weren't unfriendly either. After they sized me up, I thought it okay to approach.

I began to sense as soon as I walked up that they were worried about what appeared to be unrest on the Mexico side. Some of the people in Mexico had started shouting. One of the officers muttered, "They're always cussing at us." Was I going to be in the middle of something? I sure as hell didn't want to be around if a rock came our way.

Then I realized that there was a big party going on in Tijuana that had nothing to do with the officers at all. I told them I thought it was a celebration, but they wouldn't hear it. They were convinced it was sinister and about them. I started to hear faint blasts played on a tuba and then wafts of other instruments. I could see people playing in a park nearby. Some seemed to be dancing. Groups of young men played soccer down on the beach. People began chanting and singing. One of the officers said, "They're always trying to provoke us." They all looked askance at the dancing crowd.

Then it hit me that the crowd had gathered to celebrate Mexico's victory over France in the World Cup—the underdog really had won after all, for the first time against a major European foe. "That's a soccer party," I said, but they weren't listening. They were at the moment preoccupied with some message being sent through their helmet radios. They began to fidget. Suddenly the head officer signaled to the others. They cranked and revved their engines, jumped into place on their seats, and whizzed off the dune and down the beach at full speed. They seemed to forget I had been standing there; all I could do was step back to make sure they didn't run over my feet.

Then the dunes were empty and I was the only human being on the American side of Friendship Park. I walked toward the wall and touched it. All of the panels were numbered in paint, having been brought there from the Gulf War salvage yard and assembled in order. I took photographs through the wall, and I listened. At one point I even tried to shout over the music, "Viva Mexico!" to show my support for their team. No one heard me, and I felt shut out. My side was lonely. Mexico was where the party was, and I was locked out.

I headed down to the beach and tried to get a picture of the deteriorating end of the wall up close. As I stood focusing and framing, a soccer ball inadvertently came over the wall toward me. I thought, "Great, now I have a chance to throw a ball back to the players and maybe get a chance to interact." But before I could get to the ball, a guy about eighteen years old sidled up to the fence, glanced up to where the guards had been, then slipped between the posts and entered the United States in front of me. I couldn't believe he fit through, but it was obvious he had done it before. He hardly slowed down. In U.S. territory, he grabbed the ball and kicked it to his friends on the other side, and then slipped back into Mexico as quickly as he had come. At precisely the moment he was slipping through, he looked back toward me and I snapped his picture, my last photograph of the trip.

# THIRTY-EIGHT

# As If It Were Not There

## THE U.S./MEXICO BORDER

IT IS NOT CLEAR WHY SENATOR BARRY GOLDWATER, ARIZONA'S conservative darling, promoted an open and civil border between the United States and Mexico in 1964, the same year the Bracero program ended. There is no question he was a good promoter of commerce, and maybe his statement had something to do with the free movement of capital, a kind of precursor to NAFTA. Whatever the reason, he was horrible at fortune telling. He was quoted in 1964 in the *Tucson Daily Citizen* as follows:

> Our ties with Mexico will be much more firmly established in 2012 because sometime within the next 50 years the Mexican border will become as the Canadian border, a free one, with the formalities and red tape of ingress and egress cut to a minimum so that the residents of both countries can travel back and forth across the line as if it were not there.

He had chosen a time almost fifty years from his statement to envision the border as a free one, precisely the same time period in which I was writing this book.

Of course, his words have not come true. Today our representatives, particularly those in Goldwater's party, insist that border security be at the forefront of every discussion of immigration reform. We've gone backward, retreating

On the day Mexico beat France in the World Cup, a young man slips through the border fence into the United States to retrieve a soccer ball in order to resume his game with his friends in Tijuana.

from his predictions, and the border is more "there" than ever.

In 2013, I learned that Enrique Morones and the Border Angels (*Los Angeles de la Frontera*) encouraged border authorities to test a pilot program that will allow people to enter the Friendship Park again to communicate with their Mexican friends and family—in person. The U.S. officials were still concerned that contraband might pass between people, so they have not allowed for hands to touch, not even fingertips, but at least people may be able to talk while standing near one another.

We're still a long way from Pat Nixon's vision of what a new Friendship Park might look like, though some continue to imagine life without fences. Of course, no one in 1971 ever dreamed that the Berlin Wall would be gone. We as Americans have always known something there is that doesn't love a wall—that wants it down. We don't like being hemmed in either. We like going where we want. I believe there is a part of all of us that wants to reach across barbed wire to shake hands and hug a baby, or to thank a farmworker. Many agree with First Lady Nixon that we don't like to see a fence anywhere; that walls put up between people go against our very nature.

Of course, Mrs. Nixon's vision isn't the America I found along the border, but then again it was, in glimpses, in human stories, in lives lived like bridges rather than walls, and among the many who know we need Braceros still, not just as "strong arms" to help with our heavy lifting but also as thinkers, as neighbors with ideas. We need co-dreamers from south of the line who are ready to help imagine and build our collective future. If we remain alone behind our wall and provide no pathway toward equality, collaborations from willing newcomers will remain hidden in the shadows.

Our actions going forward, whether collaborative or not, will show the world whether we are the people of the wall or the torch of liberty, of the palisade or the lighthouse; of the land of the free or the enclosed. Right now, whether we like it or not, our wall—the largest, best-guarded, most expensive barrier ever built on this planet—underlines, perhaps undercuts, everything we believe and say we are. Now it is up to all of us to decide whether or not that is the last line, the bottom line, of our nation's story.

## ACKNOWLEDGMENTS

MANY THANKS TO MY PARENTS CLAUDETTE AND DILLARD THOMPSON for their love and support, along with the rest of my family who are always with me in spirit wherever I travel. Hope, you send me. I wouldn't have gone the first mile without you. Marshall, you're with me more than you know.

My thanks to Student Action with Farmworkers, DukeEngage on the Border, BorderLinks, *Puentes de Doble Via*, and all the organizations here in the states (particularly El Sol in Jupiter, Florida) and those along the U.S./Mexico border working for justice. Without you, this book and the hope and optimism undergirding it would not exist. Also, a thousand thanks to Sarah Boone and our many friends and hosts along the border who provided places to stay, food, ideas, encouragement, and protection along the way.

A special thank you to farmworkers from Mexico and Central America who have crossed the border to work in the farm fields of the United States: Muchísimas Gracias for the sacrifices you make to provide the food we so often take for granted. May this book help bring attention to the true meaning of your presence in our communities, and may our policies and pay soon reflect that reality.

Many friends and colleagues have helped make my work stronger. I thank the people of the Center for Documentary Studies at Duke University, the Department of Cultural Anthropology, Center for Latin American and Caribbean Studies at Duke, Latino/a Studies, The Latino Migration Project, the Center for the Study of the American South at UNC-Chapel Hill, and the Gentleman's Book and Bottle Club.

Hope Shand, Theresa May, Katharine Walton, Allan Gurganus, Paul Ortiz, Ruel Tyson, Louis Mendoza, Rob Amberg, Duncan Murrell, and John Brenner read or listened to versions of this work and gave me invaluable help on it.

Students have made such a difference in my life and writing. All of those I've taught in the courses: "Farmworkers in North Carolina," "The Politics of Food," and especially "The U.S./Mexico Border" have helped inspire this book. I want to thank especially my student assistants: Tennessee Watson, Sarah Harden, Tori Wilmarth, Alexander Stephens, Alexis Spieldenner, Abby Birrell, and Chris White, as well as all the students who read and commented on early versions of the manuscript. Also, thanks to all of those who have given a summer of their young lives to work on the border through DukeEngage, especially those who returned to Durham to start and continue Duke Students for Humane Borders, as well as those who have worked with SAF through the years. You have all been a constant inspiration. Michelle Lozano Villegas, who could be listed under all of those categories, deserves a special shout-out for guiding me to Carlos's shrine. I know all of you in your own special ways will continue building on what you have learned.

A special thank you to Marissa Bergmann for her design work and encouragement, to Zohar Nir-Amintin of Zoharworks for creating the website, to Lisa McCarthy for helping prepare my photos for publication, to Marissa B. and Junho Kim for their work on the Braceros film, to Sarah Garrahan for editing the Bracero film, and to Katharine Walton for her help with publicity. What a team!

My sincere thanks to the University of Texas Press for your unflagging help in making this book a reality. Theresa May, *un abrazo fuerte para tí.* And mil gracias to Dave Hamrick and the rest of the crew!

A final note: all of the photographs in this book and the accompanying website are mine, though I owe much to Marissa, Lisa, and Zohar for making them look as good as possible. Please see the full collection at www.borderodyssey.com.

"Annexation of Texas. Joint Resolution of the Congress of the United States, March 1, 1845." http://avalon.law.yale.edu/19th_century/texan01.asp.

Anzaldúa, Gloria. *Borderlands/La Frontera: The New Mestiza*. San Francisco: Aunt Lute, 1987.

Atkin, S. Beth. *Voices from the Fields: Children of Migrant Farmworkers Tell Their Stories*. Boston: Little, Brown, 1993.

Bank Muñoz, Carolina. *Transnational Tortillas: Race, Gender, and Shop-Floor Politics in Mexico and the United States*. Ithaca, NY: Cornell University Press, 2008.

Barndt, Deborah. *Tangled Routes: Women, Work, and Globalization on the Tomato Trail*. 2nd ed. Lanham, MD: Rowman and Littlefield, 2008.

———, ed. *Women Working the NAFTA Food Chain: Women, Food, and Globalization*. Toronto: Second Story, 1999.

Barrett, S. M. *Geronimo: His Own Story*. New York: Meridian, 1996.

Bonilla, Frank, Edwin Meléndez, Rebecca Morales, and María de los Angeles Torres, eds. *Borderless Borders: U.S. Latinos, Latin Americans, and the Paradox of Interdependence*. Philadelphia: Temple University Press, 1998.

Bouldrey, Brian, ed. *Traveling Souls: Contemporary Pilgrimage Stories*. San Francisco: Whereabouts Press, 1999.

Bowden, Charles. *Murder City: Ciudad Juárez and the Global Economy's New Killing Fields*. New York: Nation Books, 2010.

Bowden, Charles, and Molly Molloy, eds. *El Sicario: The Autobiography of a Mexican Assassin*. New York: Nation Books, 2011.

Boyle, T. C. *The Tortilla Curtain*. New York: Penguin Books, 1996.

Brinkmann, Robert, and Graham A. Tobin, eds. *Carolina del Norte*. Special issue of *Southeastern Geographer: Journal of the Southeastern Division, Association of American Geographers* 51, no. 2 (2011).

"Buffalo Soldiers and Indian Wars." http://www.buffalosoldier.net/BuffaloSold iers&ChiefVictorio.htm.

"Buffalo Soldiers and the Spanish-American War." National Park Service. http://www .nps.gov/prsf/historyculture/buffalo-soldiers-and-the-spanish-american-war .htm.

Carrico, Richard. *Strangers in a Stolen Land: Indians of San Diego County from Prehistory to the New Deal.* San Diego, CA: Sunbelt Publications, 2008.

Cather, Willa. *Death Comes for the Archbishop.* New York: Alfred A. Knopf, 1927.

Cave, Damien. "Whatever Floats Your Boat." *New York Times Magazine,* March 4, 2011.

Chasteen, John Charles. *Born in Blood and Fire: A Concise History of Latin America.* New York: W. W. Norton, 2001.

Chavez, Leo R. *Shadowed Lives: Undocumented Immigrants in American Society.* Edited by George Spindler and Louise Spindler. 2nd ed. Orlando, FL: Harcourt Brace, 1998.

"Civil War in Texas." National Park Service. http://www.nps.gov/history/seac/bro wnsville/english/index-3.htm#confederates. Last accessed July 2013.

Clothier, Patricia Wilson. *Beneath the Window: Early Ranch Life in the Big Bend Country.* Marathon, TX: Iron Mountain Press, 2005.

Coelho, Paulo. *The Pilgrimage: A Contemporary Quest for Ancient Wisdom.* New York: HarperCollins, 1998.

Contreras, Joseph. *In the Shadow of the Giant: The Americanization of Modern Mexico.* New Brunswick, NJ: Rutgers University Press, 2009.

Cory, Harry Thomas, and William Phipps Blake. *The Imperial Valley and the Salton Sink.* San Francisco: John J. Newbegin, 1915.

Dando-Collins, Stephen. *Standing Bear Is a Person: The True Story of a Native American's Quest for Justice.* Cambridge, MA: Da Capo, 2004.

Davis, Jefferson. *The Papers of Jefferson Davis.* Vol. 6, *1856–1860.* Edited by Lynda Lasswell Crist and Mary Seaton Dix. Baton Rouge: Louisiana State University Press, 1989.

De La Torre, Miguel A. *Trails of Hope and Terror: Testimonies on Immigration.* Maryknoll, NY: Orbis Books, 2009.

Deutsch, Sarah. *No Separate Refuge: Culture, Class, and Gender on an Anglo-Hispanic Frontier in the American Southwest, 1880–1940.* Oxford: Oxford University Press, 1987.

DeYonge, Dennis L., and Sandra Chisholm DeYonge. *Discover a Watershed: Rio Grande/Rio Brazo.* Bozeman, MT: The Watercourse, 2001.

"El Paso del Norte." Texas State Historical Association. http://www.tshaonline.org /handbook/online/articles/hdelu.

Emory, William H. *Report on the United States and Mexico Boundary Survey Made under the Direction of the Secretary of the Interior*. 3 vols. Washington, DC: C. Wendell, 1857–1859.

Escobar Valdez, Miguel. *El muro de la vergüenza*. Mexico City: Random House Mondadori, 2006.

Ferguson, Kathryn, Norma A. Price, and Ted Parks. *Crossing with the Virgin: Stories from the Migrant Trail*. Tucson: University of Arizona Press, 2010.

Ferriss, Susan, and Ricardo Sandoval. *The Fight in the Fields: Cesar Chavez and the Farmworkers Movement*. Orlando, FL: Harcourt Brace, 1997.

Gill, Hannah. *The Latino Immigration Experience in North Carolina: New Roots in the Old North State*. Chapel Hill: University of North Carolina Press, 2010.

González, Juan. *Harvest of Empire: A History of Latinos in America*. New York: Penguin Books, 2001.

Grant, Ulysses S. "The Mexican War—the Battle of Palo Alto—the Battle of Resaca de la Palma—Army of Invasion—General Taylor—Movement on Camargo." Chap. 7 in *Personal Memoirs of U.S. Grant*. New York: Charles L. Webster, 1885–1886. http://www.bartleby.com/1011/7.html.

Grillo, Ioan. "NGOS to Washington: Cut Military Aid to Mexico." *Global Post*. http://www.globalpost.com/dispatches/globalpost-blogs/que-pasa/ngos-wa shington-cut-military-aid-mexico.

Griswold del Castillo, Richard, and Richard A. Garcia. *César Chávez: A Triumph of Spirit*. Norman: University of Oklahoma Press, 1995.

Guthman, Julie. *Agrarian Dreams: The Paradox of Organic Farming in California*. Berkeley: University of California Press, 2004.

Hahamovitch, Cindy. *The Fruits of Their Labor: Atlantic Coast Farmworkers and the Making of Migrant Poverty, 1870–1945*. Chapel Hill: University of North Carolina Press, 1997.

Harding, Jeremy. "The Deaths Map." *London Review of Books* 33, no. 20 (October 2011): 7–13.

Heizer, Robert. *The Eighteen Unratified Treaties of 1851–1852 between the California Indians and the United States Government*. Berkeley: University of California Press, 1972.

Hellman, Judith Adler. *Mexican Lives*. New York: New Press, 1994.

Herrera, Carlos González. *La frontera que vino del norte*. Ciudad Juárez, Mexico: El Colegio de Chihuahua, 2008.

Herrera Robles, Luis Alfonso. *La Sociedad Del Abandono*. Cuidad Juárez, Mexico: El Colegio de Chihuahua, 2010.

————. *Memorias de braceros: Olvido y abandono en el norte de México*. Ciudad Juárez, Mexico: El Colegio de Chihuahua, 2012.

Hunt, Jeffery W. *The Last Battle of the Civil War: Palmetto Ranch*. Austin: University of Texas Press, 2002.

Isenberg, Andrew C. *The Destruction of the Bison: An Environmental History, 1750–1920*. Cambridge: Cambridge University Press, 2000.

Katz, Friedrich. *Imágenes De Pancho Villa*. Mexico City: Ediciones Era, 2004.

Kearney, M. K., A. K. Knopp, and A. Zavaleta. *Continuing Studies in Rio Grande Valley History*. Brownsville: Texas Center for Border and Transnational Studies, University of Texas at Brownsville and Texas Southmost College, 2010.

Las Casas, Bartolomé de. *A Short Account of the Destruction of the Indies*. New York: ReadaClassic, 2009.

Leckie, William H., and Shirley A. Leckie. *The Buffalo Soldiers: A Narrative of the Black Cavalry in the West*. Norman: University of Oklahoma Press, 2006.

Liu-Beers, Chris, ed. *For You Were Once a Stranger: Immigration in the U.S. through the Lens of Faith*. Raleigh: North Carolina Council of Churches, 2008.

Logan, Rayford W. *The Betrayal of the Negro from Rutherford B. Hayes to Woodrow Wilson*. New York: Da Capo, 1997 [1965].

"Lost in Detention." *Frontline*, PBS, 2011.

Martínez, Rubén. *Crossing Over: A Mexican Family on the Migrant Trail*. New York: Picador, 2001.

————. *The Other Side: Notes from the New LA, Mexico City, and Beyond*. New York: Vintage, 1993.

Meier, Matt S., and Feliciano Ribera. *Mexican Americans/American Mexicans: From Conquistadors to Chicanos*. New York: Hill and Wang, 1993.

"Mexico's Drug War Hits Historic Border Cantina." *All Things Considered*, NPR, 2010.

Meyer, Michael C., William L. Sherman, and Susan M. Deeds. *The Course of Mexican History*. 9th ed. Oxford: Oxford University Press, 2011.

Miller, Tom, ed. *Writing on the Edge: A Borderlands Reader*. Tucson: University of Arizona Press, 2003.

Mitchell, John Hanson. *Trespassing: An Inquiry into the Private Ownership of Land*. Reading, MA: Addison-Wesley, 1998.

Mize, Ronald L., and Alicia C. S. Swords. *Consuming Mexican Labor: From the Bracero Program to NAFTA*. Toronto: University of Toronto Press, 2011.

Morgenthaler, Jefferson. *The River Has Never Divided Us: A Border History of La Junta de Los Rios*. Austin: University of Texas Press, 2004.

Mulroy, Kevin. *Freedom on the Border: The Seminole Maroons in Florida, the Indian Territory, Coahuila, and Texas*. Lubbock: Texas Tech University Press, 1993.

Nazario, Sonia. *Enrique's Journey.* New York: Random House, 2007.

Nevins, Joseph. *Dying to Live: A Story of U.S. Immigration in an Age of Global Apartheid.* San Francisco: Open Media/City Lights Books, 2008.

Orchowski, Margaret Sands. *Immigration and the American Dream: Battling the Political Hype and Hysteria.* Lanham, MD: Rowman and Littlefield, 2008.

Orner, Peter, ed. *Underground America: Narratives of Undocumented Lives.* San Francisco, CA: McSweeney's Books, 2008.

Osorio, Rubén. *La Familia Secreta de Pancho Villa.* Alpine, TX: Sul Ross State University, 2000.

Paz, Octavio. *The Labyrinth of Solitude: Life and Thought in Mexico.* New York: Grove, 1985.

Pratt, Julius. "The Origin of 'Manifest Destiny.'" *American Historical Review* 32 (July 1927): 795–798.

Ragsdale, Kenneth Baxter. *Quicksilver: Terlingua and the Chisos Mining Company.* College Station: Texas A&M University Press, 1995.

Rascón, Alonso Domínguez. *Tierra y Autonomía.* Ciudad Juárez, Mexico: El Colegio de Chihuahua, 2011.

Regan, Margaret. *The Death of Josseline: Immigration Stories from the Arizona-Mexico Borderlands.* Boston: Beacon Press, 2010.

Reisner, Mark. *Cadillac Desert: The American West and Its Disappearing Water.* New York: Penguin Books, 1993.

Richards, Leonard L. *The California Gold Rush and the Coming of the Civil War.* New York: Alfred A. Knopf, 2007.

Rivera, Geraldo. *His Panic: Why Americans Fear Hispanics in the U.S.* London: Penguin Books, 2008.

Rivera, Juan M., Scott Whiteford, and Manuel Chávez, eds. *NAFTA and the Campesinos: The Impact of NAFTA on Small-Scale Agricultural Producers in Mexico and the Prospects for Change.* Scranton, PA: University of Scranton Press, 2009.

Rodriguez, Gregory. "El Paso Confronts Its Messy Past." *Los Angeles Times,* March 25, 2007. http://articles.latimes.com/2007/mar/25/opinion/op-rodriguez25.

Rousseau, Jean-Jacques. *A Discourse on Inequality.* Translated and with an introduction by Maurice Cranston. London: Penguin Books, 1984.

Santa Ana, Otto. *Brown Tide Rising: Metaphors of Latinos in Contemporary American Public Discourse.* Austin: University of Texas Press, 2002.

Schubert, Frank N. "The Buffalo Soldiers at San Juan Hill." Paper presented at the Conference of Army Historians, Bethesda, MD, 1998.

———. *On the Trail of the Buffalo Soldier: Biographies of African Americans in the U.S. Army, 1866–1917.* Wilmington, DE: Scholarly Resources, 1995.

Sebald, W. G. *The Emigrants*. New York: New Directions, 1997.

Segura, Denise A., and Patricia Zavella, eds. *Women and Migration in the U.S.-Mexico Borderlands: A Reader*. Durham, NC: Duke University Press, 2007.

Sheridan, Thomas E. *Arizona: A History*. Rev. ed. Tucson: University of Arizona Press, 2012.

Sonnichsen, C. L. *The Mescalero Apaches*. Norman: University of Oklahoma Press, 1973.

Soto, Carlos Badillo. *Brasas en el Desierto*. Vol. 5. Durango, Mexico: State of Durango, 1996.

Steinbeck, John. *The Harvest Gypsies: On the Road to the Grapes of Wrath*. Berkeley, CA: Heyday Books, 1988.

———. *Travels with Charley*. New York: Book-of-the-Month Club, 1995.

Street, Richard Steven. *Beasts of the Field: A Narrative History of California Farm Workers, 1769–1913*. Stanford, CA: Stanford University Press, 2004.

Student Action with Farmworkers. *Recollections of Home*. Raleigh, NC: Grassroots Press, 2000.

Thompson, Charles D., Jr., and Melinda F. Wiggins, eds. *The Human Cost of Food: Farmworkers' Lives, Labor, and Advocacy*. Austin: University of Texas Press, 2002.

Thompson, Gabriel. *Working in the Shadows: A Year of Doing the Jobs (Most) Americans Won't Do*. New York: Nation Books, 2010.

Trafzer, Clifford E. *Yuma: Frontier Crossing of the Far Southwest*. Wichita, KS: Western Heritage Books, 1980.

Underhill, Ruth M. *Papago Woman*. Prospect Heights, IL: Waveland, 1985.

Updike, John. *Endpoint and Other Poems*. New York: Alfred A. Knopf, 2009.

Urrea, Luis Alberto. *By the Lake of Sleeping Children: The Secret Life of the Mexican Border*. New York: Anchor Books, 1996.

———. *The Devil's Highway: A True Story*. New York: Back Bay Books, 2005.

Utley, Robert M. *Changing Course: The International Boundary, United States and Mexico, 1848–1963*. Tucson, AZ: Southwest Parks and Monuments Association, 1996.

Vara, Martín González de la. *Breve historia de Ciudad Juárez y su región*. Cuidad Juárez, Mexico: El Colegio de Chihuahua, 2009.

Vila, Pablo. *Identidades fronterizas*. Ciudad Juárez, Mexico: El Colegio de Chihuahua, 2007.

Weaver, John D. *The Brownsville Raid*. College Station: Texas A&M University Press, 1992.

Webb, Walter Prescott, and Eldon Stephen Banda, eds. *Handbook of Texas*. Denton: Texas State Historical Association, 1992.

Welsome, Eileen. *The General and the Jaguar: Pershing's Hunt for Pancho Villa, a True Story of Revolution and Revenge*. New York: Little, Brown, 2006.

Wooster, Robert. *Fort Davis*. Austin: Texas State Historical Association, 1994.

Zavaleta, Antonio. "The Ghosts of Historic Palmito Hill Ranch." In *Continuing Studies in Rio Grande Valley History*, edited by Milo Kearney, Anthony K. Knopp, and Antonio Zavaleta, 5–35. Brownsville: Texas Center for Border and Transnational Studies, University of Texas at Brownsville and Texas Southmost College, 2010.

*Italic* numerals indicate illustrations